Enforcement of Planning Control

Enforcement of Planning Control

C M Brand LLB

Solicitor

Longman

© Longman Group UK Ltd 1988

Published by
Longman Group UK Ltd
21–27 Lamb's Conduit Street
London WC1N 3NJ

Associated Offices
Australia, Hong Kong, Malaysia, Singapore, USA

ISBN 0-85121-409-6

British Library Cataloguing in Publication Data

Brand, Clive M.
  Enforcement of planning control.
  1. Great Britain.   Land use.   Planning.
  Legal aspects
  I. Title
  344.1064'4

Printed and bound in Great Britain by
Biddles Ltd, Guildford and King's Lynn

Contents

Preface

Enforcement of planning control is probably one of the more difficult areas of town and country planning law, but it is one which is both interesting and potentially very lucrative. The subject has generated a substantial volume of law, though this is fairly self-contained and its mastery does not depend on an in-depth knowledge of the whole town and country planning system. Its reputation for difficulty derives from the fact that the relevant provisions of the Town and Country Planning Act 1971 and the Local Government and Planning (Amendment) Act 1981, together with attendant delegated legislation, closely interlock to produce what may seem at first sight an inseparable amalgam of legislation upon which lies an equally complex layer of caselaw.

Anticipating the likely readership of this book I was particularly mindful of the need to dissect the subject into its constituent parts, so far as is reasonably possible, and to present the main features in a readily digestible form. I thus found it necessary to divide the text into sixteen chapters, rather more than would normally be required in a book of this length. My object has been to show that in most cases of enforcement action (almost 5,000 enforcement notices are issued annually) the practitioner can cope without the need to enlist specialist advice. While there will be occasions on which further advice will be necessary, these will be in the minority and should be recognisable from a study of this book.

The law which I have considered relevant is discussed as it stood on 1 October 1987.

October 1987   C M Brand

Table of Cases

xiii

Table of Statutes

Table of Statutory Instruments

Abbreviations

The 1971 Act

The Town and Country Planning Act 1971

The 1981 Act

The Local Government and Planning (Amendment) Act 1981

The Enforcement Regulations 1981

The Town and Country Planning (Enforcement Notice and Appeals) Regulations 1981 (SI 1981 No 1742)

The Enforcement Inquiries Rules 1981

The Town and Country Planning (Enforcement) (Inquiries Procedure) Rules 1981 (SI 1981 No 174) as amended by the Town and Country Planning (Various Inquiries) (Procedure) (Amendment) Rules 1986 (SI 1986 No 420)

Chapter 1

Enforcement of Planning Control

1.1 Introduction

If a client of yours is served with a copy of an enforcement notice which has been issued by the local planning authority he will probably make a visit to your office without delay, perhaps in a state of some anxiety.This is because the enforcement notice will allege that a breach of planning control has occurred and will require steps to be taken to remedy the alleged breach in a specified time. This may even involve the demolition of buildings on your client's land or total cessation of a use which is being made of the land, with obvious consequences for the value of the property and perhaps also for the client's livelihood. Faced with a situation of obvious urgency (particularly because criminal penalties are involved for failure to comply with the notice) and a client who needs advice, assurance, and the comfort of knowing that he has placed his problems in your competent hands, how are you to deal with the matter? Your mind may turn to thoughts of rights of appeal, to defending criminal proceedings, or even to challenging the validity of the enforcement notice by means of judicial review. Hopefully you will be aware that dealing with the notice requires great care and much consideration as you are being confronted with a problem which involves an area of law which has a reputation for difficulty. You must, however, act quickly in order to ensure that rights of appeal are safeguarded.

It is an uncomfortable realisation that enforcement of planning control has always been the bogey aspect of the town and country planning system. During the forty years that have elapsed since the Town and Country Planning Act 1947 came into operation on the 1 July 1948, the topic of enforcement has continually vexed the minds of local planning authorities, developers, central government, and the judiciary, as well as professional advisors. Local planning

1

authorities and central government (acting through the Secretary of State for the Environment) have encountered many difficulties in their attempts (sometimes in vain) successfully to operate the enforcement provisions of the town and country planning legislation. For their part developers have gone to great lengths to defend enforcement action with legal arguments on both procedural and substantive issues, no doubt mindful of the financial advantages of success. Inevitably the resolution of legal disputes has provided the courts with a steady flow of judicial business. The result is an impressive body of case-law which must be digested in order to gain a satisfactory working knowledge of the enforcement system.

An understanding of the case-law must, inevitably, be preceded by a knowledge of the provisions of the Town and Country Planning Act 1971 which are relevant to enforcement of planning control. Although it is well known that the 1971 Act is a complex and much amended statute, the enforcement provisions are rightly regarded as especially technical. The current scheme is based primarily upon a group of provisions in Part V of the 1971 Act, as substantially amended by the Local Government and Planning (Amendment) Act 1981. While discussion of the relevant provisions forms the basis of this book, it is as well to be aware that the enforcement aspect of the planning legislation has had something of a troubled history since its original formulation under the Town and Country Planning Act 1947. It may be helpful, therefore, before embarking on an account of the present law, to give a very brief survey of the statutory development.

1.2 Development of enforcement legislation

Enforcement law has changed considerably since its beginnings in ss 23–24 of the Town and Country Planning Act 1947, which came into force on 1 July 1948. It has, however, retained throughout two basic features: (i) that the method of enforcement is by the local planning authority exercising a discretionary power to serve an **enforcement notice** in the event of a perceived breach of planning control, and (ii) that the making of an **appeal** against the enforcement notice serves to suspend the operation of the notice until the appeal has been resolved. Important details relating to these two fundamental matters have, however, changed considerably.

Under the 1947 Act the recipient of an enforcement notice could defend himself in two ways. First, he could apply for planning permission to the local planning authority. If the application was unsuccessful he could appeal to the Minister, at that time the Minister of Town and Country Planning. Secondly, he could appeal against the enforcement notice on its merits to the magistrates' court. Both of these steps were open to the developer and the effect of taking either of them was to suspend the operation of the notice. By so doing valuable time was gained during which an unauthorised development could continue unremedied.

If no application for planning permission was made, or no appeal against the notice was made to the magistrates, the developer could still seek to defend criminal proceedings brought by the local planning authority, especially where the enforcement notice was not impeccably drafted. He could thus attempt to show that the notice contained defects which rendered it a nullity.

These arrangements, aided by a suspicious judiciary, provided developers (or perhaps more accurately their lawyers) with a field day. In the 1950's the judiciary seemed to regard planning legislation as a direct interference with private property rights and consequently (per Viscount Simonds in *East Riding County Council* v *Park Estate (Bridlington) Ltd* [1957] AC 223 at 233) required 'strict and rigid adherence to formalities' without which an enforcement notice might be declared a nullity. In another leading case of the period *Francis* v *Yiewsley and West Drayton Urban District Council* [1958] 1 QB 478 the Court of Appeal decided that not only must the enforcement notice contain accurate recitals but also that a developer could challenge the validity of an enforcement notice by means of a declaration even though he had not utilised the statutory means of defence, by way of appeal to the magistrates' court. The result, therefore, was an ineffective system of enforcement which was particularly found wanting in the case of the many unauthorised caravan sites which appeared as a result of the post-war housing shortage. For a further example of the technical approach characteristic of the period see *Cater* v *Essex County Council* [1960] 1 QB 424.

The main method chosen to remedy these problems was to ensure that an appeal against an enforcement notice could be made only to the Minister on a number of specified grounds, with a further right of appeal to the High Court on a point of law only. The Caravan Sites and Control of Development Act 1960 thus provided for the abolition of the appellate functions of the justices.

The Minister (by this time the Minister of Housing and Local Government) was also given powers (a) to correct an enforcement notice which contained an informality, defect or error rather than be forced to condemn it as invalid and (b) to grant planning permission, since by the making of an appeal the appellant was deemed to have made an application for planning permission. In addition, in order to ensure that the Minister acted as the appellate authority a privative provision was introduced (s 33(8) of the Act of 1960) which prevented the validity of an enforcement notice being challenged in any proceedings on most of the grounds on which an appeal could be made to the Minister. These changes, which were shortly afterwards incorporated into the (consolidating) Town and Country Planning Act 1962, are still major features of the enforcement system, having been re-enacted by the relevant provisions of the Town and Country Planning Act 1968, which was in turn superseded by the Town and Country Planning Act 1971.

The reforms of 1960 were not wasted by the judiciary. The turning point in approach came with the decision of the Court of Appeal in *Miller-Mead* v *Minister of Housing and Local Government* [1963] 2 QB 196 in which Lord Denning MR, Upjohn LJ and Diplock LJ used the revised legislation to set aside the constrictions imposed by the previous decisions referred to above. Lord Denning MR explained that the legislature had intervened '. . . not so much by changing the substantive law, but by altering the procedure. And in so doing, it has taken away the power of the courts to interfere on technical grounds'. The power conferred on the Minister to correct any informality, defect or error was thus identified by Lord Denning MR as the means by which, as he put it 'the legislature has disposed of the proposition that there must be a strict and rigid adherence to formalities'. Ten years later in *Square Meal Frozen Foods Ltd* v *Dunstable Corporation* [1974] 1 WLR 59 the Master of the Rolls looked back to his judgment in *Miller-Mead* v *Minister of Housing and Local Government* and commented that

Before [the Caravan Sites and Control of Development Act 1960] the procedure by enforcement notices had become greatly hampered by technical objections. I explained it in *Miller-Mead* v *Minister of Housing and Local Government*. The Act of 1960 was passed especially to do away with these technical objections and to abolish all the formalities which had surrounded enforcement notices. The object was to enable planning control to be enforced according to the merits of the case. For this purpose, it was enacted that the validity of an enforcement notice was not to be questioned by proceedings in the courts. It enacted that the only way to question the validity was an appeal to the Minister. This was a much better procedure, because it meant that planning merits and the law were considered by one and the same tribunal. If there was any technical defect in the enforcement notice, it could be amended. Moreover, if there was any breach of planning control—and yet there was a good case on the planning merits—the Minister could give planning permission in those very proceedings. Nevertheless, if there was a point of law, there was an appeal from the Minister to the High Court.

The Town and Country Planning Act 1968 made two further significant alterations. Under the previous legislation, if an unauthorised development had subsisted for at least four years it became immune from enforcement action. The 1968 Act amended this rule by excluding from its scope most developments which are classified as being in the nature of a 'material change of use' of buildings or other land. These forms of development were thus rendered vulnerable to enforcement action at any time, though provisions were included for the issue of an 'established use certificate' in respect of an act of development comprising a material change of use which had already become immune from enforcement under the previous 'four-year rule' as it was (and still is) known. The other major change initiated by the 1968 Act was to introduce a further planning instrument known as a 'stop notice'. This can be used by local planning authorities to counter the effect of making an appeal against an enforcement notice (that is to suspend its operation) and can require the alleged breach of planning control to cease as little as three days after the service of the stop notice. This procedure is, however, subject to compensation rights if the developer makes a successful appeal against the enforcement notice to the Minister (since 1970 the Secretary of State for the Environment).

Since 1968 the enforcement legislation has been the subject of changes that are more in the nature of systematic development than radical overhaul. No changes were made at all by the Town and Country Planning Act 1971, but further alterations were made in 1977 by the Town and Country Planning (Amendment) Act 1977 which extended the scope of the stop notice procedure. Subsequently, as was mentioned above, the Local Government and Planning (Amendment) Act 1981 made a number of alterations to the provisions of the Town and Country Planning Act 1971. This was achieved by using the technique of repealing the sections enacted in 1971 and substituting further sections in their place. Changes were made in a number of respects, for example by enabling the Secretary of State to make regulations supplementing the statutory requirements in relation to the content of enforcement notices. The service procedure was also changed by requiring the enforcing authority to serve copies of the notice. Of particular importance, however, are some alterations in the powers of the Secretary of State to correct or vary an enforcement notice on appeal to him and a change in the privative provisions of the 1971 Act which seek to preclude challenge to a notice except as prescribed by the Act itself.

The effect of the present scheme can perhaps be judged by the fact that the flow of case-law seems inexorable. This is largely due to the fact that the basic defects of the system have not yet been remedied. These defects are the continuing uncertainty surrounding the question of when an enforcement notice is a nullity, and the linked question of the scope of the powers of the Secretary of State on appeal to him. Thus much use is still being made of s 246 of the 1971 Act which regulates the right of appeal from the Secretary of State to the High Court on a point of law.

1.3 Enforcement today: the relevant legislation

As a result of the Local Government and Planning (Amendment) Act 1981, the current provisions regulating enforcement law are to be found mainly in ss 87, 88, 88A, 88B, 89, 90, 91, 92, 92A, 93, 94, 95, 177, 243, and 246 of the 1971 Act. These 15 sections thus comprise the basic scheme. To provide an initial sketch of the legislation the purport of each section may be summarised as follows:

s 87   Confers powers on local planning authorities to serve an enforcement notice, regulates service procedure, prescribes contents of the notice;

s 88   Provides for a right of appeal against an enforcement notice, specifies the grounds of appeal, the method of appeal, the Secretary of State's delegated legislative powers, authorises determination of the appeal, and the effect of an appeal on the enforcement notice pending its determination;

s 88A   Confers a power on the Secretary of State to (i) quash an enforcement notice, (ii) vary its terms (iii) correct any informality, defect or error;

s 88B   Enables the Secretary of State to grant planning

permission for the unauthorised development as the appellant is deemed to have made an application for planning permission;

s 89   Prescribes criminal penalties for non-compliance with an enforcement notice;

s 90   Confers powers on local planning authorities to serve a stop notice;

s 91   Confers powers on local planning authorities to enter upon land subject to an enforcement notice to execute work required; provides for recovery of expenditure incurred;

s 92   Regulates the effect of a grant of planning permission on an enforcement notice;

s 92A   Requires a register of enforcement and stop notices to be maintained by the local planning authority;

s 93   Provides that an enforcement notice remains effective despite compliance with its requirements;

s 94   Provides for application for an established use certificate;

s 95   Provides for a right of appeal against refusal of an established use certificate; confers a power on the Secretary of State to call in an application for an established use certificate;

s 177   Provides for a right to compensation if a stop notice is served but the enforcement notice on which it is dependent is subsequently quashed by the Secretary of State;

s 243   Provides that challenge to the validity of an enforcement notice can only be made by way of an appeal under s 88, unless the question of validity concerns a matter which is not a ground of appeal specified in that section;

s 246   Provides for a right of appeal from a decision of the Secretary of State to the High Court on a point of law.

At this juncture it is also desirable to give mention to two relevant items of delegated legislation which are of particular importance in the context of enforcement proceedings. These are (a) the Town and Country Planning (Enforcement Notices and Appeals) Regulations 1981 (SI 1981 No 1742) and (b) the Town and Country Planning (Enforcement) (Inquiries Procedure) Rules 1981 (SI 1981 No 1743), both of which came into force on 11

January 1982. The first of these, referred to in this book as 'the Enforcement Regulations 1981' were made by the Secretary of State under subss 87(12) and 88(5) of the 1971 Act. Their function is to add further detail to the statutory provisions governing the particulars which must be contained in an enforcement notice and also to prescribe the steps to be taken for explanation of the grounds of appeal by the parties should an appeal be made against the notice. The second of the two statutory instruments, referred to in this book as 'the Enforcement Inquiries Rules 1981' make detailed provision for the conduct of public local inquiries held pursuant to s 88(7) and s 282 of the 1971 Act. These rules (like most inquiries procedure rules) were made by the Lord Chancellor pursuant to s 11 of the Tribunals and Inquiries Act 1971 and provided, for the first time, a set of rules drafted purely for use at enforcement inquiries.

Three other items of legislation complete the statutory code. Mention was made above of the Town and Country Planning (Amendment) Act 1977. This Act amended s 90 of the 1971 Act (service of a stop notice) and also s 177, the provision which regulates the right to receipt of compensation from the local planning authority where the enforcement notice on which the stop notice is dependent is quashed on appeal to the Secretary of State. Secondly, one should note the Town and Country Planning Act 1984 which filled a gap in the enforcement code in relation to land vested in the Crown. Section 3 of the 1984 Act authorises the service with the consent of the Crown of a 'special enforcement notice' where a breach of planning control is committed on Crown land by a person who has no legal interest in the land. As a result of this enactment the special problems of enforcement which occur in relation to Crown land are explained in Chap 16. Lastly some minor changes were made by the Housing and Planning Act 1986.

1.4 Relevant ministerial communications

Like all of the important local government functions town and country planning is the subject of constant ministerial attention and frequent direction manifested in the form of Department of Environment Circulars, a number of which are particularly relevant to enforcement of planning control. Stated in chronological order the following DoE Circulars will need to be referred to:

109/77 (Welsh Office 164/77): Enforcement of Planning Control
—Established Use Certificates;
26/81 (Welsh Office 39/81): Local Government and Planning
(Amendment) Act 1981;
38/81 (Welsh Office 57/81): Planning and Enforcement
Appeals;
18/84 (Welsh Office 37/84): Crown Land and Crown Development;
20/85 (Welsh Office 49/85): Town and Country Planning Act
1971: Enforcement Appeals and Advertisement Appeals;
2/87 (Welsh Office 5/87): Award of Costs Incurred in Planning
and Compulsory Purchase Order Proceedings;
4/87 (Welsh Office 7/87): Section 90 of Town and County
Planning Act 1971: Provisions and Procedures for Stop Notices;

The most important paragraphs of these Circulars are included
in Appendix 1 to this book. While these Circulars contain useful
guidance on the operation of the enforcement system they do not
provide the statistical information which should be borne in mind
as a factor in considering the prospects of success in an appeal
against enforcement action. For this information it is necessary to
consult the annual reports of the Chief Planning Inspector, compiled jointly by the Department of the Environment, Department
of Transport and Welsh Office. The most recent of these reports,
that for 1985–6, reveals that almost 5,000 enforcement appeals are
made yearly, a figure which is thought to be about 80 per cent of
the total number of enforcement notices issued. Many do not
proceed to a determination eg because agreement is reached with
the local planning authority and hence the appeal is withdrawn. Of
those that proceed to a determination about 42 per cent of enforcement notices are quashed, about 29 per cent are varied by the
Secretary of State (by extending the period for compliance or by
altering the requirements of the notice), while a further 29 per cent
of enforcement notices are upheld without variation.

Chapter 2

Development and Breach of Planning Control

2.1 Introduction

In order for enforcement action to be competent there must first have been a breach of planning control. Section 87 of the 1971 Act gives the local planning authority a discretionary power to take enforcement action and for this purpose s 87(3) of the 1971 Act provides that there is a breach of planning control

(a) if development has been carried out, whether before or after the commencement of this Act, without the grant of the planning permission required in that behalf in accordance with Part III of . . . this Act; or

(b) if any conditions or limitations subject to which planning permission was granted have not been complied with.

Examination of this subsection shows that a number of key terms are involved. For the benefit of the reader whose knowledge of the planning jargon is limited, a short explanation of 'development', 'planning permission' and 'conditions or limitations' is included at this stage. It will then be possible to examine the scope of this subsection.

2.2 The relevant definitions

2.2.1 Development

This is the crucial term central to the whole planning system and is defined in s 22(1) of the 1971 Act as 'the carrying out of building, engineering, mining or other operations in, on, over or under land, or the making of any material change in the use of any buildings or other land'. It can be seen from this definition that the meaning of the word 'development' is capable of subdivision into two parts.

10

The first part is concerned with building and engineering activities on the land and includes mining and 'other operations'. Most acts of development falling within this part of the definition are constructional in nature, involving the building of new structures on the land. The scope of the definition is, however, very great, as illustrated by the well-known case of *Barvis* v *Secretary of State for the Environment* (1971) 22 P&CR 710. A crane 89 feet high ran on tracks but was often dismantled and loaned on hire for construction work. When not so hired, it was used by the owners of the crane on the land concerned. The court held that the crane constituted 'development' of the land despite the periodic absence of the structure from the site. In another leading case, *Buckinghamshire County Council* v *Callingham* [1952] 2 QB 515 a model village was held to be a 'structure or erection' and hence 'development' because the word 'building', in s 22(1), is further defined in s 290(1) of the 1971 Act to include 'any structure or erection'. The scope of this part of the definition is also further illustrated by *Scholes* v *Minister of Housing and Local Government* (1966) 197 EG 563 in which it was held that an act as humble as the replacement of a hedge by a fence constituted development requiring planning permission.

The second part of the definition deals with 'the making of any material change in the use of any buildings or other land'. The word 'material' is particularly important, for an act of development does not automatically follow from making a change of use in the building or land concerned: it must be a *material* change before development is involved. It is not possible to give a precise account of when a change of use is 'material' since neither the 1971 Act nor the cases give a complete answer to the question. A useful guide is that there must be a substantial difference between the new use and the old use to qualify as 'material', though it must be borne in mind that whether a change of use is a material change is one of fact and degree mixed with law. The approach to be adopted was explained by Lord Parker CJ in *Devonshire County Council* v *Allens Caravans (Estates) Ltd* (1962) 14 P&CR 444 who pointed out that 'the materiality to be considered is a materiality from a planning point of view and in particular the question of amenities'.

The meaning of the word 'development' is, therefore, to be gleaned from judicial decisions as well as from the section itself. As Lord Wilberforce once observed in *Coleshill and District Investment Co Ltd* v *Minister of Housing and Local Government* [1969] 2 All ER 525, some twenty years after the coming into force of the 1947 Act, '"Development" is a key word in the planners' vocabulary but it is one whose meaning has evolved and is still evolving. It is impossible to ascribe to it any certain dictionary meaning and difficult to analyse it accurately from the statutory definition.' It is perhaps fortunate that in this book it is not necessary to carry out an exhaustive examination; it is sufficient to be aware that cases in which the scope of the word 'development' has been placed in issue have often arisen through enforcement proceedings.

2.2.2 Planning permission

Like the word 'development' the term 'planning permission' is not fully defined by the 1971 Act. The definition section (s 290) merely states that 'planning permission' means permission under Part III of this Act. Part III of the 1971 Act is concerned with 'General Planning Control' and commences with s 22 referred to above. Very significantly s 23(1) provides that '. . . planning permission is required for the carrying out of any development of land'.

This section does not, however, specify what constitutes planning permission. Is it a formal document issued by the local planning authority following the making of a successful application for planning permission or is it a resolution passed by the council concerned? In *R v West Oxfordshire District Council ex p Pearce (CH) Homes Ltd* [1986] JPL 523 a resolution had been passed granting planning permission for the proposed development. A letter was sent to the company confirming that this was the case. Later the council declined to issue a formal notification that planning permission had been granted. Woolf J held that only a formal notification to the developer could complete the process of granting planning permission and hence the council were entitled to rescind their initial resolution prior to issuing the relevant document.

2.2.3 Conditions or limitations

If a local planning authority decide to grant planning permission after an application for planning permission has been made to them, s 29(1) empowers the local planning authority to attach 'such conditions as they think fit'. In view of the fact that failure to comply with a condition is a breach of planning control, the power to attach conditions under what appears to be a widely drafted discretionary power becomes rather significant. The discretion is not, however, an unfettered one as the doctrine of ultra vires renders illegal any conditions which exceed the powers of the local planning authority. The principles which are to be applied were stated by the House of Lords in *Newbury District Council* v *Secretary of State for the Environment* [1981] AC 578. A condition will be ultra vires and therefore illegal unless it (i) serves a purpose which is relevant to planning; and (ii) fairly and reasonably relates to the permitted development and (iii) is not unreasonable in the sense that no reasonable local planning authority exercising their power to attach conditions would impose it. Examples of conditions found to be ultra vires by the High Court include an instance where the local planning authority sought to require a housing developer to accommodate local authority tenants: *R* v *Hillingdon London Borough Council, ex p Royco Homes Ltd* [1974] QB 720 and another where a condition required the developer to lay out an estate road at his own expense and give access to the public: *Hall & Co* v *Shoreham-by-Sea Urban District Council* [1964] 1 WLR 240.

Extensive advice to local planning authorities on the use of conditions when granting planning permission is contained in Department of the Environment Circular 1/85 entitled 'The Use of Conditions in Planning Permissions'. Paragraph 11 of this Circular advises that conditions should not be imposed unless they are both necessary and effective, and do not place unjustifiable burdens on applicants. It also identifies six criteria to be used when considering the attachment of conditions to a grant of planning permission. These are whether the condition is (i) necessary (ii) relevant to planning (iii) relevant to the development to be permitted (iv) enforceable (v) precise (vi) reasonable in all other respects.

It is to be noted that the word 'limitations' does not appear in s 29(1). Indeed, in one case, *Peacock Homes Ltd* v *Secretary of State for the Environment* [1984] JPL 729, Dillon LJ said that 'the word "limitations" did not carry any technical meaning under the 1971 Act, and would seem to be surplusage in that any limitation on a planning permission would have to be imposed by way of a condition under s 29: in so far as it had any weight, however, the word "limitations" would seem apt to cover a limitation in time . . . subject to which planning permission was granted'. This view is supported by the provisions of s 30(2); if planning permission is granted subject to a requirement that the development it authorises is to be removed or discontinued after a specified period of time the grant is, by virtue of s 30(2), referred to in the 1971 Act as 'planning permission granted for a limited period'. Nevertheless the word 'limitations' has a further significance in the context of enforcement action which is explained in para **2.6** below.

2.3 Instances where no 'development' occurs

As s 87(3) is linked to the meaning of the word 'development', it is necessary to look further at s 22 since this section not only provides the statutory definition of 'development' but also specifies six instances where development is deemed not to occur. Any enforcement notice served in respect of such matters will therefore be ineffective, though an appeal against the notice should nevertheless be made to the Secretary of State. Under s 22(2) the following matters are excluded:

(a) the carrying out of works for the maintenance, improvement or other alteration of any building, being works which affect only the interior of a building or which do not materially affect the external appearance of the building and (in either case) are not works for making good war damage or works begun after 5 December 1968 for the alteration of a building by providing additional space therein below ground;

(b) the carrying out by a local highway authority of any works required for the maintenance or improvement of a road, being works carried out on land within the boundaries of the road;

(c) the carrying out by a local authority or statutory undertakers of any works for the purpose of inspecting, repairing or renewing any sewers, mains, pipes, cables or other apparatus including the breaking open of any street or other land for that purpose;

(d) the use of any buildings or other land within the curtilage of a dwellinghouse for any purpose incidental to the enjoyment of the dwellinghouse as such;

(e) the use of any land for the purposes of agriculture or forestry (including afforestation) and the use for any of those purposes of any building occupied together with land so used;

(f) in the case of buildings or other land which are used for a purpose of any class specified in an order made by the Secretary of State under this section, the use of the buildings or other land or, subject to the provisions of the order, of any part thereof for any other purpose of the same class.

The last of these six exceptions is particularly important. Under the power conferred by s 22(2)(f) the Secretary of State has made the Town and Country Planning (Use Classes) Order 1987 (SI 1987 No 764) which replaced an earlier order of 1972. The effect of the Order is to specify in a schedule a number of different classes of use (16 in all), so that a change of use from a use specified in a use class to a new use in the same use class is deemed not to involve development. The schedule is divided into four parts which group together classes of a broadly similar nature. As the 1987 Use Classes Order radically revised the previous scheme the content of many of the new classes is reproduced below.

Part A

Class A1 Shops

Use for all or any of the following purposes
- (*a*) for the retail sale of goods other than hot food;
- (*b*) as a post office;
- (*c*) for the sale of tickets or as a travel agency;
- (*d*) for the sale of sandwiches or other cold food for consumption off the premises;
- (*e*) for hairdressing;
- (*f*) for the direction of funerals;
- (*g*) for the display of goods for sale;
- (*h*) for the hiring out of domestic or personal goods or articles;
- (*i*) for the reception of goods to be washed, cleaned or repaired,

where the sale, display or service is to visiting members of the public.

Class A2 Financial and professional services

Use for the provision of
- (*a*) financial services; or
- (*b*) professional services (other than health or medical services); or
- (*c*) any other services (including use as a betting office) which it is appropriate to provide in a shopping area;

where the services are provided principally to visiting members of the public.

Class A3 Food and drink

Use for the sale of food or drink for consumption on the premises or of hot food for consumption off the premises.

Part B

Class B1 Business

Use for all or any of the following purposes
- (*a*) as an office other than a use within class A2 (financial and professional services);
- (*b*) for research and development of products or processes; or
- (*c*) for any industrial process;

being a use which can be carried out in any residential area without detriment to the amenity of that area by reason of noise, vibration, smell, fumes, smoke, soot, ash, dust or grit.

Class B2 General industrial

Use for the carrying on of an industrial process other than one falling within class B1 above or within classes B3 to B7 below.

Classes B3–B7 These contain Special Industrial Groups A–E which specify a large number of industrial processes, businesses or trades.

Class B8 Storage or distribution

Use for storage or as a distribution centre.

Part C

Class C1 Hotels and hostels

Use as a hotel, boarding or guest house or as a hostel where, in each case, no sigificant element of care is provided.

Class C2 Residential institutions

Use for the provision of residential accommodation and care to people in need of care (other than a use within class C3 (dwelling houses)).
Use as a hospital or nursing home.
Use as a residential school, college or training centre.

Class C3 Dwellinghouses

Use as a dwellinghouse (whether or not as a sole or main residence)
- (*a*) by a single person or by people living together as a family, or
- (*b*) by not more than six residents living together as a single household (including a household where care is provided for residents).

Part D

Class D1 Non-residential institutions

Any use not including a residential use
- (*a*) for the provision of any medical or health services except the use of premises attached to the residence of the consultant or practitioner,
- (*b*) as a creche, day nursery or day centre,
- (*c*) for the provision of education,
- (*d*) for the display of works of art (otherwise than for sale or hire),
- (*e*) as a museum,
- (*f*) as a public library or public reading room,
- (*g*) as a public hall or exhibition hall,
- (*h*) for, or in connection with, public worship or religious instruction.

Class D2 Assembly and leisure

Use as
- (*a*) a cinema,
- (*b*) a concert hall,
- (*c*) a bingo hall or casino,
- (*d*) a dance hall,
- (*e*) a swimming bath, skating rink, gymnasium or area for other indoor or outdoor sports or recreations, not involving motorised vehicles or firearms.

In applying the Use Classes Order particular regard should be had to art 3(1) which makes it clear that the ambit of the Order is such that in the case of every class it extends both to buildings and land. It is also noteworthy that art 3(6) excludes from the scope of the Use Classes Order the following uses: (*a*) as a theatre (*b*) as an amusement arcade or centre, or a funfair (*c*) for the washing or cleaning of clothes or fabrics in coin-operated machines or on premises at which the goods to be cleaned are received direct from the visiting public (*d*) for the sale of fuel for motor vehicles (*e*) for the sale or display for sale of motor vehicles (*f*) for a taxi business or business for the hire of motor vehicles (*g*) as a scrapyard, or a yard for the storage or distribution of minerals or the breaking of motor vehicles.

Section 22 further provides in s 22(3) that 'for the avoidance of doubt' two further matters are deemed to involve development. In the words of the subsection:

(a) the use as two or more separate dwellinghouses of any building previously used as a single dwellinghouse involves a material change in the use of the building and of each part thereof which is so used;

(b) the deposit of refuse or waste materials on land involves a material change in the use thereof, notwithstanding that the land is comprised in a site already used for that purpose, if either the superficial area of the deposit is thereby extended, or the height of the deposit is thereby extended and exceeds the level of the land adjoining the site.

2.4 Instances where no planning permission is needed

We have already seen that according to s 23(1) 'planning permission is required for the carrying out of any development of land'. By a series of complex provisions s 23(2)–(9) together provide that no planning permission is needed for various acts of development which fall within their scope. While some of these instances may seem a little obscure, others are very significant, particularly that described in paragraph (g), though paragraphs (d) and (f) below are also important. They may be summarised as follows:

(a) If land was being used on 1 July 1948 for a purpose which was not the normal use of the land, no planning permission is needed to resume the normal use, provided the resumption took place before 6 December 1968: s 23(2);

(b) If land was being used on 1 July 1948 for a particular purpose but had been used on occasions before that date for another purpose (whether regularly or not) then

(i) no planning permission is needed for the use of the land for the other purpose on occasions which occurred before 6 December 1968; and

(ii) no planning permission is needed for the use of the land for the other purpose on similar occasions after 6 December 1968 provided the land was used at least once for the other purpose after 1 July 1948 and before 6 December 1968: s 23(3);

(c) If land was unoccupied on 1 July 1948 but had been occupied at some time on or after 7 January 1937, no planning permission is needed for any use of the land which began before 6 December 1968 for the purpose for which the land was last used before 1 July 1948: s 23(4);

(d) If planning permission has been granted for a limited period, no planning permission is needed to resume the use of the land at the end of the period for the purpose for which it was normally used before the grant of planning permission was made. In applying this rule no account is taken of any use of land which took place in breach of planning control: s 23(5), (6);

(e) In applying the paragraphs (a), (b) and (c) of the above rules a modification must be made if the result would be that land could thereby be used as a caravan site without planning permission. In such a case the land must satisfy a further condition that it was used on at least one occasion as a caravan site during the period 10 March 1958 to 9 March 1960: s 23(7);

(f) If planning permission is granted by means of a development order (see para 2.5 below) subject to limitations, planning permission is not needed in order to resume the normal use of the land provided that use is a lawful use: s 23(8);

(g) If an enforcement notice is issued in respect of any land, no planning permission is needed to resume the use of the land for the purpose for which it could lawfully have been used had the unauthorised development not been carried out: s 23(9).

2.5 Instances where planning permission is deemed to be granted

There are many types of development on land which satisfy the statutory definition of 'development' in s 22(1) but which do not require to be authorised by an express grant of 'planning permission'. Development in this class is known as 'permitted development'. Under s 24 of the 1971 Act the Secretary of State is empowered to make 'development orders' for the purposes of specifying the types of development (mostly of a relatively minor nature) that can be carried out by the developer without a grant of planning permission from the local planning authority. There are several development orders but currently the most important is the Town and Country Planning General Development Order 1977 (SI 1977 No 289). This has been amended on numerous occasions: of particular importance for present purposes are alterations made in 1981, 1985 and 1987 by further statutory instruments: SI 1981 No 245, 1985 No 1101 and No 1981, and 1987 No 765. These Orders are known collectively as 'the GDO' and repay a close scrutiny. This is because in its amended form the GDO provides for 30 different classes of development for which no express grant of planning permission is needed (since planning permission is deemed to be granted), as specified in Sched 1 to the Order. This Order is presently under review and may be the subject of a consolidation, with some changes of principle, in the near future.

Although the GDO is a crucial part of the planning legislation regard should also be had to a number of special development orders, hereafter referred to as 'SDO's'. As the title implies SDO's are of special rather than general effect, being limited in their operation to specific areas or institutions. The most important of the SDO's is the Town and Country Planning (National Parks, Areas of Outstanding Natural Beauty and Conservation Areas, etc) Special Development Order 1985 (SI 1985 No 1012) as this qualifies the application of the GDO in the areas in which the SDO applies. Listed chronologically (noting relevant amendments) the SDO's are as follows:

1 Town and Country Planning (Ironstone Areas) Special Development Order 1950 (SI 1950 No 1177)
2 Town and Country Planning (New Towns) Special Development Order 1977 (SI 1977 No 665, as amended by SI 1985 No 1579)
3 Town and Country Planning (New Towns in Rural Wales) Special Development Order 1977 (SI 1977 No 815)
4 Town and Country Planning (Windscale and Calder Works) Special Development Order 1978 (SI 1978 No 523)
5 Town and Country Planning (Merseyside Urban Development Area) Special Development Order 1981 (SI 1981 No 560)
6 Town and Country Planning (London Docklands Urban Development Area) Special Development Order 1981 (SI 1981 No 1082)
7 Town and Country Planning (Vauxhall Cross) Special Development Order 1982 (SI 1982 No 796)
8 Town and Country Planning (Telecommunication Networks) (Railway Operational Land) Special Development Order 1982 (SI 1982 No 817)
9 Town and Country Planning (National Parks, Areas of Outstanding Natural Beauty and Conservation Areas, etc) Special Development Order 1985 (SI 1985 No 1012, as amended by SI 1986 No 8)
10 Town and Country Planning (NIREX) Special Development Order 1986 (SI 1986 No 812)

11 Town and Country Planning (Agricultural and Forestry Development in National Parks, etc) Special Development Order 1986 (SI 1986 No 1176)
12 Town and Country Planning (Black Country Urban Development Area) Special Development Order 1987 (SI 1987 No 1343)
13 Town and Country Planning (Teesside Urban Development Area) Special Development Order 1987 (SI 1987 No 1344)
14 Town and Country Planning (Tyne and Wear Urban Development Area) Special Development Order 1987 (SI 1987 No 1345)

2.6 Breach of planning control

With the benefit of the foregoing brief account of ss 22–24 of the 1971 Act it is possible to give further consideration to s 87(3) which contains the statutory definition of when a breach of planning control occurs. The first paragraph (s 87(3)(a)) of the subsection contemplates a breach of planning control where an act of development has occurred but there is no prior grant of planning permission authorising the development, whether expressly or by virtue of a development order. The second paragraph (s 87(3)(b)) postulates that there is a grant of planning permission but there is a failure to comply with one or more conditions or limitations subject to which the grant was made. These possibilities are now considered in turn.

2.6.1 Development without planning permission

In cases where this paragraph is involved a dispute will often arise over whether an act of 'development' has occurred which can legitimately attract an enforcement notice. In the great majority of such cases the dispute involves an alleged material change of use rather than an act of development of the operational nature. Assessing whether there has been a material change of use is often a difficult task which as has already been pointed out is a matter of fact and degree mixed with law. It is often complicated by the existence of more than one use. Although the 1971 Act does not specifically so provide, the correct method of assessing whether a material change of use has occurred requires, as an initial consideration, the determination of what is generally known as the 'planning unit'. In *Morris* v *Secretary of State for the Environment* (1975) 31 P&CR 216 Lord Widgery CJ advised that:

it is necessary to remember that the first step in deciding whether any breach of planning control has taken place is to ascertain the planning unit concerned and ask in relation to that unit whether the alleged change of use is a material one for present purposes. Once the planning unit has been ascertained, and once it is clear that a material change of use in relation to that unit has occurred, then in my judgment it is open to the planning authority to bring enforcement proceedings . . .

The planning unit, then, is the site relevant to which the materiality of the change of use must be assessed. A guide to the determination of the relevant planning unit was given by the Divisional Court in *Burdle* v *Secretary of State for the Environment* [1972] 1 WLR 1207. Bridge J said that although he did not pre-sume to propound exhaustive tests apt to cover every situation there were three categories of use which he could identify. Firstly, whenever it is possible to recognise a single main purpose of the occupier's land to which secondary activities are incidental or ancillary, the whole unit of occupation should be considered. Secondly, it may equally be apt to consider the entire unit of occupation even though the occupier carries on a variety of activities and it is not possible to say that one is incidental or ancillary to another. This would be the case where the component activities of a composite use fluctuate in their intensity but the different activities are not confined within separate and physically distinct areas of land. Thirdly, it may occur that within a single unit of occupation two or more physically separate areas are occupied for substantially different and unrelated purposes. In such a case each area used for a different main purpose (together with its incidental and ancillary activities) ought to be considered as a separate planning unit. Summarising his guide Bridge J stated that 'It may be a useful working rule to assume that **the unit of occupation is the appropriate planning unit** (author's emphasis) unless and until some smaller unit can be recognised as the site of activities which amount in substance to a separate use both physically and functionally'.

The significance of correct identification of the planning unit is that a material change of use may not have occurred when assessed in relation to a particular area of land but a contrary conclusion may be arrived at when assessed in relation to a different area. A clear illustration is provided by *Johnston* v *Secretary of State for the Environment* (1974) 28 P&CR 424 in which the question arose whether the planning unit was a whole block of 44 garages contained in a courtyard or whether there were a number of planning units to be determined in accordance with the occupation of the garages. As some of the garages had become used for vehicle repairs, was the Secretary of State correct in holding that the planning unit was the specific unit of occupation rather than the whole site and hence that a material change of use had occurred? The Divisional Court held that the conclusion reached by the Secretary of State was one which he was justified in reaching and his finding would not be disturbed. Clearly the consequence of disturbing the Secretary of State's conclusion would have resulted in him being required to reconsider the matter, which might possibly have resulted in a revised conclusion to the effect that no material change of use had occurred. This case also makes it clear that what is the correct planning unit is question of fact for the local planning authority and the Secretary of State to decide; provided the correct criteria are applied the court will not direct a reconsideration of the matter. For a further illustration see *Wood* v *Secretary of State for the Environment* (1973) 25 P&CR 303 (held that it could rarely if ever be right to dissect a single dwellinghouse and to regard one room of it in isolation as being an appropriate planning unit).

2.6.2 *Breach of condition or limitation*

Planning conditions are imposed expressly rather than by implication and their enforceability depends on the implementation of the planning permission as well as whether they are intra vires. Although the point should not be regarded as concluded, it also appears that planning conditions are ineffective if they are attached to a grant of planning permission which it is subsequently shown was not necessary to authorise the development in question: *Mounsden* v *Weymouth and Melcombe Regis Borough Council* [1960] 1 All ER 538.

With regard to breach of a limitation some further comment is needed. The power to enforce against breaches of limitations dates from the Town and Country Planning Act 1959, s 38 of which enabled local planning authorities to take enforcement action where permitted development rights are exceeded. This is needed having regard to the extent of the power granted by what is now s 24(4) of the 1971 Act which enables the Secretary of State to make development orders subject to 'such conditions or limitations as may be specified in the order'. In subsequent legislation, however, the link with GDO limitations was omitted, thus giving a wider power to the local planning authority. Apart from time-limited permissions, the context in which enforcement for breach of a limitation is most likely to occur, albeit infrequently, is the circumstance where the development authorised by an express grant of planning permission is so expressed as to impose a limitation otherwise than by a condition. Thus a grant of planning permission for a 'dwelling for an agricultural worker' is a planning permission subject to a limitation, whereas a grant of planning permission for 'erection of a dwellinghouse' subject to a condition that the occupation of the dwellinghouse is to be limited to a person employed in agriculture is a conditional grant of planning permission. Where the first formula is used the question to be considered is whether a change from agricultural occupation to non-agricultural occupation would be a material change of use: *East Suffolk County Council* v *Secretary of State for the Environment* (1972) 70 LGR 595.

Chapter 3

The Enforcing Authorities

3.1 Local planning authorities

For the most part the process of enforcement of planning control is carried out by local planning authorities. Although, as will be seen, the Secretary of State has a reserve power to take enforcement action, it is not often that this power is invoked. The term 'local planning authority' is a creation of statute which embraces both county and district councils and which acts as a convenient device for the statutory allocation of functions. Under s 1 of the 1971 Act, as amended by s 3 of the Local Government Act 1985, the local planning authority is (*a*) in London, the relevant London borough council; (*b*) in a metropolitan area, the relevant metropolitan district council; (*c*) in all other areas (ie the 'shire' counties) both the relevant county council and the relevant district council. These are both local planning authorities. In the last instance the local planning authorities do not, however, have concurrent functions; as explained below it is principally the district councils which exercise powers of enforcement.

In addition to the local planning authorities further reference is needed to National Park committees, 'special' or 'joint' planning boards and urban development corporations, although these authorities are not, strictly speaking, local planning authorities. Nevertheless as they have planning functions it is necessary to give a brief account of each type of authority.

3.1.1 National Park committees

National Parks are designated by the Countryside Commission under Part II of the National Parks and Access to the Countryside Act 1949, as amended by the Countryside Act 1968, subject to confirmation of the designation order by the Secretary of State. Ten such parks exist in England and Wales: Dartmoor; Exmoor;

the Lake District; the Peak District; Snowdonia; Brecon Beacons; Pembrokeshire Coast; Northumberland; Yorkshire Dales and North Yorkshire Moors. The administration of these areas is by means of National Park committees which comprise members appointed by the Secretary of State and by the county councils and district councils affected by the designation, pursuant to s 184 of Sched 17 to the Local Government Act 1972. These committees have most of the planning functions of county councils and district councils. Enforcement of planning control, however, is the function of the relevant county council: Local Government Act 1972 s 182(4) and Sched 17 paras 5, 6 and 20.

3.1.2 Special and joint planning boards

Under s 1(2) of the 1971 Act the Secretary of State can designate as local planning authorities two or more county councils, or two or more district councils, to act as a united area exercising the functions of a county council and district council, respectively. In such cases the Secretary of State, can, under the same provision, constitute a 'joint planning board' which by virtue of Sched 1 to the 1971 Act is a body corporate. Where this power is exercised in National Park areas the resultant joint board is known as a 'special planning board': Local Government Act 1972 s 184 and Sched 17 para 3. The power has been exercised in relation to the Lake District and Peak District National Parks: (see SIs 1973 Nos 2001 and 2061) these areas are therefore administered by the Lake District Special Planning Board and Peak District Special Planning Board, respectively. Both of these authorities have powers of enforcement of planning control: Local Government Act 1972 s 184(6) and Sched 17 paras 5, 6 and 20.

3.1.3 Urban development corporations

Urban development corporations are the product of the exercise by the Secretary of State of powers conferred on him by Part XVI of the Local Government, Planning and Land Act 1980. Section 134 of this Act enables the Secretary of State, if he considers it expedient in the national interest to do so, to designate land in any area as an urban development area, (a former limitation to metropolitan districts and inner London boroughs having been removed by s 49 of the Housing and Planning Act 1986), and to establish an urban development corporation with appropriate statutory powers to secure the regeneration of the designated area. Initially these powers were exercised on two occasions in that an urban development corporation was established for a defined area of Merseyside by the Merseyside Development Corporation (Area and Constitution) Order 1981 (SI 1981 No 481), and also for London Docklands by the London Docklands Development Corporation (Area and Constitution) Order 1981 (SI 1981 No 998). A further five such corporations have since been established; reference should therefore be made to the Trafford Park Development Corporation (Area and Constitution) Order 1987 (SI 1987 No 179), the Cardiff Bay Development Corporation (Area and Constitution) Order 1987 (SI 1987 No 646), the Black Country Development Corporation (Area and Constitution) Order 1987 (SI 1987 No 922), the Teesside Development Corporation (Area and Constitution) Order 1987 (SI 1987 No 923), and the Tyne and Wear Development Corporation (Area and Constitution) Order 1987 (SI 1987 No 924).

In order to further the statutory objective of regeneration of the urban development areas, the urban development corporations have had planning functions conferred on them by statutory instrument made by the Secretary of State pursuant to s 149 of the 1980 Act. In the words of s 149(1) the effect of conferring these powers is that '. . . an urban development corporation shall be the local planning authority for the whole or any portion of its area in place of any authority which would otherwise be the local planning authority . . .' The planning functions conferred on the first two urban development corporations are specified in the Merseyside Development Corporation (Planning Functions) Order 1981 (SI 1981 No 561), and the London Docklands Development Corporation (Planning Functions) Order 1981 (SI 1981 No 1081). Both of those orders expressly confer enforcement powers: see art 3(b) and Sched 1 to each Order. In relation to the urban development corporations established in 1987 see SI s 1987 Nos 739, 1340, 1341 and 1342.

Although the urban development corporations have enforcement powers conferred on them by the relevant Planning Functions Order they do not have the power to seek an injunction in their own name under s 222 of the Local Government Act 1972 in order to restrain a breach of planning control. In *London Docklands Development Corporation* v *Rank Hovis McDougall Ltd* [1986] JPL 825 the Court of Appeal held that as the definition of 'local authority' which appears in s 270 of the 1972 Act did not include a development corporation, the power to seek an injunction had therefore not been conferred on the corporation. It was thus necessary to invoke the assistance of the Attorney-General by obtaining a fiat to proceed by way of a relator action.

3.2 Enforcement by London borough councils, district councils and county councils

In the area of each London borough and metropolitan district there is only one local planning authority responsible for the planning of the area: see s 1(1) of the 1971 Act. Consequently each such local planning authority is solely responsible for enforcement of planning control. In the shire areas, however, the fact that the county councils and district councils co-exist means that there are two local planning authorities exercising planning functions. By virtue of s 182 of and Sched 16 to the Local Government Act 1972 the planning functions of each local planning authority are exhaustively defined. Thus by para 24(1)(b) of Sched 16, the function of enforcement of planning control is expressly conferred on the district councils. This general rule is, however, qualified by paras 24(2)–(4) of the Sched. These sub-paragraphs qualify the general rule in relation to 'county matters', the nature of which is explained below. The effect of the qualification is as follows:

(i)   If the breach of planning control relates to a county matter the district council must first consult the county council before taking enforcement action: para 24(2);

(ii) If the breach of planning control appears to the county council to relate to a county matter the county council may take enforcement action: para 24(3);

(iii) If the breach of planning control relates to a limited class of county matters (those specified as (a) to (cd) in the list which appears below) then only the county council may take enforcement action: para 24(4).

The definition of 'county matter' is obviously crucial to the determination of whether the county council has powers of enforcement. Paragraph 32 of Sched 16 to the Local Government Act 1972 specifies a list of county matters. The original list has been amended by the Local Government, Planning and Land Act 1980 s 86(4) which added several items and deleted one. As a result of the amendments county matters comprise:

(a)   the winning and working of minerals in, on or under land (whether by surface or underground working) or the erection of any building, plant or machinery
    (i)   which it is proposed to use in connection with the

winning and working of minerals or with their treatment or disposal in or on land adjoining the site of the working; or

(ii) which a person engaged in mining operations proposes to use in connection with the grading, washing, grinding or crushing of minerals;

(*aa*) the use of land, or the erection of any building, plant or machinery on land, for the carrying out of any process for the preparation or adaptation for sale of any mineral or the manufacture of any article from a mineral where

(i) the land forms part of or adjoins a site used or proposed to be used for the winning and working of minerals; or

(ii) the mineral is, or is proposed to be, brought to the land from a site used, or proposed to be used, for the winning and working of minerals by means of a pipeline, conveyor belt, aerial ropeway, or similar plant or machinery, or by private road, private waterway or private railway;

(*b*) the carrying out of searches and tests of mineral deposits or the erection of any building, plant or machinery which it is proposed to use in connection therewith;

(*c*) the disposal of mineral waste;

(*ca*) the use of land for any purpose required in connection with the transport by rail or water of aggregates (that is to say, any of the following, namely

(i) sand and gravel;

(ii) crushed rock;

(iii) artificial materials of appearance similar to sand, gravel or crushed rock and manufactured or otherwise derived from iron or steel slags, pulverised fuel ash, clay or mineral waste),

or the erection of any building, plant or machinery which it is proposed to use in connection therewith;

(*cb*) the erection of any building, plant or machinery which it is proposed to use for the coating of roadstone or the production of concrete or of concrete products or artificial aggregates, where the building, plant or machinery is to be erected in or on land which forms part of or adjoins a site used or proposed to be used

(i) for the winning and working of minerals; or

(ii) for any of the purposes mentioned in sub-para (*ca*) above;

(*cc*) the erection of any building; plant or machinery which it is proposed to use for the manufacture of cement;

(*cd*) the carrying out of operations in, on, over or under land, or a use of land, where the land is or forms part of a site where the operations or use would conflict with or prejudice compliance with a restoration condition or an aftercare condition;

(*d*) (repealed);

(*e*) the carrying out of operations in, on, over or under land, or any use of land, which is situated partly in and partly outside a National Park;

(*f*) the carrying out of any operation which is, as respects the area in question a prescribed operation or an operation of a prescribed class or any use which is, as respects that area, a prescribed use or use of a prescribed class: see the Town and Country Planning (Prescription of County Matters) Regulations 1980 (SI 1980 No 2010).

Examination of this list shows that county matters comprise, in the main, development associated with mineral working and processing. The enforcement role of county councils in these respects is further underlined by the provisions of the Town and Country Planning (Minerals) Act 1981 s 2(2) of which inserted s 1(2B) into the 1971 Act, the effect of which is to constitute each county council as a 'mineral planning authority' in common with each London borough council and metropolitan district council. The 1981 Act confers powers and imposes duties in relation to mineral development, in particular to carry out periodic reviews of mineral sites and to impose restoration and aftercare conditions on grants of planning permission involving mining operations. The 1981 Act thus provides a specific code of legislation which complements the provisions of the 1971 Act. The significance of the 1981 Act can be gauged from the observation that s 1(1) amends s 22 of the 1971 Act (containing the definition of 'development') by inserting a further provision, s 22(3A). This specifies that 'mining operations' include the removal of material of any description from a mineral-working deposit, a deposit of pulverised fuel ash or other furnace ash or clinker, and from a deposit of iron, steel or other metallic slags. It also includes the extraction of minerals from a disused railway embankment.

3.3 Powers to serve a stop notice

The authorities empowered to serve a stop notice are primarily the district councils. Where, however, the matter relates to a 'county matter' (as defined in para **3.2** above) the district planning authority may only serve a stop notice following consultation with the county planning authority. For their part, the county planning authority may serve a stop notice where it appears to them that the matter could properly be considered a county matter: para 24(2), (3). In some cases, however, only the county planning authority may serve a stop notice. These are in respect of the county matters specified in paras (*a*)–(*cd*) above: para 24(4).

In the case of both an enforcement notice and a stop notice, para 51(2) of Sched 16 provides that the validity of such notices shall not be called into question in any legal proceedings on the ground of non-consultation by the district planning authority under para 24(2) or that the county planning authority had no power to serve the notice because it did not relate to a county matter where para 24(3) or (4) applies.

In the areas of the London borough councils and metropolitan district councils, as each of these authorities are by virtue of s 1(1) of the 1971 Act the local planning authority for their respective areas, they have the same powers in relation to stop notices as they have in relation to enforcement notices.

All urban development corporations are empowered to serve a stop notice by virtue of their respective Planning Functions Orders.

3.4 Enforcement by the Secretary of State

Until the coming into force of the Local Government and Planning (Amendment) Act 1981 the Secretary of State had no reserve power to take enforcement action. Although s 276 of the 1971 Act, as originally enacted, conferred a number of reserve powers on the Secretary of State (including a power to serve a stop notice), it was deficient in this respect. Thus the 1981 Act inserted s 276(5A) into the section to enable the Secretary of State to act in default of enforcement proceedings being taken by the local planning authority. Under this provision if the Secretary of State considers it expedient to issue an enforcement notice he must first consult with the local planning authority before proceeding to issue such a notice. The effect of such action from the point of view of the recipient is the same as if the notice had been issued by the local planning authority.

Chapter 4

Restraints on Enforcement Action

4.1 Introduction

Enforcement action by a local planning authority will be ineffective in a number of circumstances, principally involving
limitation by passage of time. Although the local planning authority
are empowered to serve an enforcement notice, in the words of
s 87(1) 'Where it appears to the local planning authority that there
has been a breach of planning control . . .' there are instances in
which there is, in effect, a de facto bar to enforcement action being
taken. If such action is taken the enforcement proceedings can be
defended without undue difficulty. The best-known of these instances is where the so-called 'four-year rule' applies. There are,
however, other circumstances which require consideration and thus
the full list is as follows. These are (a) where the development first
occurred before the end of 1963; (b) where the development is one of
a number of developments protected by the passage of at least four
years since the breach of planning control first occurred; (c) where
the development is the subject of an established use certificate; and
(d) where the development attracts the operation of the principle of
estoppel. With the exception of the last of these, the protection
afforded is the result of the operation of certain statutory provisions.
These provisions are all derived from the four-year limitation period
on enforcement action which once applied (until the coming into
force of the Town and Country Planning Act 1968) to all breaches of
development control.

4.2 Development which first occurred prior to the end of 1963

Prior to the enactment of the Town and Country Planning Act
1968 all breaches of planning control were subject to a limitation
period of four years. After the passage of this period the unauthorised

development could not be controlled by means of an enforcement notice. The 1968 Act modified this principle by removing development in the nature of a material change of use from the scope of the rule, largely to overcome difficulties in applying the rule to cases involving a gradual change of use. All development which had commenced before the end of 1963, however, continued to enjoy the immunity which had been gained by 1968. This immunity is now provided for by s 87(1) of the 1971 Act which empowers local planning authorities to take enforcement action only where 'there has been a breach of planning control after the end of 1963.'

The modification of the four-year limitation period greatly simplifies the task of determining whether enforcement action is competent. Although it remains difficult in some cases to decide whether or not a change of use has become 'material' it is now unnecessary to decide exactly when this occurred because the approach which is to be taken is to compare the present use of the property with that which was being made of the property immediately before 1964. This is clearly illustrated by the decision in *Cheshire County Council* v *Secretary of State for the Environment* (1971) 222 EG 35, a case involving the gradual development of a small haulage business from 1956 to 1968. At that time the site involved also became used for the purposes of storage of containers for short periods before their despatch to their final destination. Enforcement notices were served in 1970 alleging both an intensification of the use of the land by the gradual increase in the scale of activities upon it, and also that introduction of storage of containers onto the site was of itself a material change of use. The Secretary of State upheld the appeals of the developer and quashed the enforcement notices. His decision was challenged, however, on the ground that he appeared to have looked at the history of the site in two phases before concluding that no unauthorised development had occurred, rather than by comparing the current situation with that obtaining at the end of 1963. The Divisional Court held that on construction of the decision letter the Secretary of State had in fact taken the correct approach by looking at the facts at the time of issue of the enforcement notices and comparing them with the position obtaining at the end of 1963, and hence there was no error of law on his part.

A consequence of the requirement of s 87(1) that the enforcement notice must relate to development which has taken place 'after the end of 1963' is that enforcement action cannot require a use which predates 1964 to cease completely. Thus if enforcement action is successfully taken in respect of a use which originated before 1964 but which only became the subject of a material change of use at some time after the end of 1963 then the enforcement notice cannot require total extinguishment of the use but must permit the continuance of the use at its pre-1964 level. This is known as the *Mansi* principle, based on the case of *Mansi* v *Elstree RDC* (1964) 16 P&CR 153. In this case land had been used for many years as a nursery and a number of glass houses were erected upon it. One of these became used in part for shop purposes, a 'secondary' or minor use, but which significantly expanded in 1959 and ultimately became the subject of an enforcement notice. The notice required the recipient to cease using the glass houses for shop purposes. The Minister confirmed the notice on appeal to him but the appellant applied to the High Court to have the Minister's decision overruled since it did not permit the continuation of the secondary use which had been present before the material change of use occurred. The Divisional Court agreed that the requirements of the notice were excessive. Widgery J (as he then was) stated (at p 161):

The Minister should have recognised that a notice requiring discontinuance of all sale of goods went too far and that he ought to have amended the notice . . . to make it perfectly clear that the notice did not prevent the appellant from using the premises for the sale of goods by retail, provided that such sale was on the scale and in the manner to which he was entitled in 1959.

Accordingly, the Divisional Court remitted the notice to the Minister with a direction to amend it. This principle has been applied in many subsequent cases, notably *Trevors Warehouses Ltd* v *Secretary of State for the Environment* (1972) 23 P&CR 215; *Ipswich County Borough Council* v *Secretary of State for the Environment* (1972) 225 EG 797 and *Newport* v *Secretary of State for the Environment* [1980] JPL 596 and *John Pearcy Transport Ltd* v *Secretary of State for the Environment* [1986] JPL 680. Recently, however, the court has taken the view that to direct the Secretary of State to amend an enforcement notice to secure protection of rights under the *Mansi* doctrine is a matter for the discretion of the court. It does not necessarily follow, however, that failure so to direct means that previously established rights are thereby lost for they can be continued without breach of planning control if they are in fact incidental to the lawful use: *North Sea Land Equipment* v *Secretary of State for the Environment* [1982] JPL 384.

Where a use of land first occurred before the beginning of 1964 it is prudent to obtain an established use certificate in respect of it, if possible. See further below, para **4.4**.

4.3 Immunity by passage of time: the 'four-year rule'

Some forms of development, principally those of the operational nature, continue to gain protection from enforcement action if more than four years have elapsed from the date of the breach of planning control. The forms of development which are subject to this rule are specified in s 87(4) of the 1971 Act as follows:

  (a) the carrying out without planning permission of building, engineering, mining or other operations in, on, over or under land; or

  (b) the failure to comply with any condition or limitation which relates to the carrying out of such operations and subject to which planning permission was granted for the development of that land; or

  (c) the making without planning permission of a change of use of any building to use as a single dwellinghouse; or

  (d) the failure to comply with a condition which prohibits or has the effect of preventing a change of use of a building to use as a single dwellinghouse.

It will be observed that the effect of this provision is to permit a local planning authority to take enforcement action in respect of a material change of use which first occurred more than four years before the enforcement notice is issued; the only exception is that immunity is gained where the material change of use involved concerns a change of use to use as a single dwellinghouse.

4.3.1 Calculating the four-year period

Although a local planning authority has the power to serve an enforcement notice as soon as a breach of planning control occurs, it appears that in calculating the four-year period time runs not from commencement of the development but from the time the operation is substantially complete. This is clear from *Ewen Developments Ltd* v *Secretary of State for the Environment and North Norfolk District Council* [1980] JPL 404 and from *Howes* v *Secretary of State for the Environment and Devon County Council* [1984] JPL 439. In the latter case the appellant removed a hedge which fronted onto a highway and then laid hardcore on a grassed area so that access and parking facilities could be provided for his vehicles.

Enforcement action was taken but the appellant argued that the removal of the hedge had occurred outside the four-year period and therefore he was not required to replace it. Moreover, even if he was required to take up the hardcore he could park on the grass. Hodgson J held that if the laying of the hardcore took place within the four-year period the appellant could be required not only to remove it but also to replace the hedge; the two steps were not divisible as they comprised 'a single operation of construction'. The *Ewen Developments Ltd* case also makes it clear that there is no equivalent in construction cases to the *Mansi* rule, described above, which applies only to material changes of use. Thus where embankments were constructed during a period falling partly within and partly outside the four-year period, the enforcement notice could require the removal of the whole of the development, not merely that which took place within the period of four years prior to the issue of the enforcement notice. Further, it appears from *Murfitt* v *Secretary of State for the Environment and East Cambridgeshire District Council* (1980) 40 P&CR 254 that where operational development is involved which is incidental to the implementation of a material change of use, the enforcement notice is valid even if it also requires the removal of the operational aspect of the development. This is so notwithstanding the fact that, viewed alone, the operation is protected by the four-year rule. Thus where land was covered by hardcore to provide a lorry park, the enforcement notice could require the removal of the hardcore as well as the ceasing of the use of the land for parking of the vehicles. Stephen Brown J considered in *Murfitt* that this result could be justified on the ground that s 87(7) required an enforcement notice to specify the steps needed to remedy the breach of planning control, including (under s 87(9)(*a*)) steps required for the purpose of restoring the land to its condition before the development took place.

4.3.2 *Mining operations*

Some variations on the principles which have been discussed so far apply in the case of mining operations, a form of development once described by Lord Denning MR in *Thomas David (Porthcawl) Ltd* v *Penybont RDC* [1972] 1 WLR 1526 as *sui generis*. In this case it was held that where mining operations had taken place during a period substantially in excess of four years before the enforcement notice was issued, the company could not claim the benefit of the four-year rule to permit the mining operations to continue. Lord Denning MR explained that 'In my opinion each shovelful is a mining operation' and therefore it was a separate act of development. A consequence of this approach is that no requirement can be made to restore land from which unauthorised extraction of minerals has taken place more than four years ago.

A further difference, unique to mining operations, is that the four-year period applicable to any breach of a condition or limitation attached to a grant of planning permission for mining operations does not start to run until the breach has come to the attention of the local planning authority. This modification to the normal effect of s 87(4)(b) was effected by the Town and Country Planning (Minerals) Regulations 1971, reg 4.

4.3.3 Change of use and the single dwellinghouse

Under s 87(4)(c) the four-year rule applies to the making without planning permission of a change of use of any building to use as a single dwellinghouse. In such a case it is reasonable to suppose that time runs from the moment of the commencement of the new use. It has been held, however, that the start of the four-year period can be backdated to the time when the conversion works were carried out: *Impey* v *Secretary of State for the Environment* [1983] JPL 167 and *Backer* v *Secretary of State for the Environment* (1984) 47 P&CR 149. In the latter case a small building which had formerly been used as a studio office was the subject of conversion works commencing about six years before the service of the enforcement notice and lasted approximately two years before the occupation began. The occupation was just within the four-year period, but the developer successfully appealed to the High Court against the Secretary of State's decision to uphold the enforcement notice. In the former case Donaldson LJ also accepted that works of conversion might of themselves amount to a material change of use as '. . . these matters have to be looked at in the round'.

4.3.4 Conditions and limitations

Section 87(4)(b) permits the application of the four-year rule to 'any condition or limitation which relates to the carrying out of such operations and subject to which planning permission was granted'. At first sight it is tempting to read this as applying to breach of any condition or limitation attached to a grant of planning permission for operational development. The scope of the provision depends, however, on the meaning of the words 'which relates to the carrying out of such operations'. While judicial preference appears to be to give these words wide scope it does not necessarily follow that some breaches of conditions might not be subject to successful enforcement action even after four years. If a condition is imposed on a planning permission for the construction of a dwellinghouse requiring the occupation of the dwellinghouse to be limited to a person employed or last employed in agriculture, does this relate 'to the carrying out of such operations'? Arguably it does not since the condition is concerned with subsequent use rather than with the building operations. The point does not appear to have been taken in the course of the arguments in a recent case involving agricultural occupancy *Alderson* v *Secretary of State for the Environment* (1984) 49 P&CR 307, in which the decision turned only on the validity of the condition itself.

In *Peacock Homes Ltd* v *Secretary of State for the Environment* (1984) 42 P&CR 20 the Court of Appeal took a broad view of the exemption granted by s 87(4)(*b*). In this case a warehouse was constructed pursuant to a planning permission which limited the time the warehouse was permitted to be on the site: at the end of the specified period the warehouse was to be demolished. Extensions of time were granted by further grants of planning permission but thereafter no further grants of planning permission were obtained. More than four years after the expiry of the last grant the building was still on the site, in consequence of which the local planning authority commenced enforcement proceedings some two years later. The Court of Appeal held that the enforcement notices were out of time as the key words 'which relates to' in the provision were to be interpreted in a general sense and could be taken to mean in this context 'which has to do with' and were therefore appropriate to cover the present situation; a limitation imposed by a condition such as the present could fairly be said to relate to the erection of the building which was only authorised for the limited period. Dillon LJ expressly made the point, however, without giving examples, that there may be some conditions which do not enjoy the protection of the four-year period.

4.4 Protection by means of an established use certificate

Since the general rule is that uses of land are not subject to the four-year rule (except in relation to a change of use to use as a single dwellinghouse), enforcement action can be taken at any time. It has always to be borne in mind, however, that some uses of land gained the protection of the four-year rule before the scope of the rule was altered in 1968. Thus a use could have commenced in 1962 and gained immunity by 1966. If the local planning authority decided to take enforcement action today those concerned with the land might have serious difficulties in showing that the use started before the beginning of 1964. The function of the established use certificate is to provide a ready means of evidencing uses which although **unlawful** have become established. Provision is made for application for, and issue of, established use certificates in ss 94–95 of and Sched 14 to the 1971 Act.

Under s 94(1) a use is an established use if:

(a) it was begun before the beginning of 1964 without planning permission in that behalf and has continued since the end of 1963; or

(b) it was begun before the beginning of 1964 under a planning permission in that behalf granted subject to conditions or limitations, which either have never been complied with or have not been complied with since the end of 1963; or

(c) it was begun after the end of 1963 as the result of a change of use not requiring planning permission and there has been, since the end of 1963, no change of use requiring planning permission.

If a person interested in the land considers that a use has become established he can make an application to the local planning authority for the issue of a certificate. This facility is not, however, available in relation to dwellinghouse use: s 94(2). Nor is it available in respect of an **illegal** use ie one which has continued after an enforcement notice requiring the use to cease has taken effect. In such a case the only use which is permitted is that for which the enforcement notice allows, as any previous existing use has gone: *Nash* v *Secretary of State for the Environment* [1986] JPL 128 and *Vaughan* v *Secretary of State for the Environment* [1986] JPL 840.

Details of the formalities for making such an application are to be found partially in Sched 14 but in particular in art 22 of the GDO and Sched 5 thereto. Falsified claims are to be deprecated; an applicant risks a fine of up to £1,000 (summary conviction) or an unlimited fine and up to two years imprisonment if convicted on indictment: s 94(8).

Unlike the discretion conferred upon local planning authorities to take enforcement action, in the case of an established use certificate the authority is deprived of discretion by s 94(4) which requires the local planning authority to issue a certificate in response to an application if they are satisfied that the claim is made out. Similarly if the local planning authority are not so satisfied the same provision requires that the application must be refused. Under art 22(7) of the GDO the decision should be made within eight weeks of receipt of the application unless a longer period is agreed in writing; if this period (or, as the case may be, the extended period) expires then the application is deemed to be refused: s 94(5). A right of appeal is available to the Secretary of State under s 95, provided the appeal is made within six months of the decision, or any such longer period as he may decide to allow: GDO art 22(9).

While the object of obtaining an established use certificate is clear, to ward off possible enforcement proceedings, the issue of such a certificate does not place a legal restraint on such enforcement action being initiated, it merely acts as a shield to the extent of the matters actually specified in the certificate. Although no doubt the existence of a certificate provides a de facto restraint, the shielding effect is only strictly legally operative if an appeal is made to the Secretary of State against the enforcement notice. At such stage, under s 94(7), the established use certificate is 'conclusive' in relation to the land affected by it, provided the application precedes the issue of the enforcement notice. Careful examination should be made of an established use certificate as it may not apply to the whole of the land on which a particular use has been taking place; also there may be more than one use being made of the land to which the certificate relates. The apparent shielding effect which the certificate provides may therefore be only limited, though it may in some cases even grant unexpected benefits. Thus in *Broxbourne Borough Council* v *Secretary of State for the Environment* [1979] 2 WLR 846 the rural site in question had a long association with various uses associated with timber. From 1960 it became used for storage, sorting and grading of timber in the round. In 1972 an established use certificate was issued which certified the established use as '. . . the storage, sawing, re-sawing and disposal of timber in the round and the storage, maintenance, repair and overhaul of vehicles and plant incidental thereto . . .'. The property became occupied in 1975 by a timber company which used the site as a bulk storage depot for timber planks, without handling any timber in the round and only occasional sawing took place. Having regard to the addition of concrete roadways, the Secretary of State found that the character of the site had changed from a use with rural connotations to one which had the appearance of an industrial timber yard. This change had led to the issue of an enforcement notice, but the Secretary of State decided that the established use certificate operated to protect the use enforced against and hence he quashed the notice. The local planning authority appealed against this decision to the Divisional Court. It was held, however, that it would defeat the object of an established use certificate if it was possible to go back into the history of the site to the point of investigating the factual circumstances prevailing at the time when the use became established. It was therefore necessary to interpret the established use certificate relying on the content of the document itself. Since, in this case, the established use certificate failed to specify the intensity of the use, or the precise nature of it, the result was that the site could continue to be used for the present use even if this was a more intense user than that prevailing at the date of the certificate. Summarising what he described as 'the moral' of the case, Robert Goff J said that it demonstrated that 'planning authorities should exercise great care concerning the terms of established use certificates which they issue. If a certificate is not drawn with care and expressly limited to the precise use in question, then its issue can lead to the consequence that the authority may, through its own act, find itself precluded from preventing a use for which planning permission would not have been granted simply because the certificate had been issued in terms wider than were necessary'. It is to be noted that art 22(1)(*b*) of the GDO requires that an application for an established use certificate should provide 'a description of the use in respect of which a certificate is sought (being a use subsisting at the date when the application is made)'; the Secretary of State has taken the view that this requires a specific description to be given rather than a general one such as 'light industrial purposes', see the appeal decisions, noted at [1972] JPL 121, [1974] JPL 293 and [1982] JPL 800. In the last of these the view was taken that 'general dealing in second hand goods' was too wide.

4.4.1 Scope of the procedure

The utility of the established use certificate facility is probably not limited to unlawful uses as the Secretary of State has held that such a certificate is also applicable to a lawful use, ie one which was in existence on 1 July 1948: see [1985] JPL 801. As such applications are probably comparatively rare today, attention is more likely to be directed to the scope of s 94(1)(a) which requires that the (unlawful) use 'was begun before the begining of 1964 without planning permission in that behalf and has continued since the end of 1963'. Some difficulties have been experienced in interpretation of this provision, including (a) the impact of a grant of planning permission; (b) the meaning of the word 'continued'; and (c) the effect of intensification of a use which first started before 1964. These problems are now considered in turn.

In *Bolivian and General Tin Trust Ltd* v *Secretary of State for the Environment* [1972] 1 WLR 1481 an enforcement notice was served during 1963 in respect of a petrol filling station. On appeal against the enforcement notice the Minister (as he then was) granted planning permission for a limited period. On expiration of the period an application was made for an established use certificate, which was refused by the Secretary of State. On a literal application of the legislation the use had 'begun before the beginning of 1964 without planning permission in that behalf,' but Bean J held that the provision was to be interpreted on the basis that it required an unauthorised use to have started before the beginning of 1964 and for that unauthorised use to have continued in its unauthorised condition ever since the end of 1963. It could, therefore, not apply to a case in which a grant of planning permission has been obtained.

At one time the Secretary of State considered that the word 'continued' had to be given a literal meaning, see for example the decision noted at [1979] JPL 780. This view caused an inconsistency in the legislation to become apparent in that under s 88(2)(e) of the 1971 Act it-is a ground of appeal against an enforcement notice that the breach of planning control occurred before 1964. But to require the use literally to have 'continued' since the end of 1963 until the date of the application deprives the developer of the right to obtain an established use certificate even though enforcement action can be successfully defended. A more relaxed view of the requirement that the use must have 'continued' dispenses with the need for the use to have been physically manifest throughout, and permits the two provisions to remain consistent. The Secretary of State has now adopted this approach see eg [1981] JPL 449 and will regard a use as having been continued provided it has not been superseded by another use or become lost through application of the doctrine of abandonment. In relation to the latter see the leading case of *Hartley* v *Minister of Housing and Local Government* [1970] 1 QB 413.

The third problem is the effect of an intensification of the use.

Under the provisions of s 94(3), which regulates what a certificate may certify, it does not appear to be open to the local planning authority, or the Secretary of State, to issue an established use certificate in relation to a use of land which has intensified since the end of 1963. In *Hipsey* v *Secretary of State for the Environment* [1984] JPL 805 David Widdicombe QC (sitting as a deputy judge) held that the Secretary of State was limited to issuing an established use certificate in the terms specified in the application; as the use in this case had commenced in the present form in 1969 no certificate could be issued notwithstanding the fact that the use was traceable to before 1964. Thus it would appear that there is no equivalent of the *Mansi* principle in the context of established use certificates. Reference should, however, be made to *Bristol City Council* v *Secretary of State for the Environment* (1987) *The Times*, 19 March in which Stuart Smith J held that both the local planning authority and the Secretary of State could issue a certificate in respect of a lesser use than that described in the application.

If an application for an established use certificate is successful, the certificate should be issued in the form specified by art 22(13) of and Sched 6 Part II to the GDO.

4.5 Estoppel

The extent to which a developer can rely on the principle of estoppel in resisting enforcement proceedings is still a matter for some conjecture. Claims to establish an estoppel have arisen in a variety of ways, which in turn have involved varying degrees of difficulty in determining whether there is room for the application of the concept. The common feature is that the developer relies upon a statement made by the local planning authority or an officer of the authority and then acts to his detriment on the strength of it. After a robust start in applying what is a private law principle into the public law field, followed by a period of apparent generosity in favour of the developer, judicial opinion now once again seems restrictive. Indeed, in *Brooks and Burton Ltd* v *Secretary of State for the Environment* (1976) 35 P&CR 27, Lord Widgery CJ issued a stern warning against giving further rein to the doctrine.

A graphic illustration of how an alleged estoppel might be thought to arise is provided by one of the leading cases, that of *Southend-on-Sea Corporation* v *Hodgson (Wickford) Ltd* [1961] 2 All ER 46. A proposed purchaser of a builder's yard wrote to the local planning authority asking whether it could continue to be used as such. The local planning authority replied in unequivocal terms stating that the land 'has an existing user right as a builder's yard and no planning permission is therefore necessary'. Later, after the purchase had been completed, the corporation advised that this view was misconceived and that the use should cease. Then an enforcement notice was served. The Divisional Court held that, just as an estoppel cannot be raised to prevent the carrying out of a statutory duty, so also it could not be raised in relation to the exercise of a statutory discretion, with the result that the enforcement notice took effect.

In many instances the developer can utilise the provisions of s 53 of the 1971 Act to obtain a formal determination of whether planning permission is required for a proposed development, and an authority will be bound by the determination which is given: *Wells* v *Minister of Housing and Local Government* [1967] 1 WLR 1000. Although Lord Denning MR appeared to favour the view that a response given in relation to an informal application under s 53 would also be binding, it seems from the subsequent expression of views in the Court of Appeal in *Western Fish Products Ltd* v *Penwith District Council* (1978) 38 P&CR 7 that this does not represent the conventional wisdom. Rather, the position appears to be that a local planning authority will only be bound by a determination, even if apparently of an informal nature, if it is issued following the making of an application for planning permission. This is because the Court of Appeal considered that a local planning authority could treat an application for planning permission submitted in the form required by the GDO as containing an implied application for a determination under s 53 and hence advise the applicant that planning permission was not required. If this advice is acted upon the developer would have a defence to enforcement action since the authority could not rely on lack of formalities for which the authority is itself responsible.

While it may safely be concluded that the estoppel principle has only a very limited role to play in resisting enforcement proceedings, it is nevertheless the case that in some instances the local planning authority may be bound by certain informalities of procedure. There is, therefore, a second class of case in which estoppel is relevant. In *Lever (Finance) Ltd* v *Westminster City LBC* [1971] 1 QB 222 the Court of Appeal granted a declaration to the appellant company that they were entitled to complete a development on which building work had commenced. After planning permission had been obtained the company's architect wished to revise the site layout. He contacted the local planning authority, submitted a revised plan, and was advised by telephone that as the site alterations were immaterial no further grant of planning permission was required. The effect of the alteration was that the development would be sited closer to existing properties than previously proposed. Efforts by neighbours to halt the development by persuading the local planning authority to take enforcement action proved successful. In the Court of Appeal, however, it was held that as it was a common practice of the authority to make changes in this way, and that the officer concerned had ostensible authority to advise the developer, the local planning authority was bound by his actions. Although this decision was considered 'correct on its facts' by the Court of Appeal in *Western Fish Products Ltd* v *Penwith District Council*, it was nevertheless qualified by the addition of a requirement that the developer must have some evidence to justify his reliance on the officer's statement: ostensible authority alone is not enough. The Secretary of State has subsequently decided, however, in an enforcement appeal decision noted at [1984] JPL 680, that where a long-standing practice existed permitting planning officers to approve minor amendments to proposals for which planning permission had been granted, the developer was entitled to rely on the approved variation and obtain the benefit of the exception established by the Court of Appeal in the *Lever (Finance) Ltd* v *Westminster City LBC* case.

Chapter 5

Procedural Aspects of Enforcement Action

5.1 Introduction

In this chapter an examination is made of some of the procedural aspects of taking enforcement action, in particular the issue of an enforcement notice and the process of service of copies of the notice on the owners and occupiers and other persons having an interest in the land concerned. The law which regulates the content of the notice is considered in Chap 6; together these two chapters are therefore primarily concerned with an explanation of what the local planning authority should do in order to implement a resolution to take enforcement action.

5.2 Initiating the procedure

The discretionary nature of the power to take enforcement action conferred on the local planning authority by s 87(1) indicates that the local planning authority are not under a duty to police a breach of planning control simply because they have become aware of it. Subject to s 256(5A) of the 1971 Act, which confers a reserve power to take enforcement action on the Secretary of State, the decision to enforce is entirely a matter for the authority. That there is no duty to implement the enforcement procedure was confirmed in *Perry* v *Stanborough (Developments) Ltd* (1977) 244 EG 551, despite the inconvenience thereby suffered by the plaintiff in that case. The subjective nature of the power is further underlined by the requirement that the local planning authority must consider it 'expedient' to take the necessary action.

By the same token a local planning authority act within their statutory powers if enforcement action is commenced in good faith when in fact a breach of planning control has not taken place: *Jeary* v *Chailey RDC* (1973) 26 P&CR 280. Moreover, it is not incumbent on the local planning authority to check whether a developer has exhausted any rights to which he may be entitled under the GDO. Thus in *Tidswell* v *Secretary of State for the Environment* (1976) 34 P&CR 152 the local planning authority commenced enforcement action against the operator of a Sunday market in circumstances whereby Class IV.2 of Sched 1 to the GDO (of 1973) applied. Under the GDO 14 days use as a market was permitted development, only 9 of which had been 'used up' by the developer prior to service of the enforcement notice. The Divisional Court held that there was no obligation imposed on the local planning authority to check whether the developer could bring himself within any GDO exemptions before serving the notice: it was enough that no planning permission had been granted by them and it was a matter for the developer to bring himself into any exemption which may be available to him. The Divisional Court went on to hold (on the facts of this particular case) that even though only 9 markets had been held before the enforcement notice was served, the Secretary of State had been entitled to uphold the notice, and rule that the appellant was not entitled to the exemption, when it appeared at the inquiry that the markets had been held every Sunday since their inception. This was because the GDO exemption in question authorised a 14 day use which was purely temporary, not one which was permanent and therefore unauthorised.

If enforcement action is considered expedient, the power to issue an enforcement notice is vested in the local planning authority subject to a power to delegate the function under s 101 of the Local Government Act 1972. This provision permits the authority to 'arrange for the discharge of any of their functions (*a*) by a committee, a sub-committee or an officer of the authority or (*b*) by any other authority'. Delegation of functions under the town and country planning legislation is normally made (via standing orders) to the council's planning committee, which may in turn delegate functions to officers. Whether by an oversight of drafting or otherwise, the provision does not specifically authorise the delegation of functions to the chairman of a committee, despite the common practice of 'chairman's action'. The effect therefore is that the provision does not expressly permit a committee to comprise a single member. In a case where enforcement notices were issued on the authority of the chairman of the planning committee, that of *R* v *Secretary of State for the Environment ex p Hillingdon London Borough Council* [1986] 1 All ER 810, Woolf J held that the Secretary of State had been correct to refuse to consider the developer's appeals since he had correctly regarded the notices as nullities. In another enforcement appeal, noted at [1977] JPL 604, the Secretary of State took the view that where no delegated powers existed in favour of an officer, the notice was a nullity and could not be ratified later.

5.3 Obtaining the relevant information

An enforcement notice is a heavily formalised document to which rules of considerable technicality apply for the purpose of regulating the content and the process of service of copies. In order to comply with the content and service requirements the local planning authority may need to enter onto the land to determine the use(s) which are being made of it, and to obtain details of persons interested in the land. To secure entry and to gather the necessary information the local planning authority can utilise some provisions of the 1971 Act which are of general application, not being limited to use in enforcement proceedings.

5.3.1 *Power of entry: ss 280–281*

Any person who has the written authority of the local planning authority (or of the Secretary of State) may enter onto the land at any reasonable time for the purpose of surveying it in connection with any proposal to issue an enforcement notice: s 280(1)(*c*). If it is desired to exercise this power in relation to occupied land, s 281 of the Act requires at least 24 hours notice to be given to the occupier. A person proposing to make an entry onto land pursuant to s 280 must also be prepared to produce evidence of his authority to enter if he is requested to do so: s 281(1). It is an offence wilfully to obstruct any person exercising the power of entry, punishable by a maximum fine on summary conviction of £100 (level 2 on the standard scale).

5.3.2 *Power to require information concerning interests in the land: s 284*

Under this section, as amended by s 3 of the Town and Country Planning (Amendment) Act 1977 and s 1 of and Sched 1 para 26 to the Local Government and Planning (Amendment) Act 1981, the local planning authority can serve a notice on the occupier of any premises requiring him to provide specified information. Such a notice may also be served on any person who is (whether directly or indirectly) in receipt of rent in respect of the premises. The requirements of the notice must be satisfied within 21 days, or any longer period which may be specified in the notice, time running from the date following the day of service.

The information which can be elicited under this provision is detailed in s 284(1A) as follows: (*a*) the nature of the interest in the premises of the person on whom the notice is served; (*b*) the name and address of any other person known to him as having an interest in the premises; (*c*) the purpose for which the premises are being used; (*d*) the time when that use began; (*e*) the name and address of any person known to the person on whom the notice is served as having used the premises for that purpose; (*f*) the time when any activities being carried out on the premises began. The word 'interest' is not defined by the 1971 Act, but may probably be regarded as having similar scope to the same word as it appears in s 87(5) which regulates on whom a copy of the enforcement notice must be served (see para **5.4** below).

Two offences are created by s 284(2), (3) for failure to co-operate with the local planning authority. If the notice is simply not complied with, and the recipient does not have a reasonable excuse, he is liable to a maximum fine of £400 (level 3 on the standard scale). If, however, the recipient knowingly makes a false statement in response to the notice he is liable to a maximum fine of £1,000; if convicted on indictment there is no maximum fine and a term of imprisonment for up to two years may be imposed, or both.

A similar power to require information to be given to them is also available to the local planning authority under the Local Government (Miscellaneous Provisions) Act 1976 s 16. This provision permits a notice to be served on the occupier, the freeholder, mortgagee, or lessee, or the person who is (whether directly or indirectly) in receipt of rent for the land, or the manager of the land (if any). The notice requires the recipient to provide details of his interest, and the name and address of the occupier, and details of any other person on whom a notice could have been served by the local planning authority had the authority known the relevant details. The section differs from s 284 of the 1971 Act in several respects. First, the period for compliance can be limited to 14 days beginning with the date on which the notice is served; second, the offences of failure to comply and tendering false information both carry the same maximum penalty of a fine of £2,000 (level 5 on the standard scale); lastly the range of information which can be elicited is less than that which can be required under a s 284 notice (no information can be required in relation to uses and activities). The requirements for service of notices are considered below.

Mention should also be made of s 124 of the Land Registration Act 1925. This provision allows the registrar to provide information to local authorities (and the Secretary of State) on receiving a request for assistance. The detail which can be provided is 'such particulars and information as (the local authority) are by law entitled to require owners of property to furnish to them direct'. Having regard to the privacy of the register this method should be used sparingly. As well as identifying the land the local planning authority should state the purpose, with reference to appropriate statutory provisions (in this case s 87) for which the information is required.

5.4 Issue of the notice and service of copies

In exercise of their discretionary power the local planning authority may (in the words of s 87(1)) '. . . issue a notice requiring the breach to be remedied and serve copies of the notice in accordance with subs (5) of this section'. Section 87(5) goes on to provide that 'A copy of an enforcement notice shall be served, not later than 28 days after the date of its issue and not later than 28 days before the date specified in the notice as the date on which it is to take effect (a) on the owner and on the occupier of the land to which it relates; and (b) on any other person having an interest in that land, being an interest which in the opinion of the authority is materially affected by the notice'.

These provisions therefore contemplate a two-stage process. At the first stage the local planning authority will prepare the enforcement notice and retain it in their offices. Department of the Environment Circular 26/81 entitled The Local Government and Planning (Amendment) Act 1981 explains in para 3 of the Annex that, in contrast to the position which obtained prior to the 1981 Act, there is now only one enforcement notice which will take effect on the date specified therein, and that each of the parties with an interest in the land will have to be served with a copy of the notice. The time allowed for service of copies is a maximum of 28 days, but para 5 of the Circular emphasises that this requirement should be complied with as soon as practicable and that it will be unusual for 28 days to be needed to achieve service. Even in cases where the time needed for service is comparatively short, the revised arrangements introduced by the 1981 Act overcame a difficulty illustrated by the decision in *Bambury* v *Hounslow London Borough Council* [1966] 2 All ER 532. In this case the Divisional Court held that enforcement notices relating to the same alleged breach of planning control were invalid as they were served on different days with the result that they came into effect at different times; this was inconsistent with the statutory hypothesis that there could only be one enforcement notice, not two notices differing in an essential particular.

5.4.1 Persons entitled to service of a copy of the enforcement notice

The requirement imposed by s 87(5) is to serve a copy of a notice on the owner and occupier, and any other person having an interest in the land. Who is an 'owner' or an 'occupier' for these purposes, and what is a qualifying 'interest'? Of these words only 'owner' is defined by the 1971 Act (s 290(1)) as 'a person, other than a mortgagee not in possession, who whether in his own right or as trustee for any other person, is entitled to receive the rack rent of the land, or where the land is not let at a rack rent, would be so entitled if it were so let'. It appears that this does not include a freeholder who has let at less than a rack rent: *London Corporation* v *Cusack-Smith* (1955) 5 P&CR 65.

The word 'occupier' does not extend to include everyone who is in de facto occupation of the land at the time the copies of the enforcement notice are served. On the other hand it is not necessary for persons in occupation to have a legal interest in the land to rank as an 'occupier' for the purposes of s 87(5). These propositions are based on the decisions of the Court of Appeal and of the Divisional Court in *Stevens* v *Bromley London Borough Council* [1972] 2 WLR 605 and *Scarborough Borough Council* v *Adams and Adams* [1983] JPL 673, respectively. In the former case the unauthorised development consisted of a caravan site upon which the caravan dwellers were owner-occupiers of their caravans holding licences from the site owner. It was held that whether or not a licensee is an 'occupier' is a question of fact and degree, relevant factors being whether the alleged occupier was a long-stay resident or merely transient and whether the licensee enjoyed a substantial degree of control over his caravan and the plot on which it was situated. In this instance the Court of Appeal was satisfied that the caravan dwellers were 'occupiers' and hence entitled to service.

The position of trespassers who stationed caravans in a lay-by for 18 months was considered in *Scarborough Borough Council* v *Adams and Adams*. In resisting a prosecution for failure to comply with the requirements of the notice the defendants argued that as trespassers they could not be considered occupiers of the land and that proceedings under the Town and Country Planning Act 1971 were therefore wholly inappropriate. The Divisional Court held that the local authority could serve a copy of the notice on any person they thought fit but, in any event, in this instance the trespassers were properly to be considered 'occupiers' having regard to the length of time the unauthorised encampment had lasted.

Other persons entitled to service of a copy of the notice are those who have an 'interest' which, in the words of s 87(5)(*b*), is one 'which in the opinion of the authority is materially affected by the notice'. In *Stevens* v *Bromley London Borough Council* (supra) Salmon LJ took the view (at p 611) that 'interest' is confined to a legal or equitable interest and 'does not include an interest in the loose or colloquial sense of someone being interested in the land'. The Secretary of State has, however, expressed the opinion that a prospective licensee of land which it was proposed to use as a market in breach of planning control was to be regarded as a person having an interest: see [1972] JPL 604. As will be seen, the significance of inclusion of a party within the scope of the word 'interest' is that a right of appeal against an enforcement notice can be utilised.

5.4.2 *What constitutes service?*

To comply with s 87(5) the copies of the enforcement notice must be 'served'. This process is regulated by another provision of the 1971 Act which is of general application, s 283. The section applies to all notices which have to be given or served under the 1971 Act and provides (s 283(1)) that service is achieved if (*a*) the notice is delivered to the person of the recipient; or (*b*) it is left at the usual or last known place of abode of that person, or at an address for service given by him; or (*c*) it is sent in a prepaid registered letter, or by the recorded delivery service, addressed to that person at his usual or last known place of abode, or to an address for service given by him; or (*d*) in the case of a company, by delivering it to the secretary or clerk of the company at the registered or principal office, or sending it in a prepaid registered letter, or by the recorded delivery service, addressed to the secretary or clerk at that office. To similar effect is s 233 of the Local Government Act 1972, which also provides for service of notices. This provision adds, however, that a document which has to be served on a partnership should be delivered to or posted to a partner, or a person having the control or management of the partnership business, at the address of the principal office of the partnership.

There is a presumption of delivery if the postal method of service is selected and the time of service is not critical. Under the Interpretation Act 1978 s 7, service is effected at the time at which the letter would be delivered in the ordinary course of post. Although in enforcement proceedings the time of delivery is important (since at least 28 days must elapse after completion of service of copies before the enforcement notice can come into effect) it was held in *Moody* v *Godstone RDC* [1966] 1 WLR 1085 that the time of delivery is not critical. Hence the presumption of delivery is irrebuttable by evidence that the notice did not arrive at the time which could be expected in the ordinary course of post. If the notice does not arrive at all, however, the presumption of service is rebuttable eg if the postal packet is returned marked 'gone away': *Hewitt* v *Leicester Corporation* (1969) 20 P&CR 629.

If it is chosen not to use the post there must be delivery to the person concerned or it must be left as described in s 283(1)(*b*) above. In *Borough of Morecambe and Heysham* v *Warwick* (1958) 9 P&CR 307 it was held to be sufficient service to deliver to another person at the place of business of the person on whom the notice is to be served if that other person promises to give it to the person to be served. Also in *J J Steeples* v *Derbyshire County Council* [1981] JPL 582 it was held that a notice had been 'left' (and therefore served) when placed in a box at the end of the plaintiff's path in circumstances where it was usual to place mail in the box rather than deliver it by inserting it through the letter-box of the plaintiff's house.

In some cases the local planning authority may not have succeeded in identifying all the persons entitled to service of copies of the notice, even after using the procedure prescribed by s 284. In such a case service can still be achieved by compliance with s 283(2)(*a*) or (*b*). The former paragraph applies where reasonable inquiry has been made and the name of any person having an interest has not been discovered, or that of an occupier. In such a case the notice can be addressed simply to 'the owner' or 'the occupier' (as necessary) of the premises; service is achieved if any of the methods of service described in s 283(1)(*a*)–(*c*) are used. Alternatively, under s 283(2)(*b*), if the notice is sent to the premises in a prepaid registered letter or by the recorded delivery service, or is delivered to any person on the premises, or simply attached in a conspicuous manner to some object on the premises, then service is deemed to have taken place if both the envelope and notice are marked 'Important – This Communication affects your Property', a form of words prescribed by reg 15 of the Town and Country Planning General Regulations 1976 (SI 1976 No 1419). Again reasonable inquiry must have been made before resorting to this method.

Finally, provision is made in s 283(3) for service in the case of land, part of which is not occupied. Here the copy of the enforcement notice is taken to be served on all relevant parties if it is addressed to 'the owners and any occupiers' of that part of the land and is attached in a conspicuous manner to some object on the land.

5.4.3 *Failure to comply with service requirements*

One of the issues which has featured in the case-law to which enforcement has given rise is the effect of a defect of service, or an omission to effect service on a person who is entitled to receive a copy of the notice. While careful attention to these matters is still essential, much of the scope for technical objections was removed by amendments which were made by s 16 of the Town and Country Planning Act 1968. This Act adopted the twin devices of making a defect of service a ground of appeal to the Secretary of State, and of granting the Secretary of State a power to disregard certain defects of service. Under the 1971 Act the ground of appeal is as specified in s 88(2)(*f*) ie 'that copies of the enforcement notice were not served as required by s 87(5) of this Act'. This right of appeal is available to anyone who has an interest in the land whether or not a copy of the enforcement notice has been served on him. With regard to the power to disregard defects, reference should be made to s 88A(3) of the 1971 Act. Under this provision the Secretary of State may disregard the fact that a person required to be served with a copy of the enforcement notice has not been served if no substantial prejudice has been caused to the appellant or the person who was not served. This power is examined further in Chap 7 which deals with appeals to the Secretary of State.

Two further points may be made at this juncture. First, a limited defence is available under s 243(2) to a defendant in criminal proceedings (brought under s 89(5)) who had no knowledge of the enforcement notice. Secondly, the Court of Appeal has held in *R v Greenwich London Borough Council ex p Patel* [1985] JPL 851 that judicial review is not normally available to an applicant who has not been served as the enforcement notice is not thereby rendered a nullity.

5.5 Entry in the register of enforcement notices and stop notices

As soon as practicable after the issue of an enforcement notice, and not more than 14 days afterwards, an entry must be made in this register which is compiled and maintained under s 92A of the 1971 Act. This provision, which was inserted into the 1971 Act by s 1 of and para 6 of the Sched to the 1981 Act, requires the district council or London borough council to keep a register containing the information prescribed by means of a development order. The Town and Country Planning General Development (Amendment) (No 2) Order 1981 (SI 1981 No 1569) added art 21A to the GDO of 1977 and requires the register to contain the following information about any enforcement notice which is issued in respect of any land in the area of the district council:

- (*a*) the address of the land to which the notice relates or a plan by reference to which its situation can be ascertained;
- (*b*) the name of the issuing authority;
- (*c*) the date of issue of the notice;
- (*d*) the date of service of copies of the notice;
- (*e*) a statement or summary of the breach of planning control alleged and the requirements of the notice, including the period within which any required steps are to be taken;
- (*f*) the date specified in the notice as the date on which it is to take effect;
- (*g*) information on any postponement of the date on which the notice is to take effect (due to the making of an appeal to the Secretary of State) and the date of the final determination or withdrawal of any appeal;
- (*h*) the date of service of any stop notice together with a summary of the activity prohibited;
- (*i*) the date on which the local planning authority are satisfied that steps required by the notice are complied with.

It will be seen from this list that further entries in the register will be necessary subsequent to the issue of the enforcement notice. In each case the entry must be made as soon as practicable and not more than 14 days from the occurrence of the event to which it relates. Where the enforcing authority is not the district planning authority but the county planning authority, the latter must supply the relevant information to the district planning authority for the area in which the land is situated within 14 days: art 21A(6).

If the enforcement notice is subsequently quashed by the Secretary of State on appeal to him (or if it is simply withdrawn by the enforcing authority) the relevant register entries must then be removed: art 21A(2). The county council must also keep the district council advised of such matters (within 14 days of their occurrence) so that the register can be correctly maintained.

The object of the register is to give ready access to information about enforcement proceedings without the need to make a search in the local land charges register. To this end the district council (or London borough council) must (a) include as part of the register an index of affected addresses to enable register entries to be traced; (b) keep the register at their office (except that it is permissible to keep part of the register at a place in the area of the district to which that part relates); and (c) keep the register available for public inspection at all reasonable hours without charge.

Chapter 6

Content of the Enforcement Notice

6.1 Introduction

Having examined the procedural aspects of enforcement action, attention now passes to the content of the enforcement notice itself. Much attention is always focussed on the drafting and content of a notice, not simply to determine the burden which is being imposed by the local planning authority, but more particularly to determine the strategy which is to be adopted for challenging the notice. In this connection it must be borne in mind that there is a direct link between the content of a notice and its legal effect. Although this chapter concentrates on the required content of a notice, treatment is also given to the consequences of failure to comply with the relevant provisions of the 1971 Act.

There is a substantial body of case-law dealing with the legal effect of a notice which is in some way defective; much of this authority is concerned with the question whether a notice is a 'nullity' or is 'invalid'. These concepts are explained in more detail in the next chapter but it will be appreciated that some use must be made of this jargon at this stage. All that need be said at this juncture, however, is that if a notice is **defective on its face** because it suffers from an error of omission or commission then, depending on the effect of the error, it may be regarded as a **nullity** and of no legal effect whatsoever. A notice which is **invalid** is one which is not patently defective but which contains an error and is liable to be quashed on appeal to the Secretary of State, or in some cases by application for judicial review in the High Court, the former instances being far more numerous than the latter. It is also particularly helpful to bear in mind that s 88A(2) confers a power on the Secretary of State to correct any informality, defect or error in an enforcement notice, or give directions for varying its terms, if he is satisfied that the correction or variation can be made without injustice to the appellant or to the local planning authority. Exercise of this power enables the Secretary of State to put into order an enforcement notice which is defective but is not an outright nullity.

6.2 Content of the notice and accompanying documents

In the first instance it is desirable to list the required contents of any enforcement notice as prescribed by statute and statutory instrument (the Town and Country Planning (Enforcement Notices and Appeals) Regulations 1981) followed by a more detailed description of each requirement. Great care must be exercised by the local planning authority in drafting the notice as the relevant provisions of the 1971 Act require the enforcement notice not only to require the breach of planning control to be remedied (s 87(1)) but also to 'specify' the following:

(a) the matters alleged to constitute a breach of planning control: s 87(6);

(b) the steps required by the local planning authority to be taken in order to remedy the breach: s 87(7);

(c) the period within which any step specified in the notice by the local planning authority is to be taken (different periods may be allowed for different steps): s 87(8);

(d) the reasons why the local planning authority consider it expedient to issue the notice: s 87(12)(a) and reg 3(a) of the 1981 Regulations;

(e) the precise boundaries of the land to which the notice relates, whether by reference to a plan or otherwise: s 87(12)(a) and reg 3(b) of the 1981 Regulations;

(f) the date on which the notice is to come into effect: s 87(13). Two model forms of enforcement notice, reflecting these requirements are contained in the Appendix to Department of the Environment Circular 38/81 entitled 'Planning and Enforcement Appeals' and are reproduced in Appendix 1 to this book. These model notices have been drafted to apply to either operational development or to development comprising a material change of use; the local planning authority should therefore select the form which is appropriate to the type of development with which they are concerned. No model notice appears in the Circular dealing with breach of a planning condition. In such a case the local planning authority will need to prepare a notice having regard to the model forms.

6.2.1 Accompanying documents

The notice itself must be accompanied, in accordance with s 87(12)(*b*), by an explanatory note which gives advice about the appeal procedure as applied by s 88 of the 1971 Act. The content of the explanatory note is prescribed by reg 4 of the 1981 Regulations and must include:

(*a*) a copy of ss 87–88B of the 1971 Act, or a summary which includes the information that (i) there is a right of appeal to the Secretary of State against the enforcement notice, (ii) an appeal must be made in writing to the Secretary of State before the date specified in the enforcement notice as the date on which it is to take effect, (iii) the grounds on which an appeal can be made under s 88; and

(*b*) a notification that an appellant must submit a written statement to the Secretary of State (either on giving notice of appeal or within 28 days of being required to do so by the Secretary of State) which specifies the grounds of the appeal and gives a brief statement of the facts on which he intends to reply in support of each ground of appeal.

This notice will normally take the form of provision of a copy of the DoE/Welsh Office explanatory booklet '*Enforcement Notice Appeals – A Guide to Procedure*' (revised 1985). This document is referred to in DoE Circular 20/85 entitled 'Town and Country Planning Act 1971: Enforcement Appeals and Advertisement Appeals', para 9 of Appendix 1 of which summarises the administrative procedure for service of copies of an enforcement notice. In addition to serving a copy of the enforcement notice, the local planning authority should enclose (i) a copy of the official appeal form; (ii) a further copy of the enforcement notice (and of any enclosure) which can be sent to the Secretary of State on lodging an appeal; and (iii) a copy of the explanatory booklet. A model covering letter is also printed in the Annex to Circular 38/81. Although this model letter makes reference to the fee which is payable on lodging an appeal, the local planning authority is no longer required to calculate this as the correct fee payable will be calculated by the Department of the Environment: see para 2 of Circular 20/85. The local planning authority should, however, emphasise to the recipient of the copy of the enforcement notice etc that any appeal must be **received** by the Secretary of State

before the date on which the enforcement notice is to take effect, in order to take into account the effect of the decision of Hodgson J in *Lenlyn Ltd* v *Secretary of State for the Environment* [1984] JPL 482: an appeal received on or after the relevant date is out of time.

6.3 The matters alleged to constitute a breach of planning control: s 87(6)

A general test which is applicable to the drafting of any aspect of an enforcement notice, but which is particularly pertinent to this and the next following requirement, was stated by Upjohn LJ in *Miller-Mead* v *Minister of Housing and Local Government* [1963] 2 QB 196 at 219 as follows: '. . . does the notice tell (the recipient) fairly what he has done wrong and what he must do to remedy it?' This test, which has been repeated and applied in many subsequent cases, does not, however, require an excessive degree of formalism to be achieved in drafting a notice. As Lord Denning MR put it (at p 208) in the same case, having explained that the enactment of the Caravan Sites and Control of Development Act 1960 conferred appellate jurisdiction on the Minister with powers to vary enforcement notices, '. . . the legislature has disposed of the proposition that there must be a strict and rigid adherence to formalities', a reference to the strict judicial approach previously seen in *East Riding County Council* v *Park Estate (Bridlington) Ltd* [1957] AC 223; *Francis* v *Yiewsley & West Drayton UDC* [1958] 1 QB 478, and *Cater* v *Essex County Council* [1960] 1 QB 424. Subsequently, in *Ormston* v *Horsham RDC* [1965] 63 LGR 452, Lord Denning MR said that he was 'glad that this court in *Miller-Mead* rejected all these technical considerations. It is plain from that case that an enforcement notice is not to be regarded with the strict eye of a conveyancer'.

To describe the manner in which Upjohn LJ's test has been applied regard may be had to *Eldon Garages Ltd* v *Kingston-upon-Hull County Borough Council* [1974] 1 All ER 358 in which the local planning authority had served an enforcement notice stating that it appeared to the council that 'you are contravening the provisions of the Town and Country Planning Acts by the use of the (site) by the parking of motor vehicles. . . .' and referred to s 15 of the Town and Country Planning Act 1968 which was the relevant provision in force at the time of the commencement of the enforcement action. The developer sought to obtain a declaration that the enforcement notice was a nullity on the basis that it did not specify the matters alleged to constitute a breach of planning control. Templeman J held that in order to 'specify the matters' it was not sufficient merely to state the facts as understood by the local planning authority but it was also necessary for the notice to link the facts, if only indirectly, to the statutory definition of a breach of planning control contained in what is now s 87(3). This had, however, been achieved in this case by use of the words 'unauthorised development' in that part of the notice which dealt with the steps required to remedy the breach as this could only indicate that the matter involved a development without the grant of planning permission (rather than a breach of a condition attached to a grant). The learned judge also held that it was not necessary to adhere strictly to statutory 'magic' expressions such as 'breach of planning control' or that 'they (the council) consider it expedient' to issue an enforcement notice. For a further example see *Bristol Stadium Ltd* v *Brown* [1980] JPL 107 in which the Divisional Court held that a notice was valid which described the general activity to which objection was being taken; it was not necessary to spell out precisely what the activities in question were, but that although examples were given in the notice it was not rendered defective by omission of a full list comprising further aspects of the same general activity. Lord Widgery CJ stated 'draftsmen of enforcement notices . . . should produce notices which were fair and understandable and should be notices which an ordinary person could read and fairly understand what his rights were'.

This approach to the construction of enforcement notices must be seen against a background of a long-standing requirement that the notice must make clear which part of the definition of breach of planning control stated in s 87(3) is involved, ie either development without a grant of planning permission or failure to comply with any conditions or limitations subject to which planning permission has been granted. This rule, which has the authority of the House of Lords in *East Riding County Council* v *Park Estate (Bridlington) Ltd*, in which a notice which read 'the development or other matter hereunder specified appears to (the county council) to be in contravention of planning control' was held to be invalid. This was because it did not make clear whether the breach was in contravention of development control under the 1947 Act or by virtue of previous legislation. The rule was applied by Templeman J in *Eldon Garages Ltd* v *Kingston-upon-Hull County Borough Council* who stated (at p 361) that 'the notice must make clear whether the authority is alleging that the recipient is guilty of development without planning permission or guilty of a breach of a condition subject to which planning permission was granted'. It was not necessary, however, to specify the nature of the breach in these terms 'provided that it is clear in the notice which limb is being alleged'.

More recently, however, the judiciary have not insisted on maintaining this distinction. Thus in *Rochdale Metropolitan Borough Council* v *Simmonds* [1981] JPL 191 the Divisional Court pointed out that the **nature** of the breach was not required to be specified by the 1971 Act, only the **matters** alleged to constitute the breach. Similarly, in *Scott* v *Secretary of State for the Environment* [1983] JPL 108 Mr David Widdicombe QC (sitting as a deputy judge) expressed a strong obiter dictum to the effect that the type of breach of planning control involved did not need to be specified. The matter should, however, be regarded as unconcluded at this stage.

If the notice does refer to a category of breach of planning control but the draftsman selects the wrong category, it would appear that the notice is not a nullity but may nevertheless be invalid and therefore liable to be quashed by the Secretary of State. In *Copeland Borough Council* v *Secretary of State for the Environment* (1976) 31 P&CR 403 a developer constructed a house but used roof tiles of a colour which was in breach of a condition of the planning permission. Rather than refer to this condition, the notice alleged that the roof had been constructed without permission. This therefore indicated that the local planning authority had perceived the breach of planning control to be an act of development without a grant of planning permission at all, in which case, as the Divisional Court held, the correct allegation should have been the construction of the house without planning permission. The court agreed, perhaps rather surprisingly, that the authority could draft an enforcement notice based on the unauthorised development limb of the definition of breach of planning control since a development which does not comply with a condition could in some cases be regarded as wholly unauthorised. See also *Garland* v *Minister of Housing and Local Government* (1968) 20 P&CR 93. Some minor comfort for the draftsman is, however, provided by s 243(5) of the 1971 Act which provides that it is not necessary to distinguish between conditions and limitations if the enforcement notice is based on a breach of a condition or limitation attached to a grant of planning permission.

Either (or both) of these terms can be used in an enforcement notice without fear of successful challenge to the validity of the notice.

A further consideration is whether a notice must not only select the correct part of the definition of breach of planning control, but also (in the case of unauthorised development) distinguish between development of the operational nature and development comprising a material change of use. In *Scott* v *Secretary of State for the Environment* (supra) the learned deputy judge decided that enforcement notices which had identified the correct type of breach of planning control did not need to go on to specify the relevant category of development. David Widdicombe QC stated that there was nothing in s 87 which required the category of development to be specified. He therefore stated 'If the type of breach which was referred to in s 87 did not have to be specified, then a fortiori, the category of development which was not referred to in s 87 did not have to be specified'. Where the notice incorrectly identifies the category of development it may be possible for the Secretary of State to vary its terms acting under the power conferred by s 88A(2). This possibility is discussed in the next chapter in which this important provision is examined.

6.4 The steps required by the local planning authority to be taken: s 88(7)

The full provisions of the 1971 Act dealing with the steps which must be taken extend to three subsections of s 87, though the main provision is s 87(7). In order to discuss these provisions it is necessary to set them out in full. Subsections (7), (9) and (10) of s 87 provide:

(7) An enforcement notice shall also specify
    (*a*) any steps that are required by the authority to be taken in order to remedy the breach;
    (*b*) any steps as are referred to in subs (10) of this section and are required by the authority to be taken.

(9) In this section 'steps to be taken in order to remedy the breach' means (according to the particular circumstances of the breach) steps for the purpose
    (*a*) of restoring the land to its condition before the development took place; or
    (*b*) of securing compliance with the conditions or limitations subject to which planning permission was granted, including
      (i) the demolition or alteration of any building or works;

(ii) the discontinuance of any use of land; and

(iii) the carrying out on land of any building or other operations.

(10) The steps mentioned in subsection (7)(b) of this section are steps for the purpose;

(a) of making the development comply with the terms of any planning permission which has been granted in respect of the land; or

(b) of removing or alleviating any injury to amenity which has been caused by the development.

These subsections, which were substituted by the 1981 Act, significantly altered and improved the provisions contained in the 1971 Act by giving the local planning authority more flexibility in specifying the remedial action which is to be taken. These provisions continue to place the same heavy emphasis on the remedial purpose of enforcement which was manifested by the original legislation and so tend to suggest that the local planning authority should specify steps which will secure total eradication of the unauthorised development. It is at least arguable, however, that the use of the words 'any steps' in s 87(7)(a), replacing the words 'the steps' which appeared in the 1971 Act (as originally enacted) indicate that it is within the power of the local planning authority to require less than total removal of the unauthorised development. Such 'under-enforcement' had previously received judicial approval in *Iddenden* v *Secretary of State for the Environment* [1972] 1 WLR 1433 and hence may now have been placed on a more secure statutory footing. The Secretary of State has advised in para 6 of the Annex to Circular 26/81 that the effect of the changes 'is to give local planning authorities more efficacious powers to formulate the requirements of an enforcement notice so as to bring about precisely the effect they consider appropriate to remedy a breach of planning control, instead of being limited. . . . to requiring steps which will restore the land to its prior condition or will secure compliance with planning conditions or limitations which have been breached'. Commenting on the effect of s 87(10), the Circular advises in para 8 of the Annex that the provisions 'are particularly intended to enable the local planning authority to deal effectively with the situation where unlawful development has taken place, but the authority had already granted, or are prepared to grant planning permission, provided that appropriate steps are taken to make the actual development less environmentally harmful'. The paragraph also explains that the authority could therefore require removal of only part of a building which has been constructed in excess of that approved by a grant of planning permission and describes s 87(10)(*a*) as being apt to deal with the problem which was encountered in *Copeland Borough Council* v *Secretary of State for the Environment*. Referring to s 87(10)(*b*), para 8 of the Annex goes on to state that:

Alternatively, a local planning authority might want to require the carrying out of a landscaping or tree-planting scheme; or to require the putting up of fencing; or to require the opening hours of a service establishment to be limited so as not to cause disturbance to its neighbours in the locality. Depending upon the particular circumstances, the steps which can be required by subsection (10)(*b*) of section 87 are considered apt for purposes of this sort.

6.4.1 Clarity in specifying the steps

Since the obligation on the local planning authority is to 'specify', the question of nullity for failure to comply with this requirement is again an issue of importance. In the leading case of *Miller-Mead* v *Minister of Housing and Local Government* Upjohn LJ said (at p 226) that a notice would be a nullity if 'upon its true construction the notice was hopelessly ambiguous and uncertain so that the owner or occupier . . . could not tell with reasonable certainty what steps he had to take to remedy the alleged breach'. A clear example of this rule is provided by *Metallic Protectives Ltd* v *Secretary of State for the Environment* [1976] JPL 167 in which the enforcement notice alleged breach of a condition attached to a grant of planning permission for factory premises which required that no nuisance should be caused to the residential properties in the area by reason of the omission of noise, vibration, smoke, smell, fumes, soot, ash, dust or grit. The notice required installation of 'satisfactory sound-proofing of a compressor and for all possible action to be taken to minimise the effects created by the use of acrylic paint'. Lord Widgery CJ accepted that the notice therefore imposed a continuous or open-ended obligation so that it was impossible for the enforcees to be sure that compliance had been achieved. The notice was so defective that it could not possibly be amended by the Secretary of State. Being a nullity from the start 'there is no place for it but the wastepaper basket'.

A further example, in which Upjohn LJ's dictum was directly applied, is the decision of the Divisional Court in *London Borough of Hounslow* v *Secretary of State for the Environment and the Indian Gymkhana Club Ltd* [1981] JPL 510. Two enforcement notices required those served 'to comply or seek compliance' with a planning condition requiring demolition of a building. The Secretary of State formed the view that there was a clear difference between the words 'to comply' and 'or seek compliance' and hence it was not possible for the appellants to know exactly what was being required. While the broad intention of the notices was not in doubt they were nevertheless clearly ambiguous. On an appeal by the local planning authority Ackner LJ held that the words 'or seek compliance' could not be regarded as pointless verbiage; since the recipient therefore had an alternative to actual compliance the notice was hopelessly ambiguous and uncertain. See also *Dudley Bowers Amusements Enterprises Ltd* v *Secretary of State for the Environment* (1985) 278 EG 313.

The test whether or not the notice is 'hopelessly ambiguous and uncertain' is such that some seemingly doubtful notices are not nullities. In *Ivory* v *Secretary of State for the Environment* [1985] JPL 795 a planning consent existed for livery stables but the land was additionally used for show jumping, equestrian competitions, and for lectures by famous riders. An enforcement notice was issued which required 'the use of the land for the holding of show jumping events and other equestrian competitions to be discontinued'. It was alleged that the appellant could not tell with certainty (*a*) whether demonstration of show jumping was a show jumping event; (*b*) whether the notice forbade events which were not competitions; (*c*) whether a pony club camp was an equestrian competition if participating children competed against each other in teams. Kennedy J held that although some doubtful cases could be imagined the notice was principally directed to preventing competition activities and that it was in the end a matter of fact and degree. Having regard to the background, which was known to both the local planning authority and the appellant, the wording of the enforcement notice did not fall foul of the test proposed by Upjohn LJ in *Miller-Mead* and accepted by Ackner LJ in the *Hounslow* case. See also *Rhymney Valley District Council* v *Secretary of State for Wales* [1985] JPL 27.

The knowledge which the owner or occupier of the land has of the history of the use of the land is an important factor in considering whether an enforcement notice is a nullity. This point, alluded to briefly by Kennedy J in *Ivory* v *Secretary of State for the Environment*, is well illustrated by the decision of the Court of Appeal in *Ormston* v *Horsham RDC* [1965] 63 LGR 452 in which the enforcement notice required the appellant to remove certain buildings, discontinue a car parking use, and to 'restore the land to its condition before the development' without specifying the exact nature of the steps required to achieve the restoration. Harman LJ held that the notice was not a nullity for lack of certainty. He stated (at p 455) that the appellant:

. . . knows what the land was like before he started carrying on these activities upon it and I do not see any hardship to him in being told to put it back as it was. If it merely means getting rid of the buildings and taking the cars off it, well and good; that is enough. To say it is void for uncertainty because it does not specify any further what he had got to do to restore it, seems to me to be becoming too meticulous and over-nice in these matters. Quite clearly the notice seems to me to tell him (a) what is complained of and (b) what he has to do. That is quite enough. I think the enforcement notice was perfectly good.

The courts have also recognised that in some instances that the use of vague language is to some extent inevitable. This is particularly apparent when an enforcement notice has to be drafted to accommodate and protect subsidiary rights under the principle established in *Mansi* v *Elstree RDC* (1964) 16 P&CR 153 discussed in Chap 4. Thus in *Trevors Warehouses Ltd* v *Secretary of State for the Environment* (1972) 23 P&CR 215, a case involving a material change of use of a wholesale warehouse with some incidental retail sales, to use as a retail supermarket, the enforcement notice required 'The discontinuance of the use of the . . . buildings for the retail sale of goods except to the extent to which such use was carried on prior to 1 January 1964'. Lord Widgery CJ ruled, in response to an argument that the enforcement notice was defective in that the requirement was too vague, that in view of the *Mansi* principle he was unable to decide in favour of the appellant. He stated (at p 218) that 'I see no ambiguity in the requirement as now framed, but I do see some practical difficulty in determining precisely what the extent of retail selling was . . .'. See also *Lee* v *Bromley London Borough Council* [1983] JPL 778 for a further illustration of judicial acceptance of this approach together with some guidance for solving the evidential problem.

6.5 The period within which any step is required to be taken: s 87(8)

The enforcement notice must state a specific period (in days, weeks or months, as appropriate) which is allowed for compliance with the requirements of the notice and may specify different periods for compliance with different requirements. The time allowed runs from the date on which the notice takes effect (in regard to which see further below), but there is no statutory minimum period which must be allowed. The requirement to specify the period within which any step is to be taken means that two dates and two periods will be apparent from a notice which (as is the usual case) requires steps to be taken within a single period. The dates are (*a*) the date of issue and (*b*) the date on which the notice takes effect. The periods are (*a*) the period from service to the date on which the notice comes into effect and (*b*) the period from the date of taking effect which is permitted for compliance.

Although it would seem likely that a notice which does not specify a period for compliance will be a nullity there does not appear to be any authority directly in point. It seems, however, that the courts do not insist on a period being specified in terms of days, weeks, or months if a date has been specified in the notice by which the required steps must have been carried out: *King and King* v *Secretary of State for the Environment* [1981] JPL 813. In this case Forbes J explained that what was necessary was that the requirements of the notice should be contained 'within the four corners' but this test was satisfied by simply subtracting the date of coming into effect from the date given for compliance. The difference is the 'period' for the purposes of s 87(8).

6.6 The reasons why it is considered expedient to issue the notice: s 87(12)(*a*) and reg 3 (*a*) of the 1981 Regulations

This requirement, which first formally entered the legislation as a result of the 1981 amendments, was previously the subject of non-statutory guidance issued to local planning authorities in Department of the Environment Circular 109/77 entitled 'Enforcement of Planning Control', the relevant parts of which were cancelled and replaced by Circular 38/81. Paragraph 29 of the current circular explains that the purpose of the requirement is to provide an initial means of enabling anyone who is served with a copy of an enforcement notice to understand from the outset the reasons why the local planning authority consider it expedient to issue the notice. The requirement supersedes the previous practice of issuing a covering letter explaining the reasons why enforcement action is being taken.

Although the provision of a statement of reasons why it is expedient to issue the notice is a statutory requirement, Circular

38/81 warns against the possibility that the statement might cause confusion to the recipient of a copy of a notice if the reasons are stated 'in close proximity to either the allegation of a breach of planning control, or the specification of the steps required to be taken to remedy the alleged breach. The statement of reasons why it is expedient to issue the notice might most conveniently be given in a separate annex to the enforcement notice' (para 29). In accordance with this advice the model enforcement notices contained in the Appendix to the Circular should make provision for inclusion of a statement of reasons by way of an annexe. In fact they do not.

6.7 The precise boundaries of the land: s 87(12)(*a*) and reg 3(*b*) of the 1981 Regulations

The regulation requires that the local planning authority must specify 'in' the notice 'the precise boundaries of the land to which it relates, whether by reference to a plan or otherwise'. Paragraph 31 of Circular 38/81 advises that this requirement should be discharged by attaching a plan to the notice. This is normally to be based on the Ordnance Survey, using a scale of not less than 1/2500, on which the exact boundary of the land is marked by a coloured outline. In cases where this is not sufficient for the purpose of exact identification of the boundary then the plan should be supplemented either by a brief written description or by an accurately surveyed drawing prepared on a larger scale. The model enforcement notices contained in the Appendix to the Circular provide for the boundaries of the land to be identified by reference both to an address or description of the land which is then 'shown edged [red] on the attached plan'.

6.8 The date on which the notice comes into effect: s 87(13)

This provision provides that an enforcement notice 'shall take effect on a date specified in it'. This date must not only be clearly stated in the notice and all copies of it, but must also be not less than 28 days after completion of service of the copies. The object of the requirement to specify this date is to define the period during which an appeal may be made to the Secretary of State under s 88 of the 1971 Act. It is therefore of particular importance that the date is specified and it is probable that an enforcement notice will be a nullity if the relevant date is omitted. In *Burgess* v *Jarvis and Sevenoaks RDC* [1952] 2 QB 41 an enforcement notice required a developer to demolish some houses 'within five years after the date of the service of this notice'. The Court of Appeal held that the scheme of the legislation was that two periods needed to be specified in the notice, one preceding the date on which the notice takes effect and the other succeeding that date. Although the Court of Appeal agreed that the notice was 'invalid' it is probable that the word 'nullity' would now be used to describe the effect of the omission. This does not imply, however, that there has been any subsequent change in judicial thinking, merely that this decision pre-dates the development of what has since become the conventional analysis. To like effect is *Swallow and Pearson* v *Middlesex County Council* [1953] 1 WLR 422 and *Godstone RDC* v *Brazil* [1953] 1 WLR 1102.

Chapter 7

Nullity, Invalidity and Appeals to the Secretary of State

7.1 Introduction

Once an enforcement notice has been issued and copies of it have been served, an analysis of the notice itself and of the circumstances of its issue must begin in earnest, particularly in view of the fact that rights of appeal to the Secretary of State are lost if not exercised in time. The first question to consider, however, is whether or not the notice is a nullity, since if it is a nullity, it is as Upjohn LJ stated in *Miller-Mead* v *Minister of Housing and Local Government* [1963] 2 QB 196 at p214 '. . . so much waste paper'. Clearly a purported enforcement notice which is a nullity is worthless and therefore no heed need be taken of it. It is, however, open to a recipient of a copy of an enforcement notice who believes it to be a nullity to take appropriate responsive action eg to obtain a declaration in the High Court. He should, however, be advised to appeal to the Secretary of State by the method discussed in this chapter. He need not therefore rely only on a gamble that a court of criminal jurisdiction will agree that the notice is a nullity if criminal proceedings are commenced by the local planning authority for failure to comply with its terms. It is also greatly in the interests of the landowner to take steps to challenge the notice; since an enforcement notice attaches to the land resale will be inhibited until it is withdrawn by the local planning authority or quashed.

7.2 Dealing with nullities and invalid notices: the need to appeal to the Secretary of State

Although many enforcement notices are less than perfectly drafted, it is only a small proportion that are outright nullities. To be a **nullity** a notice must be bad on its face ie that it suffers from errors of omission or commission so that it does not satisfy the legal requirements regulating the content of the notice which were explained in the previous chapter. It will be recalled that the examination of the content of an enforcement notice must take place against the background of the test enunciated by Upjohn LJ in *Miller-Mead* (at p 219) ie 'does the notice tell (the recipient) fairly what he has done wrong and what he must do to remedy it?'

Such a test means that many errors which do not create ambiguity or uncertainty will not render the notice a nullity. A notice which suffers from such defects will nevertheless be **invalid**, but some or all of the defects may be curable by the Secretary of State for the Environment acting under the corrective powers conferred on him by s 88A(2). This provision, which is of crucial importance, only comes into play, however, if an appeal is made under s 88 to the Secretary of State. Far from discouraging appeals, however, the scheme of the Act is that it is greatly to the advantage of the enforcee to appeal against an enforcement notice. This is because, otherwise than by exercising the statutory right of appeal, the means of challenging an enforcement notice is severely restricted by a privative provision contained in s 243(1)(*a*) of the 1971 Act. This provides that 'the validity of an enforcement notice shall not, except by way of an appeal under Part V of this Act, be questioned in any proceedings whatsoever on any of the grounds on which such an appeal may be brought'. It can be seen therefore that the policy of legislation is to direct disputes concerning the validity of enforcement notices to the Secretary of State in the first instance, a policy which is undoubtedly substantially achieved. A notice which is invalid stands until it is quashed by the Secretary of State. Also, the effect of making an appeal against an enforcement notice is that it is suspended until the appeal is finally determined: s 88(10).

Even in cases where it is thought that a notice is or may be a nullity, the right of appeal to the Secretary of State should be exercised as a matter of course. This is so even if proceedings are also commenced for judicial review for a declaration. This is because the Secretary of State may decide on hearing the appeal that the notice is a nullity, in which case he will decline to proceed with the matter as to do so will involve exceeding his jurisdiction. He will therefore set the notice aside. Technically the 'appeal' was not competent at all since if the enforcement notice is a nullity there is nothing to appeal against. Seeking to utilise this 'appeal' facility does, however, provide a ready and comparatively inexpensive means of achieving the desired result of ridding the land of the burden of the notice. Proceedings for judicial review may also be commenced as the privative provision in s 243(1)(*a*) has no application to nullities since the provision only applies in the case of matters which fall within the jurisdiction of the Secretary of State: *Davy* v *Spelthorne District Council* [1984] AC 262.

A notice which is not a nullity may nevertheless be invalid on a wide variety of grounds not limited to the content of the notice itself. These may include the possibilities that (i) no planning permission is needed for the alleged breach of planning control (ii) the notice is out of time where the four-year rule applies, or (iii) that the authority are estopped from taking enforcement action, to give just three examples. Here the notice looks to be satisfactory on its face but on investigation the facts do not fit the allegations. The means of challenging a notice which is considered to be invalid is dependent on the matter which gives rise to the allegation of invalidity, but in the vast majority of cases this will be by making an appeal to the Secretary of State on a number of grounds which are stated in s 88(2). In some instances an application for judicial review will be appropriate, eg if it is considered that the local planning authority have misused their powers, which, if successfully argued, will result in a grant of certiorari to quash the notice. Finally, one can defend criminal proceedings but the validity of the notice cannot be challenged on any of the grounds on which an appeal could have been made to the Secretary of State as s 243(1)(*a*) applies to preclude such a challenge. To this rule, however, there is one exception: s 243(2) permits a defendant in some criminal proceedings (those brought under s 89(5)) to rely on the grounds specified in s 88(2) provided that he can satisfy the conditions that he:

(*a*) has held an interest in the land since before the enforcement notice was issued; and

(*b*) did not have a copy of the enforcement notice served on him; and

(*c*) satisfies the court (i) that he did not know and could not reasonably be expected to know that the enforcement notice had been issued, and (ii) that his interests have been substantially prejudiced by the failure to serve him with a copy of it.

This structure for challenging invalid notices has, as its foundation stone, the right of appeal conferred by s 88. Before turning to the grounds of appeal specified in s 88(2), it may be helpful to supplement this description of how questions of invalidity should be handled with a statement of what the Secretary of State can do on receiving an appeal. He may:

(i) correct the defect which is the cause of the invalidity by exercise of powers under s 88A(2);

(ii) decline to correct the defect under s 88A(2) on the ground that to do so would effect an 'injustice'. He must therefore quash the notice.

The table on p 75 summarises the manner in which an appeal to the Secretary of State is dealt with. It incorporates the possibility that the notice is neither a nullity nor subject to a defect of drafting but the developer successfully appeals on one or more of the grounds specified in s 88(2)(a)–(h) in which case the Secretary of State will quash the enforcement notice or vary it according to the ground(s) involved. It is to the grounds of appeal to which we must therefore now turn.

7.3 Grounds of appeal to the Secretary of State

The grounds of appeal to the Secretary of State are specified in s 88(2)(a)–(h). These are as follows:

(a) that planning permission ought to be granted for the development to which the notice relates or, as the case may be, that a condition or limitation alleged in the enforcement notice not to have been complied with ought to be discharged;

(b) that the matters alleged in the notice do not constitute a breach of planning control;

(c) that the breach of planning control alleged in the notice has not taken place;

(d) in the case of a notice which, by virtue of s 87(4) of this Act, may be issued only within the period of four years from the date of the breach of planning control to which the notice relates, that that period has elapsed at the date when the notice was issued;

(e) in the case of a notice not falling within paragraph (d) of this sub-section, that the breach of planning control alleged by the notice occurred before the beginning of 1964;

(f) that copies of the enforcement notice were not served as required by s 87(5) of this Act;

(g) that the steps required by the notice to be taken exceed what is necessary to remedy any breach of planning control or to achieve a purpose specified in s 87(10) of this Act;

(h) that the period specified in the notice as the period within which any step is to be taken falls short of what should reasonably be allowed.

Decisions by the Secretary of State on an Enforcement Appeal

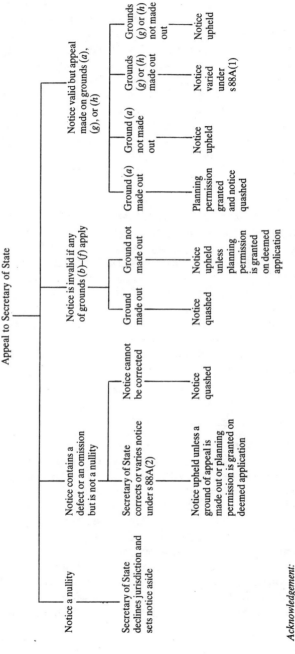

Appeal to Secretary of State

Notice a nullity	Notice contains a defect or an omission but is not a nullity		Notice is invalid if any of grounds (b)–(f) apply		Notice valid but appeal made on grounds (a), (g), or (h)			
Secretary of State declines jurisdiction and sets notice aside	Secretary of State corrects or varies notice under s 88A(2)	Notice cannot be corrected	Ground made out	Ground not made out	Ground (a) made out	Ground (a) not made out	Grounds (g) or (h) made out	Grounds (g) or (h) not made out
	Notice upheld unless a ground of appeal is made out or planning permission is granted on deemed application	Notice quashed	Notice quashed	Notice upheld unless planning permission is granted on deemed application	Planning permission granted and notice quashed	Notice upheld	Notice varied under s 88A(1)	Notice upheld

Acknowledgement:
This table is reproduced by kind permission of Malcolm Grant & Sweet & Maxwell Ltd. The original table appears in *Urban Planning Law* by Malcolm Grant (1982).

One of the less obvious aspects of enforcement law is that there is an imperfect overlap between the various matters on which an enforcement notice can be considered invalid and the grounds of appeal to the Secretary of State which are specified in s 88(2). One might be tempted to the view that the very making of an appeal to the Secretary of State always puts the validity of the notice in question. This in fact only applies in the case of grounds (b), (c), (d), (e) and (f); grounds (a), (g) and (h) are utilised on the basis that the notice is valid. It is commonly the case, however, that enforcement notices are challenged on more than one ground with the result that the question of validity is relevant in the majority of cases. It is also possible to supplement the appeal with matters which are additional to the statutory grounds eg by alleging that the issue of the notice is a misuse of the powers enjoyed by the enforcing authority.

Although ground (a) (that planning permission ought to be granted) is included as a specific ground of appeal, it should be noted that under s 88B(3) an appellant is by virtue of the appeal deemed to have made an application for planning permission for the development to which the notice relates. This provision should be read with s 32(1), (2) of the 1971 Act which makes clear that a power to grant planning permission (by the Secretary of State in the case of an appeal against an enforcement notice) includes a power to grant planning permission to retain buildings or works or to continue the use of land without complying with a condition or limitation subject to which planning permission was previously granted.

7.4 Persons entitled to appeal

The right to make an appeal against an enforcement notice is conferred by s 88(1) on 'a person having an interest in the land . . . whether or not a copy of it has been served on him'. It may be observed that this provision is inconsistent with s 87(5) which requires copies of the enforcement notice to be served on the 'owner and occupier . . . and any other person having an interest . . . which in the opinion of the authority is materially affected by the notice'. The inconsistency relates to the 'occupier'. If he has no interest in the land he cannot appeal, as occurred in *Scarborough Borough Council* v *Adams and Adams* [1983] JPL 673, a case in which trespassers in possession of land for eighteen months were held to be 'occupiers' but to have no right of appeal against the enforcement notice. The inconsistency is, however, rendered less significant by the provisions of s 4(2) of the Town and Country Planning Act 1984 which expressly grants a right of appeal to any person who by virtue of a licence in writing is in occupation both at the time of issue of the enforcement notice and at the time when the appeal is made. This is especially significant for caravan dwellers who occupy sites pursuant to site licences; prior to the amendment such occupiers were subject to prosecution for failure to comply with an enforcement notice yet had no right of appeal to the Secretary of State.

As is made clear by the express wording of s 88(1) the right of appeal is not limited to those parties on whom a copy of the notice has been served, but where there has been a failure of service an appeal is competent under ground (f). If an appeal to the Secretary of State is made the question of defective service cannot be raised in any subsequent proceedings by the appellant or by any other party irrespective of whether ground (f) was put in issue: s 110(2).

7.5 Submission of the appeal

The procedure for submission of an appeal is regulated by s 88(1), (3)–(5) and by regulations made under s 88(5). These are the Town and Country Planning (Enforcement Notices and Appeals) Regulations 1981 (SI 1981 No 1742). Of paramount importance is the requirement in s 88(1) that if an appeal is to be lodged it must be made '. . . before the date specified in the notice as the date on which it is to take effect . . .'. Since this date is a minimum of 28 days from the date of completion of service of copies of the notice, it follows that a minimum period of 28 days is available to the appellant to submit the appeal. The timing is, however, crucial in two respects. Firstly, the Court of Appeal has held in *Howard* v *Secretary of State for the Environment* [1975] 1 QB 235 that the Secretary of State has no jurisdiction to accept an appeal which is made out of time. Secondly, the last day for submission of the appeal is the day before the date specified in the notice as the date on which the notice comes into effect; the notice must be **received** by the Department of the Environment before the specified date. It is therefore not sufficient if the notice is posted before the specified date but arrives on that day: *Lenlyn Ltd* v *Secretary of State for the Environment* [1984] JPL 482. Such is the importance of lodging the appeal in time that it is a wise precaution not only to use first class post but also to telephone the

Department of the Environment shortly after you would ordinarily expect the appeal documents to have arrived in the ordinary course of post. It is also not unreasonable to suggest that the appeal be submitted sufficiently early to enable a repeat submission to be made within the limited time available if it transpires that the Department cannot confirm receipt of the first submission. Since, as described below, the minimum steps needed to secure submission of the appeal are very simple it should be possible to send the appeal documents within 14 days of receipt of a copy of the enforcement notice, trusting of course that you have been consulted promptly.

There is no prescribed form for use in submission of an enforcement appeal. There is, however, a standard form (Form DoE 14069) issued by the Department of the Environment, a copy of which will normally be supplied by the local planning authority when serving copies of the enforcement notice. If for any reason there is any difficulty in obtaining this form it is sufficient merely to write to the Department of the Environment to lodge the appeal since the bare requirement of s 88(3) of the 1971 Act is simply that 'An appeal under this section shall be made by notice in writing to the Secretary of State'. It is not necessary to state the grounds of appeal or the facts on which reliance is made in support of the appeal, though these details must be supplied later in accordance with the requirements of s 88(4), (5) and the Enforcement Regulations of 1981. It will be noted that the standard form invites the appellant to state both the grounds of appeal and the facts on which he relies. The requirement of the legislation is, however, that the appellant must submit these details by a written statement either at the time of lodging the appeal or within 28 days of being requested to do so by the Secretary of State: reg 5 of the 1981 Enforcement Regulations. This provision requires that a statement must be made specifying the grounds of appeal and 'stating briefly the facts on which he proposes to rely'. The Secretary of State can, however, consider other grounds of appeal in order to do justice to the appellant: *Chelmsford RDC v Powell* [1963] 1 WLR 123.

Equally careful attention must be given to the time limit for submission of the statement as s 88(6)(*a*) enables the Secretary of State to dismiss the appeal if the appellant fails to comply with the requirements of s 88(4), (5) within the 28 day period. Furthermore, if the appellant has selected more than one ground of appeal but submits a statement of facts within the 28 day period which is incomplete (due to a failure to state facts applicable to each of the grounds on which the appeal is made) the Secretary of State may determine the appeal without regard to the grounds of appeal which are unsupported by facts: s 88(9). It is customary for the Secretary of State to give a week's notice of intention to exercise the powers conferred by s 88(6) or s 88(9): Circular 38/81 para 35.

The address for submission of an appeal using the standard appeal form is printed on the form itself. If, however, it is necessary to submit the appeal by letter the following address should be used:

Department of the Environment
(PLUP 2)
PO Box 326
Bristol
BS99 7XF

For appeals relating to land in Wales:

The Secretary
The Welsh Office
Cathays Park
Cardiff
CF1 3NQ.

Once an appeal has been made which complies with the requirements described above the effect on the notice is that it is of no effect pending the final determination or the withdrawal of the appeal: s 88(10). This suspending effect applies to all parties even if only one party chooses to appeal where more than one has been served with a copy of the enforcement notice.

7.6 The appeal fee

Wherever an appeal is made against an enforcement notice the appellant is deemed to have made an application to the Secretary of State for planning permission for the development to which the notice relates: s 88B(3). Since planning applications are subject to a system of fees, a planning fee is payable in respect of the deemed application to the Secretary of State. The system of planning fees is a complex one; it is regulated by the Town and Country Planning (Fees for Applications and Deemed Applications) Regulations 1983 (SI 1983 No 1674) as amended by the Town and Country Planning (Fees for Applications and Deemed Applications) (Amendment) Regulations 1987 (SI 1987 No 101).

Although it is not appropriate to explain the fees system in this book, the reader may care to consult Brand and Williams *Planning Law for Conveyancers* 2nd edn (Longman) for a succinct account. Although the correct sum must be remitted, in the majority of cases the amount payable is not punitive.

For present purposes the main points of importance are (i) who determines what fee is payable, and (ii) when must it be paid? Prior to 1 October 1985 it was the practice for the enforcing local planning authority to advise those on whom copies of an enforcement notice are served of the fee which would be payable if the right of appeal is exercised; the appellant would be expected to pay this fee on giving written notice of appeal. A change in procedure was effected pursuant to Circular 20/85 which advises that the Department of the Environment (or Welsh Office, as appropriate) will calculate the fee and notify the appellant accordingly. The Circular does not explain when the fee must be paid, nor the procedure followed by the Department in the event of non-payment. By analogy with the position which applies in the case of applications for planning permission, it is submitted that the Secretary of State need not decide on the deemed planning application until the fee is paid. It would appear, however, that he is not prevented from otherwise determining the appeal against the enforcement notice.

As is emphasised by para 3 of Appendix 1 to Circular 20/85, the fee is charged in respect of the consideration of the deemed application, not for consideration of the appeal generally. This means that the fee will be refunded if (i) the appeal is withdrawn by the appellant prior to the public inquiry (or site inspection in the case of a written representations appeal), or (ii) the enforcement notice is withdrawn by the local planning authority, or (iii) the appeal succeeds on any of the grounds (*b*)–(*f*) (except if the appeal involves the stationing of a residential caravan on the land) or (iv) the appeal is rejected by the Secretary of State as invalid, or is dismissed for lack of submission of facts to support the grounds of appeal or (v) the enforcement notice is quashed by the Secretary of State for failure by the local planning authority to submit prescribed information or (vi) the enforcement notice is found to be invalid or to contain a defect which the Secretary of State cannot correct on appeal.

7.7 Powers of the Secretary of State to correct or vary the terms of an enforcement notice

Returning to the question of validity of the enforcement notice, what is the position if the notice contains a defect in its terms but which does not render it a nullity? The notice is nevertheless invalid and is, in theory, liable to be quashed by the Secretary of State. But the Secretary of State has a power to correct an enforcement notice under s 88A(2), thereby enabling him to save a notice which might otherwise have to be quashed on a technicality. This power was first granted in 1960 by s 33(5) of the Caravan Sites and Control of Development Act 1960 and under that provision could be applied to any 'informality, defect or error' which was not 'material'. This power was interpreted by Lord Denning MR in *Miller-Mead* v *Minister of Housing and Local Government* to mean that the Secretary of State 'can correct errors so long as, having regard to the merits of the case, the correction can be made without injustice'; an injustice occurs when the required correction 'goes to the substance of the matter'. The amendments to the 1971 Act effected by the 1981 Act incorporated this interpretation into the legislation and the use of the word 'material' was thereafter omitted. The provision now reads as follows:

. . . the Secretary of State may correct any informality, defect or error in the enforcement notice, or give directions for varying its terms, if he is satisfied that the correction or variation can be made without injustice to the appellant or to the local planning authority.

7.7.1 The power to correct

Minor errors, even if there are several, do not render the notice a nullity and should therefore be capable of correction by the Secretary of State. In *Patel* v *Betts* (1977) 243 EG 1003 the enforcement notice contained three minor errors. It recited (i) that a breach of planning control had occurred after a date which had not yet passed (ii) did not use the word 'material' in referring to the breach of planning control as comprising a material change of use, and (iii) did not identify which of the ground floor rooms in the property concerned was the subject of the alleged breach of planning control. There was no appeal to the Secretary of State and these errors went uncorrected. In subsequent criminal proceedings for failure to comply with the notice it was alleged that the notice was invalid. The Divisional Court held that each of the errors was capable of correction by the Secretary of State without any injustice. Even though the Secretary of State had not exercised this power (since no appeal to him had been made) as he could have done so the notice was a valid one.

Where an appeal is made to the Secretary of State it is his duty to exercise his powers to correct any defects in the enforcement notice if this can be done without injustice. Lord Widgery CJ so held in *Hammersmith London Borough Council* v *Secretary of State for the Environment* (1975) 30 P&CR 19 in which the Secretary of State had declined to exercise his power to correct a notice which had used the term 'guest house' instead of the more appropriate term 'lodging house'. The Divisional Court held, on appeal by the local planning authority, that the Secretary of State was perfectly entitled to substitute the most appropriate label for the form of development which had attracted the enforcement notice. As this could be done without injustice the matter was remitted to the Secretary of State for further consideration.

Notwithstanding the duty to exercise the power under s 88A(2), the court has also issued a guideline that the power is a 'distinctly limited' one. In *Royal Borough of Kensington and Chelsea* v *Secretary of State for the Environment and Mia Carla Ltd* [1981] JPL 50 the enforcement notice as originally drafted alleged 'a material change in the use of the garden of the said land to a use for the purposes of a restaurant'. At the inquiry it became clear that the appropriate allegation was one of material change of use due to the intensification of the restaurant use. The Secretary of State refused to correct the notice, a decision which was challenged by the local planning authority. The Divisional Court agreed that the Secretary of State had properly declined to exercise the power since to do so would have produced a totally different enforcement notice.

Where the Secretary of State amends the scope of the notice by purporting to give the notice wider effect than as originally drafted, it will rarely qualify as a correction falling within the scope of s 88A(2). An example is *TLG Building Materials* v *Secretary of State for the Environment* [1981] JPL 513. In this case the enforcement notice required the use of land for storage of building materials to cease. The use of the land had been carried on in association with a builders merchants business which was operated from adjacent premises. The notice should therefore have described the unauthorised use as a builders merchants yard. The Secretary of State corrected this error on appeal, but in the Divisional Court Donaldson LJ said that 'it was beyond a mere formality to call upon somebody to stop using some land for the storage of building materials and to amend it to the much wider concept of prohibiting use as a builders merchants yard'. Summarising his view of the matter he concluded that 'any wider condemnation—if that was the right word—in an enforcement notice must be material except in somewhat exceptional circumstances'. In the same case Hodgson J further observed that if the Secretary of State decided to alter the planning unit described in the enforcement notice this would almost always be a material alteration outwith the power conferred s 88A(2). The enforcement notice in issue in *Sanders* v *Secretary of State for the Environment* [1981] JPL 593 was, however, capable of correction even though it involved enlarging its scope. Land had been used for storing and cutting up of scrap metal and for the repair of boilers. This last use was not mentioned in the enforcement notice but had been placed in issue during the inquiry. As this use was a composite mixed use, or (to use more colloquial language) 'part and parcel' of the uses referred to in the notice, so that it could not be carried on independently of storing and cutting metal, the correction to the notice had not caused an injustice to the appellant. See also *Scurlock* v *Secretary of State for Wales* (1976) 33 P&CR 202.

Just as any enlargement of the scope of the notice is likely to cause injustice, any reduction in the scope is unlikely to go to the substance of the matter and will therefore fall within the scope of the power conferred by s 88A(2). Thus in *Burner* v *Secretary of State for the Environment and the South Hams District Council* [1983] JPL 459 the enforcement notice identified the breach of planning control as the 'stationing' of caravans on the site in question without referring to the purpose for which the stationing had taken place; without alleging an unauthorised use it was not clear what was the breach of planning control which the local planning authority required the appellant to remedy. The Secretary of State deleted the word 'stationing' and substituted the word 'storage'. Glidewell J held that this could be achieved under the subsection since no injustice was involved in cutting down the notice to prevent a use of the land which was of a lesser ambit than that which was originally specified. A contrary decision was reached, however, in *Dunton Park Caravan Site Ltd* v *Secretary of State for the Environment* [1981] JPL 511 where the Secretary of State reduced the scope of the notice from a site extending to 67 acres to one only one-tenth of that size. The effect of so doing was to distort the relevance of the findings of fact and prevented the appellants from arguing their case on the general issue as to the scope of existing storage rights.

Less clear is the question whether s 88A(2) enables the Secretary of State to correct defects which are relevant to the specification of the breach of planning control. The rule that the notice must, in specifying the breach of planning control, distinguish between development without planning permission and failure to comply with a breach of a condition or limitation attached to grant of planning permission (para **6.3**) has been undermined by recent expressions of judicial opinion eg in *Rochdale Metropolitan Borough Council* v *Simmonds* [1981] JPL 191 and in *Scott* v *Secretary of State for the Environment* [1983] JPL 108. Whilst it is possibly the case that failure to include an appropriate statement in the enforcement notice may not render the notice a nullity, an incorrect statement will render it invalid. As Lord Lane CJ put it in *Kerrier District Council* v *Secretary of State for the Environment* [1981] JPL 193: 'If on the facts of any particular case a planning authority put the case in the wrong pigeon-hole the enforcement notice would be set aside' and hence s 88A(2) could not be invoked to save it. A similar result was also achieved in solving the problem which arose in *H T Hughes & Sons Ltd* v *Secretary of State for the Environment* [1985] JPL 486. Here Hodgson J quashed an enforcement notice which had incorrectly alleged a breach of planning control 'after the end of 1963' instead of alleging that a breach had occurred within the last four years in a case where the four-year limitation period applied. He held that the Secretary of State did not have power under s 88A(2) to correct the notice because the defect went to the substance of the matter. This was because the misrecital involved reference to the wrong limitation period: had the appellant been aware that he could have made out a case for immunity he might have been able to take advantage of it. The loss of that opportunity would have resulted in an injustice.

It seems that a correction can be made where the notice has properly identified the nature of the breach as development without a grant of planning permission but which has either omitted or made an incorrect reference to the relevant part of the definition of development. This occurred in *Scott* v *Secretary of State for the Environment* in which one of the several enforcement notices issued by the local planning authority alleged a breach of planning control by the stationing of touring caravans on the land without stating whether this constituted a material change of use or an operational development. The Secretary of State cured this omission acting under s 88A(2). Mr David Widdicombe QC (sitting as a deputy judge) held that the category of development did not need to be specified, and that even if he was wrong in so holding, the Secretary of State had been empowered to correct the notice as no one was misled by the alteration and hence no injustice was thereby effected. The same deputy judge also decided the similar case of *Wealden District Council* v *Secretary of State for the Environment* [1983] JPL 234, a case involving the unauthorised stationing of a caravan but in which the local planning authority had stated in the enforcement notice that this constituted a material change in the use of the land. As the caravan in question had been converted to a permanent structure by removal of its wheels, axles and springs the Secretary of State took the view that the notice was invalid as it should have referred to operational development and that it could not be saved by exercise of the power of correction. The learned deputy judge held that the change required in this case fell outside the ambit of a 'correction' and could be more suitably described as a 'variation'. As the Secretary of State had not considered the possibility that a variation could be made under s 88A(2) the notice was remitted to him for further consideration. Mr David Widdicombe QC made it clear, however, that the variation needed in this case could be made without injustice though this would not often be the case.

7.7.2 *The power to vary*

The power of the Secretary of State to 'vary' the terms of an enforcement notice is also contained in s 88A(2) and its exercise is subject to the same test, ie that the Secretary of State must be satisfied that variation can be made 'without injustice to the appellant or to the local planning authority'. Prior to the 1981 Act the power to vary was less extensive being limited to variations 'in favour of the appellant'. This distinction occasionally required the court to construe a variation as a correction. Thus in *Morris* v *Secretary of State for the Environment* (1975) 31 P&CR 216 the omission of one word from a notice prohibiting activities associated with an unauthorised use of land for garage purposes was considered by the Secretary of State to be a mere oversight by the local planning authority and he varied the notice accordingly. As such the variation was clearly not in favour of the appellant who sought to have the notice quashed by the High Court. The Divisional Court held that although the Secretary of State had used the word 'variation' he had in fact merely corrected the notice and that no injustice had been suffered by the appellant.

The recasting of the Secretary of State's power to vary has greatly increased the scope for keeping a notice alive that would formerly have been quashed as invalid. Mr David Widdicombe QC (sitting as a deputy judge) pointed out in *Wealden District Council* v *Secretary of State for the Environment* that 'variation in this context was clearly a wider term than correction' but he added that to satisfy the description 'variation' it was necessary that there 'must be sufficient continuity of identity between the notice before and after the change'. He declined, however, to issue an opinion on the exact distinction between the two words. In *Harrogate Borough Council* v *Secretary of State for the Environment* [1987] JPL 288 Webster J also considered that '. . . it was neither necessary nor desirable to attempt to define either a correction or a variation for the purposes of the Act, nor to draw any fine line of distinction between the two words . . .'. The important considerations were first that neither a correction nor a variation could be made under s 88A(2) unless the Secretary of State was satisfied that the alteration could be made without injustice. The second consideration was that no alteration could be made which was wider or more fundamental than what could properly be described as a variation.

While the full extent of the Secretary of State's power to vary has yet to be developed by case-law, the use previously made of the power has been largely in the contexts of (i) variation arising from a successful appeal to the Secretary of State on the grounds specified in s 88(2)(*g*) and (*h*), and (ii) protection of established use rights. The power to vary is hence often utilised in order to reduce the steps required by the notice to remedy the breach of planning control, or to extend the time which is permitted for compliance. With regard to protection of established use rights, the enforcement notice must safeguard such rights in accordance with the principle established in *Mansi* v *Elstree Rural District Council* (1964) 16 P&CR 153. If a notice does not do so it can be varied under this power. If the Secretary of State does not vary the notice to protect established use rights the appellant may apply to the High Court under s 246 of the 1971 Act whereupon the court can direct the Secretary of State to reconsider the matter.

While the Secretary of State is under a duty to protect established use rights, he can also exercise a discretion to vary a notice to include a provision relevant to an ancillary use: *Haigh* v *Secretary of State for the Environment* [1983] JPL 40. In this case McCullough J summarised a line of authority developed subsequent to the *Mansi* decision. After referring to *Williams* v *Ministry of Housing and Local Government* (1967) 18 P&CR 514; *Monomart (Warehouses) Ltd* v *Secretary of State for the Environment* (1977) 34 P&CR 305; *Day* v *Secretary of State for the Environment* (1979) 78 LGR 27; *Newport* v *Secretary of State for the Environment* (1980) 40 P&CR 261, *Cord* v *Secretary of State for the Environment* [1981] JPL 40 and *North Sea Land Equipment* v *Secretary of State for the Environment* [1982] JPL 384, he stated that:

An enforcement notice offended if it prohibited an established use. Care had therefore to be taken to ensure that an enforcement notice was so worded as to preserve such uses. If it purported to prohibit an established use it had to be amended. Where an enforcement notice did not prohibit an established use it was not necessary to say in terms that a use ancillary thereto was preserved, because this was implied by law. However, it was often desirable to say so, even although it might not be necessary. This was a matter which the Secretary of State might want to consider and which it will be his duty to consider, if submissions to this effect were made to him. Such consideration was desirable because disobedience to an enforcement notice was a criminal offence and the citizen to whom it was directed was entitled to know, as far as these things may reasonably be made plain to him, which activities may, and which activities may not, amount to disobedience.

7.8 Power of the Secretary of State to disregard defects of service

One of the grounds of appeal to the Secretary of State specified in s 88(2) against an enforcement notice is that copies of the notice have not been served as required by s 87(5) of the 1971 Act: s 88(2)(*f*). Where a copy of the notice has not been served as required the appellant can thereby allege that the notice is invalid and hence it is potentially liable to be quashed by the Secretary of State on appeal to him. Such a claim can in many instances be overcome by use of the power granted to the Secretary of State by s 88A(3). The provision (which is a re-enactment of s 88(4)(*b*) of the 1971 Act, as originally drafted) is as follows:

Where it would otherwise be a ground for determining such an appeal in favour of the appellant that a person required to be served with a copy of the enforcement notice was not served, the Secretary of State may disregard that fact if neither the appellant nor that person has been substantially prejudiced by the failure to serve him.

It seems that it is not often that the Secretary of State will conclude that substantial prejudice has occurred due to a defect of service. In *Skinner and King* v *Secretary of State for the Environment*

[1978] JPL 842 a number of enforcement notices were served in relation to a site which comprised several buildings. The owner received a notice relating to the whole site and the occupiers of the buildings, who were tenants, each received a notice relating to their particular building. No copies were served. The Secretary of State held on appeal against a notice served on a tenant that the site owner had not been substantially prejudiced by the failure of the local planning authority to serve a copy on him as he considered there was insufficient evidence to substantiate such a claim. In the Divisional Court Lord Widgery CJ held that the Secretary of State's decision should be upheld as a site owner who received an enforcement notice in relation to a tenanted property would go to the site to find out what the individual tenants were up to. Moreover, the site owner had a 'safety net' in that he could not be successfully prosecuted for failure to comply with the requirements of his tenant's notice if a copy had not been served on him. He was therefore not substantially prejudiced. The Divisional Court also held that in cases where an appeal is made on the ground specified in s 88(2)(f) the decision of the Secretary of State should stand unless it could be shown that there was no evidence upon which that conclusion could be based, or, alternatively, it was shown that the Secretary of State had proceeded on an erroneous principle by leaving out of consideration a relevant factor or including an irrelevant factor.

Most of the reported enforcement appeal decisions have resulted in an unsuccessful challenge on this ground. Regard may be had to the decisions reported at [1974] JPL 248 (no prejudice where market stall holders were not served but the effect of the notice was explained by the landowner); [1979] JPL 693 (no prejudice where one notice was incorrectly addressed but in fact delivered by the Post Office to the correct address, another not delivered at all but a copy was sent to the appellant's agent who supplied the appellant with a further copy); [1974] JPL 41 (no prejudice where co-owner not served). Substantial prejudice was held to have occurred, however, in the appeal noted at [1983] JPL 271 (copies not served on owner-occupiers of caravans where the breach of planning control concerned a colour condition).

Once the question of defective service of a copy of the enforcement notice has been put in issue by appeal to the Secretary of State under s 88(2)(f), any further proceedings are precluded by s 110(2). This subsection provides that neither the appellant nor any other person shall be entitled to claim that the notice was not duly served on the person who appealed. Therefore its effect is to place a further restriction on the scope for litigation over questions of service, but the provision will not apply in the absence of an appeal to the Secretary of State. Hence it remains possible for the appellant to challenge the notice by proceedings for judicial review and claim that the notice is a **nullity** due to the defect of service. It would appear, however, following the decision of the Court of Appeal in *R* v *Greenwich London Borough Council ex p Patel* [1985] JPL 851 that the prospects of success in such proceedings are very limited. The decision in this case needs to be compared with that in a leading Scottish case, *McDaid* v *Clydebank District Council* [1984] JPL 579 to appreciate the scope, if any, for success in such proceedings. In *McDaid*, the local planning authority issued a series of enforcement notices relating to land used as a scrapyard. Copies were served on the occupiers but not on the owners, even though the local planning authority knew who the owners were. As a result of the omission the owners did not appeal to the Secretary of State as they did not discover the existence of the notices until after they had come into effect. The Court of Session held that it was open to the appellants to challenge the enforcement notice on the ground that it was a nullity, despite the statutory scheme, which directs appeals to the Secretary of State. This is because the privative provision of the legislation (see s 243(1) of the 1971 Act, which contains the equivalent provision applicable to England and Wales) only applies to parties who are in a position to exercise the statutory right of appeal. Since the enforcing authority were in unexplained default they could not shelter behind the privative clause; the enforcement notice was therefore a nullity.

In the *Patel* case the council mistakenly but reasonably believed that Mrs Patel was the owner of a property which in fact belonged to her brother-in-law to whom she paid a fee for its use. An enforcement notice was issued in respect of a development carried out by Mrs Patel but this was ignored; it was only at the stage of prosecution that the local planning authority discovered that she did not own the land as the prosecution under s 89(1) was doomed to failure having been mounted against a non-owner. The council then resolved to exercise the power of entry conferred by s 91 of the 1971 Act in order to remove the offending structure. The true owner then became aware of the proceedings and sought judicial review to obtain an order of prohibition to restrain the council from demolishing the structure alleging that failure to serve a copy of the notice on him rendered the notice a nullity. The application failed. The Court of Appeal adopted a different approach to that of the Court of Session in the *McDaid* case and held that the key provision of the 1971 Act in this case was s 243(2). This enables a person charged with an offence under s 89(5) (which unlike s 89(1) does not depend on service of a copy of the notice) to challenge the validity of the enforcement notice on any of the grounds specified in s 88(2) in defence to a prosecution, provided that (inter alia) he can satisfy the court that he did not know and could not reasonably be expected to know that the enforcement notice had been issued and that his interests have been substantially prejudiced by the failure to serve him with a copy of it. The Court of Appeal therefore construed the provisions of s 243 to preclude proceedings by way of judicial review to have an enforcement notice declared a nullity.

While the decision in *Patel* does provide strong authority for the view that a defect of service does not render a notice a nullity it is pertinent to note that Neill LJ stated (at p 855) that 'there might of course be cases where the validity of an enforcement notice was challenged on some ground other than those contained in the relevant paragraphs of s 88(2). In such cases s 243 has no application'. This impliedly permits a developer to seek judicial review if, acting in bad faith, the local planning authority deliberately failed to serve a copy of a notice on a relevant party. As Neill LJ's point raises the general question of the availability of judicial review it is to this topic that we therefore now turn.

Chapter 8

Nullity, Invalidity and Judicial Review

8.1 Introduction

Notwithstanding the heavy emphasis placed on the right of appeal to the Secretary of State as a means of challenging an enforcement notice, it is nevertheless important to bear in mind that the notice may be challengeable on ordinary principles of administrative law. Indeed this may be the only remedy available to a person on whom a copy of the enforcement notice has been served but who cannot appeal to the Secretary of State for lack of an 'interest' in the land which is required by s 88(1), as occurred for example in *Scarborough Borough Council* v *Adams and Adams* [1983] JLP 673. The notice may be a nullity due to a patent defect or it may be invalid due to some vitiating factor rendering it ultra vires the council which issued it eg that the motivation for issuing it was bad in law. In such circumstances it may be considered desirable to determine the issue by means of an application for judicial review rather than rely only on the statutory right of appeal to the Secretary of State, if available.

It has already been observed in the opening paragraphs of Chap 7 that the 1971 Act includes a provision which directs most challenges to the validity of an enforcement notice to the Secretary of State in the first instance. Section 243(1)(*a*), generally referred to as 'the privative provision', is of such importance in the present context that its terms are restated here. It provides: 'Subject to the provisions of this section (*a*) the validity of an enforcement notice shall not, except by way of an appeal under Part V of the Act, be questioned in any proceedings whatsoever on any of the grounds on which such an appeal may be brought'. The main issues which now need to be examined are (i) what is the scope of this

provision? and (ii) in what circumstances might an application for
judicial review be successful?

8.2 The scope of s 243 in civil proceedings

The operation of s 243 depends on the effect of the words
'. . . on any of the grounds on which such an appeal may be
brought'. Does this mean that no challenge can be made to the
validity of the notice except by making an appeal under s 88, or
does it leave open the possibility that a challenge can be made in
the courts on grounds other than those specified in s 88(2)(a)–(h)?
Any doubts that may have existed in relation to this point were
dispelled by the House of Lords in *Davy* v *Spelthorne Borough
Council* [1984] AC 262. In this case Lord Fraser explained that
'[T]he effect of s 243(1)(a) is to prohibit the bringing of appeals on
any of the grounds to which it relates before the High Court and,
in accordance with s 88(1), to substitute the Secretary of State as
the forum for deciding such appeals'. He later continued:

S 243(1)(a) provides that the validity of an enforcement notice shall not be
questioned in any proceedings whatsoever 'on any of the grounds on
which such an appeal may be brought'. The words 'such an appeal' are a
reference back to an appeal under Pt V of the 1971 Act, and they mean in
effect the grounds specified in s 88(2). But s 243(1)(a) does not prohibit
questioning the validity of the notice on other grounds. If, for example,
the respondent had alleged that the enforcement notice had been vitiated
by fraud, because one of the appellants' officers had been bribed to issue
it, or had been served without the appellants' authority, he would indeed
have been questioning its validity, but not on any of the grounds on which
an appeal may be brought under Pt V.

While this passage makes it clear that s 243 is not entirely
'watertight' an examination of the case-law reveals that the provision is nevertheless very effective in preventing litigation in the
High Court which is directed to the validity of the notice. Two
Court of Appeal cases illustrate this point. In *Jeary* v *Chailey Rural
District Council* (1973) 26 P&CR 280 the appellant had failed to
exercise the statutory right of appeal to the Secretary of State.
After criminal proceedings had been taken the appellant issued a
writ claiming that the enforcement notice was a nullity on the
ground inter alia that the development which the enforcement
notice sought to control was the subject of existing use rights. It
was hence claimed that if s 243 was operated strictly it would
deprive the appellant of those rights, but the Court of Appeal

roundly declared (per Orr LJ at p 284) that 's 243 cannot . . . be construed as directed only to groundless challenges of an enforcement notice but must be read as directed also to preventing the assertion of vested rights'. Secondly, in *Square Meal Frozen Foods Ltd* v *Dunstable Corporation* [1974] 1 WLR 59, the Court of Appeal considered whether s 243 prevented the appellant from seeking a declaration that a threatened enforcement notice would be invalid on the ground that an existing grant of planning permission was sufficiently wide in scope to encompass the prospective development which it was alleged would be unauthorised. Lord Denning MR was of the opinion that s 243 applied not only to proceedings started after the service of an enforcement notice but also to proceedings started before the enforcement notice has been served—at any rate when one is anticipated. The Master of the Rolls further opined that even if s 243 did not apply the court should in exercise of its discretion prevent the application from proceeding further as the matter was best dealt with by the Secretary of State. He stated at p 65 that '[T]he Minister can deal with everything quite comprehensively. And, if a point of law does emerge there is an appeal to the High Court. That procedure is much to be preferred to the decision of an isolated question of a summons'.

Since in both of these cases a ground of appeal mentioned in s 88(2)(*a*)–(*h*) would have been put in issue had an appeal been made to the Secretary of State (ground (*d*) in the *Jeary* case and ground (*b*) in the *Dunstable* case) it can be seen that s 243 is an effective bar where reliance is sought to be placed on one of the statutory grounds, but outside the period for making an appeal to the Secretary of State. Where, however, the ground of appeal does not relate to a matter referred to in s 88(2), s 243 will not operate. It was on this basis that Roskill LJ was able to distinguish *Square Meal Frozen Foods Ltd* v *Dunstable Corporation* in *Flashman* v *Camden London Borough Council* (1979) 130 New LJ 885. In this case the council had manifested a desire to terminate a tenancy of a property which was being used for a business purpose as well as for the appellant's residence. The council disapproved of the business activity taking place in council property although they had been aware of this use at the time of acquisition of the freehold reversion. The tenant obtained a declaration that his tenancy was a protected one as the Landlord and Tenant Act 1954 applied. The council then resolved to take enforcement action against the tenant, but before the notice was served the tenant commenced proceedings for a declaration that his user was permitted under the 1971 Act and an injunction to restrain service of the enforcement notice. In response to the council's application to have the action struck out the tenant therefore claimed that the challenge to the validity of the anticipated enforcement notice was based on the ground that it was ultra vires (and also that there was evidence to support an estoppel argument) and that it was not barred by s 243. Since neither of these grounds are mentioned in s 88(2) it was held that the application could proceed as it was clearly open to argument that s 243 was inoperative and that it was wrong to apply the section so as to strangle the appellant's action at birth.

8.3 The scope of s 243 in criminal proceedings

Although a full examination of the criminal aspects of enforcement must await Chap 11 it is opportune to consider whether s 243 also bars questions of validity being raised in criminal proceedings. Although the point had been considered in *Findlow* v *Lewis* [1963] 1 QB 151, currently the leading case is the Court of Appeal decision in *R* v *Smith (Thomas George)* (1984) 48 P&CR 392 in which a prosecution took place for failure to comply with a notice which required discontinuance of use of land as a scrapyard, in respect of which no planning permission had been granted. No appeal was made to the Secretary of State against the notice, a copy of which was duly served on the owner. On prosecution in the Crown Court the defendant claimed that the use of the land had started before the end of 1963 and hence the notice was invalid. This defence corresponds to the ground of appeal to the Secretary of State which appears in s 88(2)(e). The Crown Court judge held that no evidence could be given in relation to this matter. On appeal to the Court of Appeal, Mann J held that the word 'proceedings' in s 243(1)(a) includes criminal proceedings and therefore the prosecution could not be defended on any of the grounds on which an appeal could have been made to the Secretary of State. The Court of Appeal made it quite clear, however, that the preclusive effect of s 243 is limited to the grounds specified in s 88(2). Thus Mann J referred to *Davy* v *Spelthorne Borough Council* (supra) and *Scarborough Borough Council* v *Adams and Adams* (supra) in support of the proposition that a prosecution can be defended on other grounds. Reference should also be made to *Prosser* v *Sharp* [1985] JPL 717 for further authority on this point. A clear example of the operation of s 243(1) is also provided by another Court of Appeal case, *R* v *Keeys* (1987) *The Times*, 17 June. In this case is was held that where a defendant does not claim that there has been any change in the use of land since the issue of the enforcement notice he is prevented by s 243(1) from raising by way of defence the argument that he was not in fact using the land in the manner alleged in the notice. If he was allowed to do so he would in effect, be making a retrospective challenge to the validity of the notice. Finally, it should hardly need stating that if the enforcement notice is a nullity it is totally ineffective and hence a defendant is entitled to argue accordingly; s 243 does not operate to protect nullities.

The effect of s 243(1)(*a*) on criminal proceedings is subject to one statutory qualification which appears in s 243(2). This provides that s 243(1)(*a*) does not apply where a prosecution is brought under s 89(5) of the 1971 Act (failure to comply with an enforcement notice requiring a use of land to be discontinued). The defendant in such a case can defend the prosecution on any ground, including those stated in s 88(2) if he can satisfy the condition that (*a*) he has held an interest in the land since before the enforcement notice was issued; (*b*) a copy of the notice was not served on him; (*c*) he satisfies the court (i) that he did not know and could not reasonably be expected to know that the enforcement notice had been issued, and (ii) that his interests have been substantially prejudiced by the failure to serve him with a copy of it.

8.4 In what circumstances might an application for judicial review be successful?

This is one of the more difficult questions raised by enforcement law and it is doubtful whether a totally satisfactory answer can be given, either in a few paragraphs or in a detailed exposition. While the subject does not entirely defy analysis difficulties are raised by an inconsistency in use of jargon by the judiciary, particularly in relatively early cases, the words 'nullity', 'invalid', 'ultra vires' or simply 'bad' being used without adequate definition. Also, although the judgments given in *Miller-Mead* v *Minister of Housing and Local Government* [1963] 2 QB 196 are extremely helpful in understanding the concepts of nullity and invalidity and have enabled a degree of certainty to be achieved, nevertheless the subject has also to be seen in the rather more fluid administrative law context. Since the key concept in administrative law is ultra vires, and that questions of public law must be pursued by means of an application for judicial review under RSC Ord 53 and s 31 of the Supreme Court Act 1981 rather than by an ordinary action begun by writ (see *O'Reilly* v *Mackman* [1983] 2 AC 237) it is inevitable that the less crystallised and more flexible concepts of administrative law have permeated and to some extent blurred the distinctions made in *Miller-Mead*. As a result the word 'nullity' now seems to be used in a wider class of case than the 'patent defect' class identified in that case.

Although it can be safely asserted that an enforcement notice which is a nullity can be described as ultra vires, some caution is now needed in applying the ultra vires label in relation to notices which have in these pages hitherto been described as 'invalid'. It is suggested, however, that some light has been thrown on this problem by the opinion of Lord Fraser expressed in *Davy* v *Spelthorne Borough Council* [1984] AC 262 that, referring to the word 'validity' in s 243(1)(a), he said that 'the word "validity" is evidently not intended to be understood in its strict sense—it is used to mean enforceability'. This indicates that the label of ultra vires should not necessarily be attached to an enforcement notice which is invalid (in the sense of unenforceable) but can rightly be attached to an enforcement notice which is invalid for some other reason eg that it was issued in bad faith. This is made clear by the Court of Appeal decision in *Jeary* v *Chailey Rural District Council* (supra) in which Orr LJ explained that a local planning authority act within their powers if an enforcement notice is issued which is based upon a false basis of fact. This is because s 87(1) of the 1971 Act, which confers the powers on the local planning authority to take enforcement action, does not impose a precondition to the commencement of such proceedings that a breach of planning control should have taken place: all that is necessary is that it must **appear** to the local planning control that a breach has occurred.

Given that the scope for judicial review is qualified by s 243(1)(a) and that the matters mentioned in s 88(2) are, to adopt Lord Fraser's terminology, largely concerned with the enforceability of the notice, it is submitted that the following examples comprise the residue of matters which are susceptible to judicial review on the ground that they render an enforcement notice ultra vires in the sense that this term is used in administrative law.

8.4.1 Nullity

Subject to the application of Upjohn LJ's test in *Miller-Mead* v *Minister of Housing and Local Government* that the notice must tell the recipient 'fairly what he has done wrong and what he must do to remedy it', a notice which does not 'specify' the matters referred to in s 87(6), (7), (8), (12) and (13) as explained in Chap 6 is a nullity. For examples of cases where an application has been made direct to the High Court to obtain a declaration that it is a nullity see *Burgess* v *Jarvis and Sevenoaks Rural District Council* [1952] 2 QB 41; *Swallow and Pearson* v *Middlesex County Council* [1953] 1 WLR 422; *Eldon Garages Ltd* v *Kingston-upon-Hull County Borough Council* [1974] 1 All ER 358.

8.4.2 Invalidity

An enforcement notice is ultra vires and invalid in each of the following circumstances:

  (i) Lack of jurisdiction to issue the notice. In *Scarborough Borough Council* v *Adams and Adams* [1983] JPL 673 Waller LJ stated that it was open to an enforcee to challenge the notice on the ground that the local planning authority had no jurisdiction to issue it. For an example see *R* v *Secretary of State for the Environment ex p Hillingdon London Borough Council* [1986] 1 All ER 810.

  (ii) Improper exercise of discretion. This encompasses the possibility that the council have taken into account irrelevant matters in resolving to take enforcement action. Thus, for example, the council in *Flashman* v *London Borough of Camden* (1979) 130 New LJ 885 could not take into account its previous failure to recover possession of the property. In *Davy* v *Spelthorne Borough Council* [1984] AC 262 Lord Fraser identified fraud as invalidating a notice: clearly this would involve an improper motivation for the issue of the notice and hence would have a vitiating effect.

  (iii) Misrecitals in the notice. At one time it was thought that misrecitals rendered an enforcement notice invalid, eg *Francis* v *Yiewsley and West Drayton Urban District Council* [1958] 1 QB 478. Having regard to the Secretary of State's power to correct an enforcement notice under s 88A(2) where the correction can be made without injustice, the taint of invalidity and hence ultra vires extends only to the small number of cases where the notice cannot be rectified, eg *Kerrier District Council* v *Secretary of State for the Environment* [1981] JPL 193 and *H T Hughes & Sons Ltd* v *Secretary of State for the Environment* [1985] JPL 486.

(iv) Estoppel. Where an appellant claims the benefit of an estoppel he will normally claim that the effect of the estoppel is that planning permission is not needed for the development in question or that planning permission already exists. Such a claim should be made by way of an appeal under s 88(2)(b) or (c) rather than by way of an application for judicial review, since s 243(1)(a) will apply to prevent challenge to the validity of the notice in the High Court. There is, however, a limited class of case in which the developer may be able to claim that the local planning authority are estopped **from taking enforcement action**, as distinct from being estopped from denying that a particular defence is available to the developer. That limited class, based on a representation by the local planning authority that no enforcement action will be taken, does not fall within s 243. For an example of an attempt to obtain declaratory relief, albeit unsuccessful, see *Western Fish Products Ltd* v *Penwith District Council* (1978) 38 P&CR 7.

8.5 Applying for judicial review

Section 31 of the Supreme Court Act 1981 places on a statutory footing part of the revision of RSC Ord 53 which was effected in 1977 by statutory instrument (see SI 1977 No 1955, as amended by SIs 1980 No 2000 and 1982 No 1111). The provisions regulating applications for judicial review are therefore now contained in s 31 and RSC 1965 (SI 1965 No 1776), as amended by the above instruments) Ord 53 rules 1–14.

The section provides (s 31(1)) that an application to the High Court for an order of mandamus, prohibition, certiorari, or a declaration or injunction 'shall be made in accordance with rules of court by a procedure to be known as an application for judicial review'. Specific provision is made for declaration and injunction in s 31(2) in that these remedies are available if an application for judicial review has been made and the High Court considers that it would be just and convenient for the declaration to be made or the injunction granted having regard to (a) the nature of the matters in respect of which relief may be granted by orders of mandamus, prohibition or certiorari; (b) the nature of the persons and bodies against whom relief may be granted by such orders; and (c) all the circumstances of the case. Any of the five remedies can be claimed either in the alternative or in addition to any other remedy (r 2). Under r 7 it is within the jurisdiction of the court to award damages to a successful applicant if a claim for damages has been included in the application and provided that damages could have been awarded had the matter in respect of which damages are claimed been the subject of an ordinary action.

One of the distinctive features of judicial review is that leave of the High Court is necessary before any application can be made (r 3). Under this rule the application for leave is made ex parte to a judge by means of filing in the Crown Office a notice in Form 86A and an affidavit verifying the facts relied on. The notice is required to contain a statement of (a) the name and address of the applicant; (b) the relief sought and the grounds upon which it is sought; (c) the name and address of the applicant's solicitors; and (d) the applicant's address for service. The application is normally determined by the judge without a hearing unless the applicant has requested to be heard. If leave is refused it is possible to renew the application after giving notice of intention to do so in Form 86B within 10 days of notification of the refusal; the renewed application will come before a judge sitting in open court. Where a hearing was held in relation to the initial application for leave no appeal is available: r 13. In determining whether to grant leave the judge must have regard to r 3(7) which directs that leave shall not be granted unless the court considers that the applicant has a 'sufficient interest' in the matter to which the application relates.

The requirements of leave and of 'sufficient interest' are of such importance that they appear in s 31(3). Lord Diplock explained in *R v Inland Revenue Commissioners ex p National Federation of Self-Employed and Small Businesses Ltd* [1982] AC 617 that the object of the requirement of leave to apply for judicial review is to 'prevent the time of the court being wasted by busybodies with misguided or trivial complaints of administrative error, and to remove the uncertainty in which public officers and authorities might be left as to whether they could safely proceed with administrative action while proceedings for judicial review of it were actually pending even though misconceived'. It appears from the same case that 'sufficient interest' is a mixed question of fact and law in which particular regard is to be had to the relationship between the applicant and the matter giving rise to the application. In the context of enforcement proceedings there can be little doubt that a person who has an interest in the land would have the necessary locus standi to satisfy s 31(3) and r 3(7).

The limitation aspect of an application for judicial review is distinctly more generous than that applicable to an appeal under s 88. In this instance r 4 provides that the application 'shall be made promptly and in any event within three months from the date when grounds for the application first arose unless the Court considers that there is good reason for extending the period within which the application shall be made'. This rule is, however, subject to a qualification imposed by s 3(6) of the Supreme Court Act 1981 which enables the High Court to refuse to grant leave to make the application (or to grant relief on hearing the application itself) if the Court considers that there has been 'undue delay' in making the application and it considers that the granting of the relief sought would be likely to cause substantial hardship to, or substantially prejudice the rights of, any person or would be detrimental to good administration. See *R* v *Stratford-on-Avon District Council ex p Jackson* [1985] 1 WLR 1319 for judicial interpretation of these limitation provisions.

Once leave has been granted the application for judicial review must be made within 14 days; this is achieved by making an originating motion to a judge sitting in open court: r 5(2). Notice of the motion must be served on all persons directly affected and an affidavit giving details of those served must be filed before the motion is entered for hearing. Normally a period of 10 days must elapse from service of the notice of motion before the hearing takes place: r 5(4).

Where it is considered that an enforcement notice is a nullity or invalid the usual remedy will be to obtain a declaration to that effect. Since a declaration can be obtained in civil proceedings otherwise than by making an application for judicial review, does this mean that there is no need to invoke the judicial review procedure at all? In *O'Reilly* v *Mackman* [1983] 2 AC 237 the House of Lords ruled that where the application for a declaration raises questions of public law rights due to the actions of a public authority then, as a general rule, the action should proceed by way of an application for judicial review rather than by ordinary action. To permit matters of public law to be raised by an ordinary action would evade the requirement of leave. This would be an abuse of the process of the court and contrary to public policy. The House of Lords accepted in *O'Reilly* v *Mackman* that a possible exception to the general rule could be made if an issue of public law was raised as a collateral point in an action which was essentially founded in private law. The extent of this possible exception was amplified soon afterwards in a case involving an enforcement notice, *Davy* v *Spelthorne Borough Council* [1984] AC 262. In this case the local planning authority entered into an agreement with the developer to the effect that the developer would not appeal against an enforcement notice which the authority were contemplating serving provided that the notice would not be enforced for three years. The notice was duly served and in accordance with the agreement no appeal was made to the Secretary of State. Before the three year period expired the developer issued a writ alleging that the agreement was ultra vires and claiming damages against the council for having negligently advised him concerning his right of appeal, as the developer considered that he could have appealed successfully. The council sought to have the proceedings struck out as an abuse of the process of the court alleging that the matter should proceed by way of judicial review. The House of Lords held that the claim did not abuse the process of the court because the developer's action for damages was based in tort and hence no issue of public law was involved. Adopting the words used in *O'Reilly* v *Mackman* by Lord Diplock the negligence claim was not concerned with 'the infringement of rights to which the plaintiff was entitled to protection under public law' because the validity of the enforcement notice was not being placed in issue.

Chapter 9

Enforcement Appeals and Inquiries

9.1 General

When an appeal against an enforcement notice has been successfully lodged with the Secretary of State in accordance with s 88 of the 1971 Act and reg 5 of the Enforcement Regulations of 1981 (see Chap 7), together with the correct fee, the appeal will then proceed to a determination. In the majority of cases this will involve the Secretary of State convening a public local inquiry since most enforcement appeals involve disputes over questions of fact which can only be conveniently established through the forum of an inquiry. Some enforcement appeals can, however, be dealt with by means of each party making written representations to the Secretary of State, a procedure which has advantages in being quicker, less complex and expensive, though to some appellants (those who seek to take advantage of the suspension of the effect of the enforcement notice) its rapidity might be seen as a disadvantage. Although some references are made to this procedure in the course of this chapter it is the subject of separate consideration in the final paragraphs.

A right of audience prior to the determination of the appeal is guaranteed by s 88(7). This provides that '. . . the Secretary of State, shall, if either the appellant or the local planning authority so desire, afford to each of them an opportunity of appearing before, and being heard by, a person appointed by the Secretary of State for the purpose'. In granting the opportunity of appearing before a 'person appointed' (a member of the planning inspectorate) the Secretary of State is empowered by s 282 to convene a public local inquiry. He is not obliged to do so, however, as the Secretary of State may grant the parties the opportunity of appearing informally before a planning inspector, though only a minority of cases are resolved in this way.

The procedural aspects of public local inquiries are regulated by the Town and Country Planning (Enforcement) (Inquiries Procedure) Rules 1981 (SI 1981 No 1743) ('the Enforcement Inquiries Rules 1981'); these Rules apply irrespective of whether the appeal is to be determined by the Secretary of State or by the person appointed by the Secretary of State to chair the inquiry. Most enforcement appeals are determined by the 'person appointed' under jurisdiction conferred by Sched 9 of the 1971 Act and the Town and Country Planning (Determination of Appeals by Appointed Persons) (Prescribed Classes) Regulations 1981 (SI 1981 No 804) (as amended by the Town and Country Planning (Determination of Appeals by Appointed Persons) Regulations 1986 (SI 1986 No 623). These regulations also determine the classes of enforcement appeals which are decided by a planning inspector following submission of written representations.

9.2 Pre-inquiry procedure

Although the standard appeal form (Form DoE 14069) requires that the grounds of appeal must be stated by the appellant and that the details of the facts on which the appellant is relying should also be supplied, these details can be withheld until a notice is received from the Secretary of State requesting this information. After receipt of the notice in the form of a written request, the appellant has 28 days in which to specify the relevant grounds and give a brief account of the facts: reg 5 of the Enforcement Regulations 1981. This information is forwarded by the Secretary of State to the local planning authority, to which an onus to respond passes under reg 6. Not later than 28 days before the date fixed by the Secretary of State for the inquiry (or any shorter period which may be agreed in writing between all three parties), the authority must serve a **statement** on the Secretary of State and the appellant which (i) indicates the submissions which will be put forward on the appeal; (ii) contains a summary of the authority's response to each ground of appeal pleaded by the appellant; and (iii) states whether the authority would be prepared to grant planning permission for the development alleged in the enforcement notice to have been carried out and particulars of any conditions which they would wish to attach to any such grant. The Secretary of State may further require the authority to provide details of the persons on whom a copy of the enforcement notice has been served, together with a copy of the enforcement notice itself. If such a request is made it must be complied with not later than 14 days after receipt of the request: reg 8. Failure by either party to comply with the requirements of regs 5 and 6 may lead to the Secretary of State dismissing the appeal or quashing the enforcement notice under s 88(6)(*a*), (*b*). In this respect see Circular 38/81 paras 35 and 39.

Apart from the matters contained in regs 5, 6 and 8 of the Enforcement Regulations 1981, the provisions regulating pre-inquiry procedure are contained in the Enforcement Inquiries Rules 1981, rules 4–6. Under r 4(1) a written notice must be given by the Secretary of State (or the inspector if the appeal is to be determined by the inspector) to the local planning authority and the appellant of the date of the inquiry giving at least 42 days notice of the inquiry with details of the date, time and place at which it will be held. This period may be reduced if the parties to the appeal agree. The Secretary of State will advise the parties under r 5 of the identity of the inspector if the appeal is to be determined by him (ie the 'person appointed'), though no timetable applies to this requirement.

Publicity for the forthcoming inquiry may be required by the Secretary of State under r 4(2). Although no timetable is specified in the 1981 Rules, he may require the authority to take one or more of the following steps:

(*a*) publish in one or more local newspapers a notice of the forthcoming inquiry;

(*b*) serve notice of the inquiry on such persons or classes of persons as he may specify;

(*c*) post notice(s) of the inquiry near to the land in conspicuous places. A site notice may also be required to be posted on the land itself if it is under the control of the appellant. Such a notice must be visible to and legible by the public and must be in position for such period as the Secretary of State specifies: r 4(3).

9.2.1 Pre-inquiry exchange of statements

Under r 6 of the 1981 Rules provision is made for the parties to serve copies of documents which are to be used in evidence at the inquiry. In the case of the local planning authority this also involves issuing the appellant with a statement relating to certain views or opinions on which they also seek to rely. Thus, if appropriate, the local authority must, at least 28 days before the inquiry, serve on the appellant a statement to the effect that they will rely on any of the following written views or opinions expressed in writing by a government department or a local authority:

   (i) a view as to the expediency of issuing the enforcement notice;

  (ii) an opinion on any of the terms of the enforcement notice;

 (iii) a view as to whether planning permission should be granted for the development to which the enforcement notice relates.

Any such statement served under this rule must include a copy of the expression of view or opinion. Equipped with this information, the appellant can make a written request under rr 9(1) and 10(1) to the Secretary of State, for a representative of the department concerned (or of a local authority) to be present at the inquiry respectively. This request must be made at least 14 days before the inquiry. If duly made the Secretary of State is then obliged by rr 9(2) and 10(2) to make appropriate arrangements, including (where necessary) procuring the presence of a representative of that department, or transmitting the request to the local authority.

With regard to other documents (including maps and plans) which are to be referred to at the inquiry, or put in evidence, the local planning authority must, at least 28 days before the inquiry serve a list of these documents on the appellant. The list must include notice of the times and place at which these documents can be inspected; if the appellant decides to inspect them a reasonable opportunity must be given for him to do so and where practicable to take copies of them.

The obligation on the appellant under the Enforcement Inquiries Rules 1981 is slightly different. Under r 6(5) the appellant must, if required to do so by the Secretary of State, give to the local planning authority a written statement of the **submissions** he proposes to put forward at the inquiry. This statement must be accompanied by a list of any documents (including maps and plans) which the appellant intends to refer to or put in evidence at the inquiry. If the authority wish to inspect these documents and take copies of them, a reasonable opportunity must be given to enable the authority to do so. While a requirement is not often made by the Secretary of State under this rule, the power it confers is appropriate where information previously received from the appellant is unclear or inadequate. There appears to be no sanction (ie dismissal of the appeal) if the appellant does not comply.

9.3 Inquiry procedure

Subject to specific requirements contained in the Enforcement Inquiries Rules 1981 (and of the rules of natural justice) the inspector has a discretion conferred by r 11(1) to determine the procedure which is to be followed. The rules do, however, specify the order in which the evidence is to be given, subject to a discretionary power considered further below. They also specify who has the right of appearance at the inquiry. Under r 8 a right of audience is granted to (i) the appellant (ii) the local planning authority (iii) any person on whom the Secretary of State required notice of the inquiry to be served under r 4(2) (iv) the county council, if the enforcement notice was served by the district council (and vice versa) (v) the following bodies in cases where any of them has responsibility for the area in which the land is situated: (*a*) the National Park Committee (*b*) the joint or special planning board (*c*) the new town development corporation (*d*) the urban development corporation (*e*) the enterprise zone authority. Other parties may only appear at the discretion of the inspector. Such 'third parties' will often include neighbours, preservation societies or the parish council. In order to avoid repetitive evidence being given by such parties r 8(4) permits the inspector to allow one or more persons to appear for those who have a common interest. Third parties who have a contribution to make to the inquiry are normally granted audience without question. They will normally be heard after the main parties but it is possible to hear their evidence first if the inspector exercises his discretionary power to permit them to do so, with the agreement of the appellant: r 11(2). Having regard to this reference to r 11(2) it will be apparent that the appellant has the right to be heard first. He also has the right of final reply.

Both the appellant and the local planning authority are entitled to call evidence and cross-examine witnesses, though all other parties are entitled to do so only so far as the inspector permits. Evidence is admitted at the discretion of the inspector (this may therefore include hearsay evidence (see *T A Miller Ltd* v *Minister of Housing and Local Government* [1968] 1 WLR 992)) and he may require evidence to be given on oath pursuant to s 250(2) of the Local Government Act 1972 (applied by s 282(2) of the 1971 Act); this power is often exercised in enforcement inquiries. Evidence may be oral or documentary; it is normal for each witness to prepare and read a proof of evidence and be cross-examined on it. In taking evidence the inspector is authorised by r 11(5) to allow the appellant or the local planning authority to alter or add to the submissions contained in any statement which was served under r 6, the list of documents, or pre-inquiry submissions made under the Enforcement Regulations 1981. Such alterations or additions must only be permitted so far as is necessary to determine the questions of controversy between the parties and an adequate opportunity must be given to the other party to consider the matter. In some cases this may even involve adjournment of the inquiry. Any late alteration or additions should therefore be avoided, not only because of the possibility of an adjournment, but because costs may be awarded against the party making the alteration or addition.

There are two restrictions on evidence which can be given at the inquiry. First, the inspector is required to exclude evidence which would be 'contrary to the public interest' (r 11(4)). Second, a limitation is placed on cross-examination of evidence given by a member of a government department who is present at the inquiry pursuant to a request made by the appellant to the Secretary of State under r 9. While such a witness is required by r 9(2) to state the reasons for any view or opinion on which the local planning authority has chosen to rely, no cross-examination can be made which requires the witness to answer a question which, in the opinion of the inspector, is directed to the merits of government policy. This rule does not, however, apply to a witness who represents a local authority at the inquiry (ie an authority other than the authority which issued the enforcement notice).

While the inquiry proceedings will be conducted at the inspector's discretion and within the legal framework established by the 1981 Rules, it may be helpful to include a brief note on the procedure commonly adopted, including the making of a site inspection. Regard should also be had to the code of Good Practice at Planning Inquiries issued as Appendix F to the Chief Planning Inspector's Report for 1985–86. (It is printed at Appendix 2 to this book.) As the appellant will normally begin the proceedings he will often open his case by making an initial address to the inspector which outlines the main points of his case, giving emphasis to identifying the issues. These matters can then be examined in detail by calling witnesses and taking them through their proofs of evidence. After they have been cross-examined by the local planning authority the opportunity of re-examination can be taken if desired. Witnesses must be prepared to answer questions put to them by the inspector which may be posed at any time during their appearance and after the process of examination, cross-examination and re-examination is complete. After the appellant's witnesses have been heard he should not only cross-examine the local planning authority's witnesses but also gather further points which became apparent from the proceedings for inclusion in his closing submissions.

An opening address by the local planning authority will often not be necessary as the issues will have already been identified by the appellant. Instead, emphasis will be placed by the authority on the closing address which will be made following the hearing of their witnesses using the same procedure as for the appellant witnesses. Third parties will then normally give their evidence. These will commonly support rather than oppose the authority's case and are subject to cross-examination by the appellant.

The parties will normally place particular emphasis on their closing submissions to the inspector, who will often note them in full. They should be limited to essential points revealed by the evidence which has been given during the course of the inquiry, thereby inviting a conclusion favourable to the case being made. The opportunity should also be taken at this stage to make submissions on points of law which may need to be considered in determining the appeal. These should, of course, be detailed rather than a summary.

Site inspection is regulated by r 12 of the 1981 Rules which empowers the inspector to make an unaccompanied visit to the site before or during the inquiry. He may also make a site inspection after the inquiry has closed and must do so if so requested by either party during the course of the inquiry. Such an inspection will be accompanied by the parties. Should any evidence be revealed by a site inspection which has not been placed before the inspector during the course of the inquiry, he should invite the parties to comment on it if it is to be taken into account in determining the appeal or included in a report to the Secretary of State: *Fairmount Investments Ltd* v *Secretary of State for the Environment* [1976] 1 WLR 1255. Failure to do so is a breach of the requirements of natural justice.

9.3.1 Onus and standard of proof

Despite the fact that the local planning authority has alleged a breach of planning control the onus in an enforcement appeal lies on the appellant to disprove the breach: *Nelsovil* v *Minister of*

Housing and Local Government [1962] 1 WLR 404. This is particularly relevant to appeals on grounds (*b*), (*c*), (*d*), (*e*) and (*f*) of s 88(2). Where, on an appeal on ground (*d*) (the four-year rule) the appellant claims immunity from enforcement action, he must show that the unauthorised development commenced more than four years before the enforcement notice was issued: *Parker Brothers (Farms) Ltd* v *Minister of Housing and Local Government* (1969) 210 EG 825. The standard of proof which is required is the balance of probabilities: *LWT Contractors Ltd* v *Secretary of State for the Environment* [1981] JPL 815 and *Thrasyvoulou* v *Secretary of State for the Environment* [1984] JPL 732.

9.4 Post-inquiry procedure

The procedure which is to be followed after the inquiry has closed depends on whether the decision on the appeal is to be made by the Secretary of State or whether the decision is to be taken by the inspector, known as a 'transferred appeal'. By s 88(11) of the 1971 Act, a scheme for determination of appeals by appointed persons contained in Sched 9 is applied to enforcement appeals, thereby permitting such appeals to be determined by inspectors. They are therefore given powers similar to those of the Secretary of State, and a decision reached by an inspector is treated as that of the Secretary of State: Sched 9 para 2(3). Where an appeal would ordinarily fall to be determined under Sched 9 by the inspector, the Secretary of State may nevertheless direct under Sched 9 para 3 that it shall be determined by the Secretary of State. The appeals which fall to be determined as transferred appeals are detailed in the Town and Country Planning (Determination of Appeals by Appointed Persons) (Prescribed Classes) Regulations 1981 (SI 1981 No 804), as amended by the Town and Country Planning (Determination of Appeals by Appointed Persons) Regulations 1986 (SI 1986 No 623). Under reg 3(*b*) decisions on all appeals against enforcement notices under s 88 of the 1971 Act are transferred to inspectors, except appeals by statutory undertakers relating to operational land or proposed operational land. These are reserved for decision by the Secretary of State by reg 4(*b*).

9.4.1 Inspector's report

The distinction between transferred and non-transferred appeals is immediately apparent at the post-inquiry stage as r 13 of the 1981 Rules requires a report to be compiled by the inspector and submitted to the Secretary of State if the appeal is not a transferred appeal or if the Secretary of State has made a direction under Sched 9 para 3 of the 1971 Act withdrawing the appeal from decision by the inspector. This report must include the inspector's findings of fact, his conclusions of fact, and his recommendations, if any, or his reason for not making any recommendations. The Secretary of State is not bound by the report and must therefore exercise his discretion as he sees fit giving such weight to the inspector's findings and recommendations as he considers appropriate: *Nelsovil Ltd* v *Minister of Housing and Local Government* [1962] 1 WLR 404. There is no equivalent procedure to the compilation of a report in the case of transferred appeals.

9.4.2 New evidence

In a minority of enforcement appeals new evidence may become available after the inquiry has closed and before a decision is made on the appeal. Under r 14(1) of the 1981 Rules, provision is made for dealing with new evidence and also for the possibility that the Secretary of State may disagree with the inspector's recommendation because he differs from the inspector on a finding of fact. Thus if the Secretary of State differs from the inspector on a finding of fact, or after the close of the inquiry takes into consideration any new evidence (including expert opinion on a matter of fact) or any new issue of fact (not being a matter of government policy) which was not raised at the inquiry, and as a result is disposed to disagree with the recommendation he must adopt the following procedure. First he must notify the parties of his disagreement and the reasons for it. Then he must grant the appellant and local authority an opportunity of making written representations within 21 days; in the case of new evidence (or a new issue of fact) he must also allow the parties the opportunity of requesting that the inquiry be re-opened.

Transferred appeals are subject to a similar rule contained in r 14(2). Thus if the inspector proposes to take into consideration any new evidence (including expert opinion on a matter of fact) or any new issue of fact (not being a matter of government policy) which was not raised at the inquiry and which he considers material to his decision he must notify the parties of the substance of the matter and grant them an opportunity of making written representations within 21 days. The parties also have the right to request that the inquiry be re-opened. Whether or not the appeal is a transferred one the inquiry must be re-opened in response to such a request: r 14(3).

9.4.3 Determination of the appeal

The powers of the Secretary of State (and of the inspector in a transferred appeal) in determining the appeal are contained in s 88A(1). This provides that 'On determination of an appeal under s 88 . . . the Secretary of State shall give directions for giving effect to the determination, including, where appropriate, directions for quashing the enforcement notice or varying its terms'. Thus every enforcement appeal will result in a direction to quash the notice or to uphold it and may also lead to a direction by the Secretary of State to vary its terms. The scope of the power to vary the terms of the enforcement notice (or to correct any informality, defect or error in the notice) is conferred by s 88A(2); this power was considered in detail in Chap 7.

These powers are supplemented by a power to grant planning permission under s 88B. Since every enforcement appeal is, by virtue of s 88B(3), deemed to give rise to an application for planning permission for the development to which the notice relates, powers are conferred on the Secretary of State to determine the deemed application. Under s 88B(1) the Secretary of State may:

(a) grant planning permission for the development to which the enforcement notice relates or for part of that development or for the development of part of the land to which the enforcement notice relates;

(b) discharge any condition or limitation subject to which planning permission was granted;

(c) determine any purpose for which the land may, in the circumstances obtaining at the time of the determination, be lawfully used having regard to any past use of it and to any planning permission relating to it.

In exercise of these powers the Secretary of State must have regard to the provisions of the development plan so far as material to the subject matter of the enforcement notice, and to any other material considerations. If he decides to grant planning permission this may include permission to retain or complete any building or works on the land, or to do so without complying with a condition subject to which planning permission was previously granted. Where the Secretary of State decides to discharge a condition or limitation under s 88B(1)(b) he may substitute a further condition or limitation which may be more or less onerous: s 88B(2).

The power conferred by s 88B(1) to grant planning permission is linked to the terms of the enforcement notice. The notice delineates the scope of the power and hence the Secretary of State cannot grant planning permission for other development. Hence a decision to grant planning permission for the use of land for the 'parking of motor vehicles' when the enforcement notice had related only to 'parking of motor coaches' was held to exceed the power granted by the provision: *Richmond upon Thames London Borough Council* v *Secretary of State for the Environment* (1972) 224 EG 1555.

Where the Secretary of State discharges a condition and substitutes another he will (*a*) quash the notice, (*b*) discharge the condition attached to the original grant of planning permission, and (*c*) add a fresh condition to the original grant. Lord Widgery CJ pointed out in *Dudley Borough Council* v *Secretary of State for the Environment* [1980] JPL 181 that the same result could be achieved by utilising the power granted by s 92 of the 1971 Act and making a conditional grant of planning permission, which under that section would supersede the enforcement notice. Whether this alternative method is chosen is a matter for the Secretary of State, as is the choice between extending the period for compliance with the requirements of the notice (eg to permit a use of land to continue for a stated period) by varying the terms of the enforcement notice instead of making a temporary grant of planning permission for the same period: *Molddene Ltd* v *Secretary of State for the Environment* [1979] JPL 177.

9.4.4 Notification of decision

The decision of the Secretary of State or in the case of a transferred appeal the appointed person, is communicated by letter. In the case of a transferred appeal r 16(1) requires the inspector to give a written notification of his decision, with reasons, to the appellant, the local planning authority, and to any person who appeared at the inquiry and has asked to be notified of the decision. Copies of any documents, photographs or plans referred to in the decision letter will not be supplied but can be inspected if a request to do so is given to the Secretary of State within six weeks of the notification of the decision.

Where the appeal has been determined by the Secretary of State the same parties have to be notified of the decision as in transferred cases. The recipients, of the decision letter will receive in addition, however, a summary of the inspector's conclusions and recommendations or a copy of the inspector's report to the Secretary of State. If the decision letter is accompanied only by a summary, a copy of the report can be obtained by making a written request to the Secretary of State within one month of the date of the decision (ie the date of the decision letter): r 16(2), (3). This should always be done where the appeal has failed as the report will require scrutiny and will be of importance to any appeal that might be made to the High Court under s 246 of the 1971 Act on a point of law. The report itself will not include the documents, photographs or plans that are appended in the report though, as in the case of transferred appeals, these can be inspected on making a request in that behalf to the Secretary of State within six weeks of notification of the decision or supply of the inspector's report whichever is the later: r 16(4).

Particular attention should be given by the parties to the reasons for the decision contained in the decision letter. A statement of reasons which is unclear or inadequate is a common ground for appeal to the High Court as this will be a breach not only of the 1981 Rules but also of s 12 of the Tribunals and Inquiries Act 1971. In *Hope* v *Secretary of State for the Environment* (1975) 31 P&CR 120 Phillips J expressed the view (at p 123) that '. . . the decision must be such that it enables the appellant to understand on what grounds the appeal has been decided and be in sufficient detail to enable him to know what conclusions the inspector has reached on the principal important controversial issues'. This case was the subject of a further inquiry and a further challenge was made to the decision of the Secretary of State: in *Hope* v *Secretary of State for the Environment* [1979] JPL 104, Sir Douglas Frank QC (sitting as a deputy judge) added that 'the reasons given must be such as not to leave in the mind of an informed reader such real and substantial doubt as to the reasons for his decision and as to the matters which he had and had not taken into account'. See also *Givandan & Co Ltd* v *Minister of Housing and Local Government* (1967) 18 P&CR 88. It should be borne in mind, however, that 'It is no part of the court's duty to subject the letter to the kind of scrutiny appropriate to the determination of a contract or statute' per Forbes J in *Seddon Properties Ltd* v *Secretary of State for the Environment* (1978) 248 EG 950.

9.5 Recovery of costs

The parties to an enforcement appeal must normally bear their own costs of preparing for and participating in the inquiry. An award of costs can, however, be made by the Secretary of State in exercise of powers under s 250(5) of the Local Government Act 1972, which is applied to inquiries by s 282(2) of the 1971 Act. Although these provisions do not restrict the power to award costs, the Secretary of State has advised in Circular 2/87 (Welsh Office 5/87) entitled 'Award of Costs Incurred in Planning and Compulsory Purchase Order Proceedings' that an award of costs will only be made if he is satisfied that the party against whom costs are sought has behaved unreasonably. This restates the advice formerly contained in DoE Circulars 73/65 and 69/71, though the 1987 circular is more specific in explaining when a party can be considered to have behaved unreasonably. If an award of costs is sought the application should be made to the inspector at or before the close of the inquiry itself: Circular 2/87 para 26, though a subsequent application can be made if good reasons can be shown for not having made the application at the earlier stage. The claim itself is conducted by written submissions: para 27. Third parties are expected to bear their own costs, though para 25 of the Circular advises that an award of costs can be made for or against third parties in 'exceptional circumstances'. This is identified as unreasonable conduct relating to procedure at the inquiry which causes unnecessary expense eg due to an adjournment.

In the case of an appeal which is to be determined by the Secretary of State, r 13 of the 1981 Rules requires the inspector to report on the application for costs to the Secretary of State and draw his attention to any matter which appears to him to be relevant to the decision. A recommendation on the matter can also be included in the report.

The power to award costs is not limited however to Secretary of State inquiry cases as the power also applies to transferred inquiry cases by virtue of s 49 and Sched 11 para 8 to the Housing and Planning Act 1986. Written representations cases are also included by virtue of para 9 of Sched 11.

Unreasonable behaviour committed by another party must have taken place before an award can be made in favour of the applicant. Circular 2/87 makes it clear in para 6 that before an award of costs can be made the alleged unreasonable behaviour must have caused the applicant to incur expense unnecessarily, either (i) because it should not have been necessary for the case to come before the Secretary of State for determination, or (ii) because of the manner in which another party has conducted his part of the proceedings. Some examples of grounds for awarding costs against the appellant or the local planning authority in enforcement proceedings are as follows:

9.5.1 Awards against local planning authorities

1 Unreasonable issue of an enforcement notice. The local planning authority is expected to exercise care to ensure that an enforcement notice takes full account of relevant case law and of planning policy and advice stated in Circulars. Moreover, in enforcement cases the Secretary of State will need to consider whether the planning authority had reasonable grounds for concluding that there had been a breach of planning control and also the adequacy of their stated reasons (as required by reg 3 of the Town and Country Planning (Enforcement Notices and Appeals) Regulations 1981) why enforcement action was considered expedient in the particular circumstances. For example, it will generally be regarded as unreasonable for a planning authority to have issued an enforcement notice when their sole reason for doing so is the absence of a valid planning permission for the particular development enforced against and it is concluded on appeal that there is no significant planning objection to the alleged breach of control: para 14.

2 Handling of the enforcement proceedings. If the local planning authority have refused a request from the appellant to discuss the possibility of granting planning permission (including a conditional permission) for the development alleged in the enforcement notice, or have refused to provide information which they could be reasonably expected to provide. An award of costs may be made if the appeal might otherwise have been avoided: para 16.

3 Failure to undertake reasonable investigations to establish whether or not there has been a breach of planning control, by, for example, making inquiries of the owner and the occupier of the premises, and consulting their own records for information about any previous planning consents. Failure to undertake reasonable investigations of this nature may provide grounds for an award of costs if it results in an appeal to the Secretary of State which might otherwise have been avoided: para 17.

4 Conduct of the appeal. Costs may be awarded if the local planning authority withdraw the enforcement notice in the course of the proceedings, or where they have been un-

necessarily prolonged by lack of co-operation in settling agreed facts or supplying relevant information: para 18.

5 Failure to comply with procedural requirements leading to an adjournment of the inquiry because of serious prejudice to the appellant eg if submissions are made on matters not included in the pre-inquiry statement: para 19.

9.5.2 Awards against appellants

1 Unreasonably making an appeal. If it is obvious that the appeal against the enforcement notice has no reasonable prospect of success, having regard to policy statements and judicial decisions: para 20.

2 Handling of the enforcement proceedings. The appellant must comply with procedural requirements and hence a failure to provide an adequate pre-inquiry statement or introduction of a new ground of appeal may be considered unreasonable behaviour, particularly if expenses are incurred due to an adjournment. In addition costs can be awarded against an appellant who is wilfully unco-operative, for example, by refusing to explain the grounds of appeal, or by refusing to discuss the appeal, if the planning authority are thereby put to unnecessary expense: para 21.

3 Withdrawal or failure to pursue the appeal. If the appellant withdraws his appeal so soon before the inquiry date that there is insufficient time to inform other parties and their witnesses, an award may be made covering the attendance costs of all other parties: para 22.

If an award of costs is made the sum awarded is the amount necessarily and reasonably incurred and will exclude any indirect costs, eg due to the effects of delay. Once awarded, the measure is determined by agreement between the parties following submission of details of costs to the party against whom the award has been made. In default of agreement the party to whom costs have been awarded can refer the matter to a Master of the Supreme Court Taxing Office for a determination.

If an award of costs is not made, where one has been requested, the Secretary of State's decision can be the subject of an application for judicial review in the same way as any other administrative decision: *R* v *Secretary of State for the Environment ex p Wild* [1985] JPL 753.

9.6 Written representations

An alternative to the holding of a public local inquiry (or of informal appearance before a planning inspector) is to make written representations to the Secretary of State, a method which can be employed if the appellant and local planning authority are both willing to waive the right of audience granted by s 88(7). In the case of the appellant this can be indicated to the Secretary of State on the standard appeal form DoE 14069 in response to a question in that behalf.

Where the written representations procedure is to be used the procedure prescribed by the Enforcement Regulations 1981 (see para **9.2** above) will apply with minor modifications. While reg 5 applies (submission of statement of grounds of appeal and facts which are to be relied on) to all enforcement appeals, a modification is made to reg 6 which deals with the statement made by the local planning authority. Where no inquiry is to be held reg 6(2)(*b*) provides that the local planning authority's statement must be served on the Secretary of State not later than 28 days from the date on which the notice is sent by him to the authority requiring the statement (normally at the same time that the making of the appeal is notified). Of particular importance in the present context, however, is that reg 7 of the 1981 Regulations (which is inapplicable where an inquiry is held) must be complied with. This requires the local planning authority to give notice of the appeal to the occupiers of properties in the locality of the appeal site and to any other persons who in the opinion of the authority are affected by the alleged breach of planning control. This notification is not in prescribed form but must include the following information:

(*a*) a description of the alleged breach of planning control;

(*b*) a statement of the reasons why the local planning authority consider it expedient to issue the enforcement notice;

(*c*) the grounds on which the appellant appealed against the enforcement notice; and

(*d*) a statement that interested persons may submit comments in writing to the local planning authority within a period specified in the notification.

Any responses to this notification procedure will be submitted to the Secretary of State not later than submission of the authority's statement under reg 6. As with inquiry procedure, the statement made by the local planning authority under reg 6(2)(*b*) must summarise the response of the authority to each ground of appeal pleaded by the appellant and a statement whether they would be prepared to grant planning permission for the development alleged in the enforcement notice, together with any conditions which they would wish to attach to such a grant.

The precise procedure which is to be followed on a written representations appeal once regs 6(2)(b) and 7 of the 1981 Regulations have been complied with is in need of clarification by the Department of the Environment. This is because guidance formerly contained in Parts I and II of Circular 38/81 (which was applicable to planning as well as enforcement appeals) was withdrawn when further guidance was issued in Circular 18/86. Unfortunately the latter circular is expressly limited to planning appeals, with the result that the Department may have inadvertently created a small lacuna. In view of this observation the following two paragraphs must be regarded as tentative, though they reflect the intention of the Department to expedite the appeal process.

Once the local planning authority have submitted their statement the Secretary of State will transmit a copy of it (and the submissions of any interested parties) to the appellant who should submit any observations to the Department within two weeks. If negotiations are taking place between the appellant and the local planning authority this period can be extended if a written request is sent to the Department and an extension of time is granted.

The appeal will be decided on the basis of the documents submitted pursuant to this procedure as it is intended that no further submissions should be made unless there is insufficient evidence on which to decide the appeal. There will then follow a site visit by the inspector; this will only involve the parties if access is needed to the site. A decision should then be issued within a period of four weeks from the date of the site visit.

9.6.1 Notification of decision

As with inquiry cases, the decision of the Secretary of State, or, in the case of a transferred appeal, the inspector, is communicated by letter. As there is no equivalent to the Enforcement Inquiries Rules 1981 there is no delegated legislative provision requiring reasons to be given for the decision unless requested by appellant or local planning authority. In *Westminster City Council* v *Secretary of State for the Environment* [1984] JPL 27, Mr David Widdicombe QC (sitting as a deputy judge) expressed the view that s 12 of the Tribunals and Inquiries Act 1971 applied and he observed that this provision applies to all transferred appeals by virtue of para 7 of Sched 9 to the 1971 Act. Reasons should therefore be given pursuant to the section if a request is duly made on or before notification of the decision. In *Sir George Grenfell-Baines v Secretary of State for the Environment* [1985] JPL 256 Woolf J went further and considered that there was a general duty to give reasons. In practice, reasons are always given in written representations appeals and therefore the main interest is in their clarity and adequacy. In this respect Woolf J was of the opinion that it would often be possible for an inspector to give a much shorter decision than would be practicable when there had been an inquiry and oral evidence. Frequently it would not be necessary for the inspector to set out his findings of fact expressly, or it might be clear from the nature of the representations that no such findings were necessary. Equally it might be possible for the inspector to incorporate the submissions which had been made in writing into his decision letter, hence avoiding the necessity of recording many matters which might otherwise have to be set out in it in order to make it intelligible.

Although a decision letter issued following the submission of written submissions may be less lengthy than one issued following an inquiry, the reasons given by the inspector must reach the same standard of intelligibility and completeness: *Westminster City Council v Secretary of State for the Environment* (supra). Mr David Widdicombe QC stated that the fact that the written representations procedure was employed was not a ground for relaxing the standards previously established by the judiciary. Thus it is not enough for the inspector to state 'I have considered the written representations' for he must show that he has considered the essence of the appellant's case: *Shepperton Builders Ltd v Secretary of State for the Environment* [1979] JPL 102.

If a decision letter does not contain a sufficient or intelligible statement of reasons the Secretary of State (or in the case of a transferred appeal, the inspector) will commit an error of law. As such the error is capable of being the subject of an appeal to the High Court under s 246 of the 1971 Act. Appeals to the High Court under s 246 on this and other grounds are not uncommon and it is to this important section that attention now passes.

Chapter 10

Appeal to the High Court

10.1 Introduction

Once an appeal against an enforcement notice has been progressed through the procedure described in Chap 9, leading to a decision issued by the Secretary of State under s 88A, a further right of appeal is available under s 246. While most enforcement appeals will not be the subject of litigation under this section, it is nevertheless a crucial provision as it enables the parties to the appeal to challenge the decision of the Secretary of State on a point of law; many of the cases discussed in this book have been the subject of this procedure. The remedy is available irrespective of whether the decision was transferred to the inspector, and irrespective of whether the appeal was decided following submission of written representations.

If an appeal under s 246 is successful the result is that the matter is remitted to the Secretary of State for rehearing and determination. The High Court has no power to quash an enforcement notice under this provision but the Secretary of State may (following consideration) decide to do so, or to hold a new public local inquiry if the application arose from a procedural defect.

10.2 Use of s 246 procedure

The section has a scope which is slightly wider than enforcement notice appeals as it extends, in addition, to two other matters which in the interests of clarity and brevity have been excluded from this book. These matters are listed building enforcement notice appeals and appeals relating to enforcement of duties to replace trees, the latter item being the concern of s 246(1A). Shorn of material which is not relevant to the present context the provisions of s 246(1) are as follows:

s 246(1) Where the Secretary of State gives a decision in proceedings on an appeal under Part V of this Act against
(a) an enforcement notice;
the appellant or the local planning authority or any other person having an interest in the land to which the notice relates may, according as rules of court may provide, either appeal to the High Court against the decision on a point of law or require the Secretary of State to state and sign a case for the opinion of the High Court.

The persons who have the right of appeal under this section are therefore the principal parties to the appeal and any other person having an 'interest' in the land. No definition of 'interest' appears in the section but reference can be made to the discussion at Chap 7 (para **7.4**) in connection with the right of appeal under s 88, with which this provision is consistent. Other parties such as neighbours are therefore excluded but they are not without a right of appeal as it is to s 245 of the 1971 Act that such parties must look. This provision is discussed in para **10.6** below. Unlike an applicant under s 245, an appellant under s 246 need not be a 'person aggrieved'.

Section 246 can only be employed where the Secretary of State 'gives a decision in proceedings on an appeal'. Thus where the Secretary of State declines to accept jurisdiction on an enforcement notice appeal because it is out of time the decision can only be challenged by judicial review rather than under s 246: *Lenlyn Ltd* v *Secretary of State for the Environment* [1984] JPL 482. The same applies to cases where the Secretary of State declines jurisdiction on the ground that the notice is a nullity: *Rhymney Valley District Council* v *Secretary of State for Wales* [1985] JPL 27, but apparently s 246 applies where the Secretary of State has erroneously ruled that the notice is not a nullity: *Dudley Bowers Amusement Enterprises Ltd* v *Secretary of State for the Environment* (1986) 278 EG 313.

Most decisions taken by the Secretary of State will fall within the category of 'a decision in proceedings on an appeal' and therefore subject to s 246. This includes cases where the Secretary of State does not proceed with an appeal because the appellant does not provide the grounds of appeal and the facts upon which he is relying when called upon to do so by the Secretary of State under reg 5 of the Enforcement Regulations 1981. As will shortly be seen, an appellant has only 28 days in which to challenge such a decision under s 246; if he fails to do so he cannot claim that the Secretary of State wrongly rejected his appeal as a defence in criminal proceedings: *Button* v *Jenkins* [1975] 3 All ER 585, *Horsham District Council* v *Fisher* [1977] JPL 178 and *Wain* v *Secretary of State for the Environment* (1978) 39 P&CR 82.

The section contemplates two possible means of testing the point of law raised by the appellant, and for rules of court to specify the relevant procedures. In fact the Rules of the Supreme Court (SI 1965 No 1776) only make provision for an appeal to the High Court. Thus the latter part of s 246(1) under which an appellant can require the Secretary of State to state and sign a case for the opinion of the High Court is presently redundant: in *Hoser* v *Ministry of Housing and Local Government* [1963] Ch 428 it was held that in the absence of rules of court the appellant had no right of election as to the procedure to be followed. A procedure is prescribed for appeals to the High Court which is contained in RSC Ords 55 and 94 of which a principal feature is that only 28 days are allowed for the making of such an appeal.

10.2.1 Effect of appeal on the enforcement notice

Where an appeal has been made to the Secretary of State under s 88, it was observed in Chap 7 (see para **7.2**) that the effect of s 88(10) is that the enforcement notice 'shall be of no effect pending the final determination . . . of the appeal'. What constitutes the 'final determination' for these purposes? Is it when a decision has been given on the s 88 appeal or does the enforcement notice remain of no effect pending the outcome of an appeal under s 246? In *Garland* v *Westminster London Borough Council* (1970) 21 P&CR 555 Bridge J expressed the view (at p 558) that the time of final determination must 'at the latest be the time when an appeal, whether to the Minister or from the Minister to this court or from this court to the Court of Appeal, has been dismissed and the time for appealing further has expired without such further appeal having been instituted'. Applying this dictum an enforcement notice would remain suspended by a s 246 appeal, and would also be suspended during the time available for making such an appeal, even if none is actually made. The period for compliance specified in the notice will then begin to run. The Divisional Court has subsequently decided, however, in *Dover District Council* v *McKeen* [1985] JPL 627 that the suspensive effect of s 88(10) is limited to the s 88 appeal only and comes to an end on the day when the Secretary of State issues his decision upholding the notice. If the local planning authority then prosecute for failure to comply with the notice notwithstanding that an appeal under s 246 is being made the courses open to the appellant to take are to seek an adjournment of the prosecution proceedings or to seek an order under RSC Ord 55 r 3(3) in interlocutory proceedings in the High Court that the appeal under s 246 should operate as a stay on any proceedings under the enforcement notice: *London Parachuting Ltd* v *Secretary of State for the Environment* [1986] JPL 279.

10.3 Procedure for appeal under s 246

The procedural requirements for making an appeal under s 246 are to be found principally in RSC Ords 55 and 94. Under RSC Ord 55 r 4 the time limit for making an appeal is 28 days from the date on which notice of the decision is given to the appellant. In *Ringroad Investments Ltd* v *Secretary of State for the Environment* (1979) 30 P&CR 99 the appellants entered their appeal on the twenty-eighth day after receiving a decision letter from the Secretary of State. The letter had been posted on the day prior to its receipt and the question arose whether time should be calculated from the date of receipt or from an earlier point in time. The Divisional Court rather reluctantly held that the application was out of time and that the court was bound by the previous authority of *Minister of Labour* v *Genner Iron and Steel Co (Wollescote) Ltd* [1967] 1 WLR 1386. The point is, however, not conclusively settled as the Court of Appeal considered obiter in *Griffiths* v *Secretary of State for the Environment* [1983] 2 AC 51 that the 28 day period should run from the date on which the decision letter is received. In that case the House of Lords took a robust view in their interpretation of s 245 of the Act which uses the words 'action . . . taken' by the Secretary of State, rather than the words 'notice . . . was given' which appear in RSC Ord 55 r 4.

An appellant who is out of time must seek an extension under RSC Ord 3 r 5. Although the court has a broad discretion to grant an extension of time the Court of Appeal warned in *Smith* v *Secretary of State for the Environment* (1987) *The Times*, 6 July that Ord 3 r 5 did not provide an easy escape route for practitioners who failed to conduct their clients cases with reasonable expedition. In that case the Court of Appeal upheld a refusal to grant an extension of time when the applicant had merely set out the chronology of events which had resulted in delay without giving any reasons which would tend to excuse it.

The method of making the appeal is by originating motion: Order 94 r 12. The originating motion (which must specify the grounds of appeal) is entered in the Crown Office within the permitted 28 day period and notice of the motion must be served (also within the 28 day period) on the Secretary of State and the local planning authority. If the appeal is brought by the local planning authority they must serve notice of the motion on the person who appealed to the Secretary of State under s 88. In either case the s 246 appellant must also serve notice of the motion on any other person who was served with a copy of the enforcement notice: r 12(3).

As evidence in a s 246 appeal is submitted by affidavit under Ord 94 r 3, arrangements are also made for filing and service of copies. The affidavit which supports the application made by the appellant must be filed in the Crown Office within 14 days after service of the notice of motion and a copy must (a) be filed in the Crown Office, together with any exhibit, for the use of the Court (r3(4)); and (b) be served on the respondent to the proceedings, together with any exhibit (r 3(2)). If the proceedings are opposed the respondent is required by r 3(3) to file an affidavit in the Crown Office within 21 days after service on him of the appellant's affidavit, together with a copy of it and any exhibit, and to serve the same on the appellant.

A further procedural matter is contained in Ord 55 r 7(4). This provision (which is of general application) places an appellant under a duty to apply to the inspector who chaired the public local inquiry for a signed copy of any note made by him during the proceedings and to provide this for the use of the court. In a case in which the appellant sought to obtain this evidence, *Weitz v Secretary of State for the Environment* (1983) 43 P&CR 150, in order to support an application under s 246 in which it was alleged that the inspector had erred in law in failing to deal with a substantive issue raised at the inquiry, Woolf J observed that Ord 55 r 7(4) had not previously been applied in this type of appeal. He then decided that appellants need not comply with this requirement, nor was it necessary for the inspector's note to be made available to the appellant. Although Woolf J accepted that there might be unspecified exceptional circumstances demanding the production of the inspector's note, as the appeal was on a point of law (rather than of fact) there was no need to require more than the inspector's report to the Secretary of State, or, in a transferred appeal, his decision letter. As will be seen below some exceptions have been established which are consistent with the ruling given by Woolf J; these are considered below in the context of the scope of s 246. Once the procedural steps have been complied with, the hearing will take place before a single judge of the Queens Bench Division. The court may, however, direct that the matter should be heard and determined by a Divisional Court in accordance with Ord 94 r 12(2A).

10.4 The scope of s 246

At this stage it is appropriate to consider the nature of the matters that can be the subject of an appeal to the High Court under the section. It is to be emphasised that the provision is concerned to provide a means of challenging the Secretary of State's decision on a s 88 appeal, but only on a point of law. Prima facie, therefore, issues of fact cannot be put in issue by this procedure, a matter made clear by the Divisional Court in *Green* v *Minister of Housing and Local Government* [1967] 2 WLR 192. In this case the appellant had been unsuccessful in resisting an enforcement notice while seeking to rely on the application of the four-year limitation rule. After the decision was issued further evidence became available which the appellant submitted cast doubt on the findings of the inspector. In dismissing the appeal Widgery J (as he then was) commented that it was 'a very bold argument that a section giving a power to appeal on a point of law can in fact result in a complete rehearing of the facts together with the admission of new evidence'. He made it clear, however, that fresh evidence might need to be admitted if the court was faced with a question of jurisdiction or a question of procedure adopted by the Secretary of State when it was necessary to find out precisely what the Secretary of State had done and on what grounds he had done it.

Just as fresh evidence will normally be excluded, so also will an examination of evidence which has been submitted to the inquiry. This will take place, however, if the error of law alleged by the appellant is that the inspector reached a conclusion that no reasonable inspector could have reached and there is sufficient evidence from the affidavits and grounds for the appeal contained in the originating motion to justify an examination of uncontroverted evidence placed before the inspector: *Forkhurst* v *Secretary of State for the Environment* (1982) 46 P&CR 89. Hodgson J in this case also issued guidance on the relevance of Ord 55 r 7(4) to s 246 appeals. He stated (at p 102) that the rule only applied '. . . when the appellant wished to place before the court all the material that had been before the inspector either because . . . the decision letter did not itself contain a record of the evidence or because a ground of appeal was that the inspector's record was so inaccurate that the appellant was entitled to supplement his record'.

It would appear from the many reported cases involving s 246 that the majority of appeals do not succeed, though many are made more in hope than expectation of success. Thus in *Donovan* v *Secretary of State for the Environment* (1987) *The Times*, 4 July, Otton J held that no error of law occurred when the Secretary of State had upheld an enforcement notice where the complaint was that the local planning authority had chosen to take enforcement action only against the appellant, in circumstances when they were aware of other traders who were also in breach of planning control. In another recent case, *ELS Wholesale (Wolverhampton) Ltd* v *Secretary of State for the Environment* (1987) *The Times*, 5 May, it was made clear that it was not a ground of appeal under s 246 that the inspector had paid insufficient heed to certain factors or failed to take sufficient account of certain matters, or that the evidence to support his findings was inadequate. Such complaints amount in substance to a claim that the inspector has failed to rely on the evidence or factors concerned to the extent that the appellant would have wished. The Divisional Court did make it clear, however, that if there was no evidence to support a finding of fact or that a material consideration has been left out of account, questions of law could be raised and hence could be the subject of a s 246 appeal.

It is the case, however, that a sizeable proportion of s 246 appeals do succeed. The following cases provide a few illustrations of instances where the matter has been remitted to the Secretary of State for rehearing and determination. It seems that planning inspectors often fall into error in identifying the correct planning unit: *Burdle* v *Secretary of State for the Environment* [1972] 1 WLR 1207; *Wood* v *Secretary of State for the Environment* (1973) 25 P&CR 303; *De Mulder* v *Secretary of State for the Environment* [1974] QB 792; *Barling Ltd* v *Secretary of State for the Environment* [1980] JPL 594; *TLG Building Materials Ltd* v *Secretary of State for the Environment* [1981] JPL 313, *Duffy* v *Secretary of State for the Environment* [1981] JPL 811. Exercise of the power to correct or vary the terms of an enforcement notice is also a fertile source of litigation: *Hammersmith London Borough Council* v *Secretary of State for the Environment* (1975) 30 P&CR 19; *Dunton Park Caravan Site Ltd* v *Secretary of State for the Environment*

[1981] JPL 511; *H T Hughes & Sons Ltd* v *Secretary of State for the Environment* [1985] JPL 486. Errors of law which occur during inquiry proceedings should also be appealed under s 246 eg *Thrasyvoulou* v *Secretary of State for the Environment* [1984] JPL 732.

10.5 Powers of the court

If an appeal is successful the powers of the court are as provided by the Rules of the Supreme Court 1965. Section 246(3) of the 1971 Act authorises rules of court to be made to provide for remitting the matter for rehearing and determination by the Secretary of State. Order 94 r 12(5) duly provides that 'if the Court is of the opinion that the decision appealed against was erroneous in point of law, it shall not set aside or vary that decision but shall remit the matter to the Secretary of State with the opinion of the Court for rehearing and determination by him'. These provisions make it clear that the court has no power to quash a decision of the Secretary of State from which the appeal has been made; it is for the Secretary of State to act in accordance with the court's opinion which may lead to the enforcement notice being quashed by him or a new inquiry being held. The whole matter is remitted to the Secretary of State and hence he is not bound by any aspect of his previous determination. Thus in *Newbury District Council* v *Secretary of State for the Environment* (1987) *The Times*, 2 July, Kennedy J held that even if the Secretary of State had already granted planning permission under s 88B(1), he was entitled to come to a different decision on rehearing and determination. Since the application under s 246 made by the local planning authority had been successful the whole matter was to be determined afresh and hence it was not the case that the developer could claim the benefit of any planning consent previously granted by the Secretary of State on the s 88 appeal.

It appears that the High Court has no discretion under s 246 if an error of law is established. As Ord 94 r 12(5) uses the words 'shall remit' it seems that the court is under a duty to remit the matter to the Secretary of State even if the error of law is slight. The Court of Appeal has expressed the view that the matter should always be remitted if there was any possibility however slight, that the Secretary of State may have been influenced by it: *LTSS Print and Supply Services Ltd* v *Hackney London Borough Council* [1975] 1 WLR 138 at p 142 (Goff LJ).

10.6 Relevance of s 245

Most of the decisions which can be taken by the Secretary of State under the 1971 Act are challengeable in the High Court under s 245, rather than under s 246. The latter section is one of a small number of provisions which provide an appeal facility in respect of a decision by the Secretary of State which cannot be conveniently channelled through the facility provided by s 245. Nevertheless, as will now be explained, s 245 is relevant in a limited respect to decisions taken by the Secretary of State under s 88.

Under s 88B(1) the Secretary of State is empowered to grant planning permission for the development to which the enforcement notice relates, or for part of that development, or for the development of part of the land to which the enforcement notice relates. He can also discharge any condition or limitation subject to which planning permission was granted. Such a decision is brought within the scope of s 245 of the 1971 Act by s 245(3).

The remedy which s 245 offers is not unlike that of s 246 but is couched in rather different terms. It enables the local planning authority or any 'person aggrieved' by the decision of the Secretary of State to question the validity of his decision on the grounds that:

(a) it is not within the powers of the Act; or
(b) that any relevant requirements have not been complied with.

Any challenge in the High Court under this section must be made within six weeks of the action being taken; time runs from the date when the Secretary of State's decision letter is typed, signed on his behalf, and date-stamped: *Griffiths* v *Secretary of State for the Environment* [1983] 2 AC 51. On an application being made under this section the High Court is empowered by s 245(4) to (i) suspend the operation of the Secretary of State's decision until the matter has been finally determined, and (ii) if satisfied that the application succeeds on the ground that the Secretary of State's decision is not within the powers of the Act, or that the applicant has been substantially prejudiced by a failure to comply with any relevant requirements, the High Court may quash his decision. While a person who has an interest in land may challenge a decision of the Secretary of State given under s 88B(1) by using s 245 it seems that he can, in the alternative use s 246: *Gill* v *Secretary of State for the Environment* [1985] JPL 710. The remedy under s 245 is the more appropriate, however, to such a case and is of particular relevance to a party who lacks locus standi to appeal under s 246, such as a neighbour. Such a party will normally qualify as a 'person aggrieved' see *Bizony* v *Secretary of State for the Environment* [1976] JPL 306 and *Hollis* v *Secretary of State for the Environment* [1983] JPL 164.

Chapter 11

Prosecution for Non-Compliance with an Enforcement Notice

11.1 Introduction

The criminal sanctions for failure to comply with an enforcement notice are contained in s 89 of the 1971 Act. This section creates a number of offences (four in all) by (i) drawing a distinction between different types of default in compliance with an enforcement notice and (ii) by prescribing that failure to comply with an enforcement notice following an initial conviction is a further offence. The main provisions are s 89(1), (4) and (5).

Under s 89(1) where:

> . . . a copy of an enforcement notice has been served on the person who, at the time when the copy was served on him, was the owner of the land to which the notice relates then, if any steps required by the notice to be taken (other than the discontinuance of a use of land) have not been taken within the period allowed for compliance with the notice, that person shall be liable on summary conviction to a fine not exceeding £2,000 or on conviction on indictment to a fine.

The further offence with which this provision is associated is contained in s 89(4). This provides for a further fine not exceeding £200 for each day on which the requirements of the enforcement notice remain unfulfilled, with an unlimited fine if convicted on indictment.

While s 89(1) and (4) are concerned with enforcement notices which require steps to be taken on the land other than discontinuance of a use of the land, s 89(5) is much wider in scope. It contains two offences in the same sub-section and provides as follows:

> Where, by virtue of an enforcement notice, a use of land is required to be discontinued, or any conditions or limitations are required to be complied

with in respect of a use of land or in respect of the carrying out of operations thereon, then if any person uses the land or causes or permits it to be used, or carries out those operations or causes or permits them to be carried out, in contravention of the notice, he shall be guilty of an offence, and shall be liable on summary conviction to a fine not exceeding £2,000 or on conviction on indictment to a fine; and if the use is continued after the conviction he shall be guilty of a further offence and liable on summary conviction to a fine not exceeding £200 for each day on which the use is so continued, or on conviction on indictment to a fine.

This provision therefore applies not only to uses of land but also failure to comply with any conditions or limitations subject to which planning permission has been granted for any form of development. While these provisions are examined in this chapter, together with defences available to a prosecution, it is desirable at this stage to deal with a preliminary issue, namely when a prosecution by the local planning authority becomes competent.

11.2 The point in time at which an offence is committed

If the enforcee, having received a copy of the enforcement notice, decides simply to ignore the notice and does not utilise the right of appeal to the Secretary of State under s 88, he will put himself at risk of prosecution as soon as the period allowed for compliance with the notice has expired. But it is in cases where an appeal is made to the Secretary of State that more difficult questions arise, flowing from the effect of s 88(10) which provides that the enforcement notice 'shall be of no effect pending the final determination or the withdrawal of the appeal'. Clearly while the enforcement notice is ineffective there can be no question of prosecution.

If an appeal is withdrawn before determination by the Secretary of State the notice becomes effective again. Where the date of withdrawal is subsequent to the date on which the notice is to come into effect the enforcee will have the full period specified for compliance available to him. He nevertheless runs the risk of prosecution where an appeal made by another person interested in the land is withdrawn but the enforcee has no notice of the fact that the notice has once again become active. In *South Cambridgeshire District Council v Stokes* [1981] JPL 594 a landlord was prosecuted under s 89(1) in circumstances where his tenant, who had appealed against the enforcement notice, had subsequently withdrawn his appeal. The defendant had successfully argued in the Crown Court that as he had not known that the appeal had been withdrawn he did not know the date on which the notice had once again become effective. The

Divisional Court allowed the appeal of the local planning authority and held that since the defendant knew of the enforcement proceedings it was incumbent upon him to make enquiry of the local planning authority of the progress of the appeal, as he had to take proper care to inform himself. The Divisional Court doubted whether it was an essential ingredient of the mens rea of the offence but even if this was the case, it was subject to the rider that the enforcee had to take proper care to inform himself of any facts which would make his conduct lawful or unlawful.

Where no withdrawal takes place, at what point in time, in the words of s 88(10) does a 'final determination' of the appeal occur? As an appeal can be made from the Secretary of State, is it necessary to add on a further period of 28 days from the date of his decision in order to allow for the possibility that an appeal might be made to the High Court under s 246? Despite a strong obiter dictum of Bridge J in *Garland* v *Westminster London Borough Council* (1970) 21 P&CR 555 at p 558 to the effect that such an allowance should be made, the Divisional Court decided in *Dover District Council* v *McKeen* [1985] JPL 627 that on construction of the legislation no such allowance should be made and that therefore a person who had failed to comply with the requirements of an enforcement notice within the period specified by the notice was properly convicted when an information was laid within the following 28 days. The Divisional Court held that s 88(10) applied only to the appeal to the Secretary of State and not to any subsequent appeal under s 246.

Once the Secretary of State has decided an appeal in favour of the local planning authority, the effect of the *Dover* decision is that criminal proceedings can commence as soon as the period for compliance with the notice has expired. If, however, an appeal is made under s 246 the appropriate course of action for the appellant is to make an application in interlocutory proceedings under RSC Ord 55 r 3(3) that the making of the appeal should operate as a stay on any proceedings on the enforcement notice pending determination of the appeal: *London Parachuting Ltd* v *Secretary of State for the Environment* [1986] JPL 279, in which the Court of Appeal approved the *Dover* decision. Alternatively, if a prosecution does proceed, a request for adjournment of the hearing can be made pending the outcome of the s 246 appeal.

11.3 The nature of the offences

Until the decision of the House of Lords in *Chiltern District Council* v *Hodgetts* [1983] 1 All ER 1057 some uncertainty had existed over the question whether the offences in s 89 are single offences or continuing offences which repeat themselves every day the enforcement notice is not complied with. This was particularly relevant to the question whether an information was bad for duplicity, for if a new offence was committed every day an information which alleged failure to comply with an enforcement notice 'on and since' a particular date would be invalid. Earlier authorities can be summarised by stating that s 89(1) was thought to create a 'once and for all' offence: *St Albans District Council* v *Norman Harper Autosales Ltd* (1978) 35 P&CR 70; s 89(4) was thought to create a continuing offence: *Tandridge District Council* v *Powers* [1982] JPL 645; s 89(5) (first offence) was thought to create a continuing offence: *Parry* v *Forest of Dean District Council* (1977) 34 P&CR 209; and s 89(5) (second offence) was also thought to create a continuing offence: *R* v *Chertsey JJ, ex p Franks* [1961] 2 QB 152.

The information in *Chiltern District Council* v *Hodgetts* alleged a contravention of s 89(5) in that the respondent had failed to comply with an enforcement notice requiring a use of land and buildings to cease. The information alleged that default had taken place 'on and since 27 May 1980'. The lower courts considered themselves bound by *Parry* v *Forest of Dean District Council* and dismissed the information. The House of Lords held, however, that it was not an essential characteristic of a criminal offence that any prohibited act or omission, in order to constitute a single offence, should take place once and for all on a single day. It may take place, whether continuously or intermittently, over a period of time. The House of Lords thus held that all the offences in s 89 are single offences, albeit those created by s 89(4) and s 89(5) (second offence) are committed over a period of time. So far as the drafting of the information was concerned the 'on and since' formula used by the local planning authority was approved, though the House of Lords expressed a preference for charging an offence under s 89(5) (first offence) by using two specified dates. These would usually be the date when compliance with the enforcement notice first become due and a date not later than the date when the information was laid (or an earlier date if the enforcement notice was complied with after the date for compliance but before the information was laid).

One difficulty to which the interpretation of s 89 may yet give rise is the question of further prosecution of the persistent offender. If he is convicted for an initial offence and for a further offence, since both are single offences is it possible to obtain a further conviction if the breach of planning control remains unremedied? This is particularly relevant to s 89(4) which appears to indicate that the offence cannot be charged afresh. This potential problem which had been influential in the decision of the Divisional Court in *Tandridge District Council* v *Powers* which held that s 89(4) created a continuing offence, remains unresolved and was not considered by the House of Lords in *Chiltern District Council* v *Hodgetts*. Nevertheless it may still be possible for the defendant to be charged with a fresh offence under s 89(4) by an information which refers to different periods in which the required steps have not been taken.

11.4 The scope of s 89(5) – meaning of 'causes or permits'

Whereas s 89(1) applies only to a person who is the owner of land subject to an enforcement notice, s 89(5) applies to 'any person' who uses land or causes or permits it to be used in contravention of such a notice. Moreover, liability under s 89(5) attaches to any person who uses the land or causes or permits a contravention of the notice irrespective of whether a copy of the enforcement notice has been served on him. The provision therefore encompasses tenants, squatters and trespassers notwithstanding that in the case of those lacking an interest in the land they have no right of appeal to the Secretary of State: *Scarborough Borough Council* v *Adams and Adams* [1983] JPL 673.

If an enforcement notice has been issued and served in respect of a breach of planning control (comprising a material change of use) which has been caused by a trespasser, the local planning authority will often prosecute both the owner and unauthorised occupier of the land under s 89(5) for failure to remedy the breach. In such a case does a landowner who does not take legal action to recover possession of his property or resort to self-help 'cause or permit' the use of the land in contravention of the notice? In *Ragsdale* v *Creswick* [1984] JPL 883 a trespasser remained in possession of the land with a caravan for about two years. The defendant landowner made many efforts to persuade the trespasser to leave, falling short of legal proceedings. The local planning authority prosecuted the trespasser on at least one occasion as being 'any person' who 'causes or permits' the breach of planning control to continue. Although a conviction was obtained, the local planning authority decided to take no further action and they proceeded instead against the landowner, as the trespasser had still failed to vacate the land. The Divisional Court held that whether a person 'causes or permits' a use of land to continue is essentially a question of fact for the magistrates' court to decide after taking into account all the circumstances of the case, but the fact that legal proceedings had not been instituted for possession did not automatically render the defendant guilty of the offence.

This decision is consistent with some other instances which have arisen from prosecutions under the Caravan Sites and Control of Development Act 1960. Under s 1 of that Act it is an offence to 'cause or permit' land to be used as a caravan site without a site licence; decisions under the 1960 legislation are therefore of direct relevance in the present context. The most graphic of these is *Test Valley Investments Ltd* v *Tanner* (1964) 15 P&CR 279 in which a site which was owned by the appellant company became occupied by approximately 30 gipsies, who comprised a floating population. No attempt was made by the company to obtain a site licence and the company was successfully prosecuted for this default. The company then commenced proceedings in the county court to obtain injunctions against the trespassers but because of the floating population at the site these proved ineffective. Proceedings were brought for a second offence and the magistrates again convicted the appellant company on the basis that the company had 'permitted' the use of the site, since no attempt was made physically to evict the trespassers. On appeal to the Divisional Court the company claimed it was not reasonable to resort to the remedy of self-help. The court held that (per Lord Parker CJ at p 282): '. . . if the only steps that can be taken are steps which in all the circumstances are unreasonable you cannot be said to permit because you do not take those unreasonable steps'. In this instance it was found to be 'wholly unreasonable' to resort to the remedy of self-help, as a breach of the peace was predictable. The general principle to be applied, however, was stated by Lord Parker CJ (at p 281): '. . . a man may be said to permit something, not merely if he gives permission but if he fails to take what in the cases have sometimes been called proper steps and in other cases adequate steps to prevent that which it is said he is permitting'. Reference should also be made to the decision in *Bromsgrove District Council* v *Carthy* (1977) 30 P&CR 34 (Divisional Court held that whether legal action should have been taken was only one factor to be taken into consideration in deciding whether an offence had been committed by the defendant).

These cases illustrate problems which arise from the presence of trespassers on the land. Different considerations apply where the land is subject to a tenancy and the owner is unable to gain possession due to the tenant's security of tenure. In such a case the landlord will not commit an offence under s 89(5) if he is not in a position to discontinue the unlawful use. In *Johnston* v *Secretary of State for the Environment* (1974) 28 P&CR 424 a landlord of some domestic garages which were let to individual tenants received an enforcement notice requiring the ceasing of the use of the garages for repair purposes within 28 days. The landlords alleged that since the tenants were protected by the Landlord and Tenant Act 1954 it was impossible to regain possession within the time mentioned in the notice and that the notice should therefore have specified no particular time for compliance. The Divisional Court held that only the occupiers were at risk of prosecution under s 89(5) as (per Lord Widgery CJ at p 427) '. . . it is only a person who is in a position to determine the unlawful use and who, notwithstanding the notice, either continues to use the land in defiance of it or causes or permits some other person to do so who is at risk at all'. Thus the period for compliance with the enforcement notice in this case was effective only against the occupying tenants; since it was ineffective against the owners it was a misconceived argument that the period should be extended.

It is to be noted that an owner of land who is prosecuted under s 89(1) for failure to take any steps required by an enforcement notice, may not be able to shelter behind a protected tenant. This is because ss 91(3) and (4) of the 1971 Act, together with reg 16 of the Town and Country Planning General Regulations 1976 (SI 1976 No 1419) apply s 289 of the Public Health Act 1936 to the planning legislation. This provision enables an owner of premises to make a complaint to the magistrates' court that a person having an interest in the land is preventing the owner from taking steps required by an enforcement notice. If the court is satisfied on hearing the complaint, an order can be made requiring that person to permit the steps to be taken.

Finally, the use of the alternative words 'causes or permits' in s 89(5) calls for accuracy in drafting the information. In *Waddell* v *Winter* (1967) 65 LGR 370 the defendant placed a caravan on land which he owned and proceeded to live in it without obtaining a site licence under the Caravan Sites and Control of Development Act 1960. He was charged with the offence of 'permitting' the use of the land as a caravan site but he argued that since he used the site himself he was not 'permitting' its use. This argument succeeded before the magistrates, and in the Divisional Court, where Lord Parker CJ pointed out that 'The offence of permitting is committed when someone is allowed to do something as a matter of permission and not as a matter of authority or mandate from the occupier'. If however, the defendant had been charged with 'causing' the use of the land as a caravan site he would properly have been convicted.

11.5 Defending a prosecution

In typical enforcement proceedings by the time the local planning authority have decided to prosecute under s 89 the breach of planning control will have subsisted for many months. The enforcee will have exhausted his right of appeal to the Secretary of State and the notice will have been upheld. The last resort is therefore for the defendant to attempt to defend the prosecution if the requirements of the notice have still not been observed. Sometimes the process will be accelerated by the omission of an appeal by the enforcee. In less typical circumstances the enforcee will not have a right of appeal at all due to lack of an interest in the land (see Chap 7).

The scope for defending a prosecution is comparatively slim, unless it is proposed to attack the enforcement notice on the ground that it is a nullity and therefore of no effect. The main problem is that the privative effect of s 243(1) applies in criminal proceedings, so that it is not possible to question the validity of the enforcement notice on any of the grounds on which an appeal could have been made to the Secretary of State under s 88. These matters are considered more fully below after discussion of the following matters:

11.5.1 Limitation

The Magistrates' Court Act 1980 provides (in s 127(1)) that an information or complaint shall not be tried or heard unless proceedings are commenced within six months of the offence being committed. Where, however, the offence is an indictable one triable either way s 127(2) qualifies the limitation rule by excluding such offences, irrespective of the court in which the information is tried. Bearing in mind that all the offences in s 89 of the 1971 Act are, since *Chiltern District Council* v *Hodgetts* (supra) single offences, the qualification in s 127(2) (first introduced by s 18 of the Criminal Law Act 1977) is especially pertinent. The effect is that limitation cannot be pleaded as a defence.

11.5.2   The statutory defence on change of ownership

A very limited statutory defence applies in s 89(1) cases where the owner of the land has sold the land before the expiration of the period for compliance with the notice. In such a case, under s 89(2), the defendant should give the prosecution not less than three clear days' notice of his intention to plead this defence. He should also lay an information before the magistrates. If he complies with these requirements he is entitled to have the subsequent owner brought before the court. To complete the defence he must then prove (i) that the failure to take the steps specified in the enforcement notice was attributable (in whole or in part) to the default of the subsequent owner and (ii) that he took all reasonable steps to secure compliance with the notice: s 89(3). If he is able to establish these matters he must be acquitted, and the subsequent owner may be convicted.

While these provisions make it clear that ownership is critical to a prosecution under s 89(1), it is not necessary for the local planning authority to provide proof of ownership on the date on which the copy of the enforcement notice is served if there is evidence of ownership at an earlier date. The local planning authority will normally have determined the question of ownership prior to issuing the enforcement notice and service of copies of it, having used the statutory methods for procuring such information described in Chap 5. Armed with evidence of ownership at a prior date it is to be presumed in favour of the local planning authority that the defendant was also the owner at the time of service of the copy of the enforcement notice unless there is evidence to the contrary: *Whitfield* v *Gowling* (1974) 28 P&CR 386.

Apart from the limited defence available under ss 89(2) and (3) to a prosecution under s 89(1), the defendant in criminal proceedings brought under that provision is reduced to disputing questions of fact eg that a copy of the notice was not served on him or that the steps required by the notice have been complied with, or that he has been charged under the wrong part of s 89 (see *R* v *Jefford* [1986] JPL 912). What he cannot do is to dispute the validity of the enforcement notice unless he can find a reason for doing so which is not one of the grounds of appeal to the Secretary of State listed in s 88(2). This is because s 243(1), with one exception affecting prosecutions under s 89(5), precludes a challenge to the validity of the notice in any legal proceedings, if the challenge is based on a s 88(2) ground. This problem has already been examined in Chap 8, in which the authorities on the preclusive effect of s 243(1) were examined in both a civil and criminal context. It may be pointed out afresh, however, that the Court of Appeal in *R* v *Smith (Thomas George)* (1984) 48 P&CR 392 ruled that s 243(1) applies to criminal proceeding under s 89 and was not (as had been argued in that case) limited to applications for judicial review. It is, however, significant that the Court of Appeal asserted that in criminal proceedings the defendant could rely on non-s 88(2) grounds. These other grounds are slowly being developed by the judiciary and include the same matters in respect of which an application for judicial review could be made. Particular reference should therefore be made to *Davy* v *Spelthorne Borough Council* [1984] AC 262 and *Scarborough Borough Council* v *Adams and Adams* [1983] JPL 673 for some indications of when a prosecution might be successfully defended. These cases have identified lack of jurisdiction to issue the notice, and improper exercise of discretion by the local planning authority as the main considerations.

The one exception to the preclusive effect of s 243(1), affecting prosecutions under s 89(5) is contained in s 243(2). This provision applies where the defendant can satisfy the conditions that (*a*) he has held an interest in the land since before the enforcement notice was issued, and (*b*) that a copy of the enforcement notice was not served on him. If he can satisfy the court that he did not know and could not reasonably be expected to know that the enforcement notice had been issued, and that his interests have been substantially prejudiced by the failure to serve him with a copy of it, he can challenge the notice on any ground including those listed in s 88(2).

In view of the preclusive effect of s 243(1) on most of the grounds on which an enforcement notice might be considered invalid, there remains the possibility that the defendant can escape conviction on the ground that the notice is a nullity. Since an enforcement notice which is a nullity is totally ineffective it is clearly open to the defendant to attack the notice on the ground that it is defective on its face ie that it fails to meet the requirements discussed at length in Chap 5.

11.6 Offences by corporations

In many instances the defendant to a prosecution under s 89 will be an incorporated body rather than an individual. In such a case not only can the corporation be convicted and fined in the normal way, but also can those responsible for the affairs of the corporation. Under s 285(1), if an offence committed by a corporation has been committed with the consent or connivance of, or is attributable to neglect by a director, manager, secretary or other similar officer, or any person purporting to act as such, that person is also guilty of an offence. Thus both the corporation and the responsible officers can be convicted of the same offence. Where the defendant corporation is a nationalised body, the members of the corporation responsible for its management are 'directors' for the purposes of this provision: s 285(2).

Chapter 12

The Power of Entry

12.1 Introduction

Quite apart from the possibility that the local planning authority might prosecute for non-compliance with the requirements of an enforcement notice under s 89, the authority are also empowered to enter upon the land and themselves take the steps which are required by the enforcement notice. This power, which is only infrequently invoked, is conferred by s 91 of the 1971 Act, as amended by the Local Government and Planning (Amendment) Act 1981. It only applies, however, to the case in which the enforcement notice identifies particular steps to be taken, as distinct from one which merely requires a specific use of land to cease.

The power of entry is also expressly limited by s 91(1) in respect of (a) the time when the power can be exercised; (b) the steps which can be taken on the land by the local planning authority; and (c) against whom the local planning authority may proceed to recover their expenses. The provision is as follows:

If, within the period specified in an enforcement notice for compliance therewith, or within such extended period as the local planning authority may allow, any steps which by virtue of section 87(7)(a) of this Act are required by the notice to be taken (other than the discontinuance of a use of land) have not been taken, the local planning authority may enter the land and take those steps, and may recover from the person who is then the owner of the land any expenses reasonably incurred by them in doing so.

12.2 Time when the power can be exercised

No entry can be made on the land until the period specified in the enforcement notice in accordance with s 87(5) has expired. As s 87(8) permits different periods to be specified for different steps to be taken it is presumably open to the local planning authority to exercise the power of entry selectively as each specified period expires. It must also be borne in mind that s 89(6) empowers the local planning authority to grant an extension of time for compliance with the notice: s 91(1) clearly requires any such extension to be taken into account by the local planning authority. It seems likely that if an extension is involved, the extension can only be granted once and only within the original period specified in the notice, though the extension may be for any fixed period of time: *St Albans District Council* v *Norman Harper Autosales Ltd* (1977) 35 P&CR 30. If the local planning authority purport to grant an extension after the specified period has expired this will probably not bind the local planning authority: *Joyner* v *Guildford Corporation* (1954) 5 P&CR 30 (county court).

The 1971 Act does not specify that any warning must be given or that a notice of proposed entry must be served. Having regard, however, to the possible consequences of exercising this remedy (demolition of property followed by a financial charge) a prudent local planning authority would bear in mind the requirements of natural justice. Hence it would be a wise precaution to notify those interested in the land of the intention to exercise this power. Where, as will be the normal case, copies of the enforcement notice have been duly served on those interested in the land it is unlikely that the local planning authority must grant a hearing: *R* v *Greenwich London Borough Council ex p Patel* [1985] JPL 851. The position is different however where there has been a failure of service; this is considered further below (see para **12.5**).

A warning must be given, however, in the circumstances to which ss 93(3) and (4) apply. These provisions enable the local planning authority to exercise the power conferred by s 91 where any buildings or works have been reinstated or restored (in breach of planning control) following demolition or alteration of them pursuant to an enforcement notice. If the local planning authority propose to enter and take any steps specified in the enforcement notice they must first give at least 28 days written notice of their intention to the owner and occupier of the land.

12.3 The steps which can be taken

Section 91(1) uses the words '. . . steps which by virtue of s 87(7)(*a*) of this Act are required by the notice to be taken . . .' Reference to s 87(7)(*a*) shows that this provision requires the enforcement notice to contain the '. . . steps which are required by the authority to be taken in order to remedy the breach'. These steps are to be distinguished from those referred to in s 87(7)(*b*) which are the steps (if any) which are required by the local planning authority to be taken in order to make the development comply with the terms of any planning permission which has been granted in respect of the land or for removing or alleviating any injury to amenity which has been caused by the development. Accordingly, the local planning authority are not empowered by s 91(1) to carry out all the requirements of an enforcement notice unless those requirements all fall within the category of steps identified by s 87(7)(*a*).

In the exercise of the power the local planning authority are not bound to carry out all the steps which are required by the enforcement notice to remedy the breach of planning control; the power can therefore be under-exercised. In *Arcam Demolition and Construction Co Ltd* v *Worcestershire County Council* [1964] 2 All ER 286 the enforcement notice required demolition of certain buildings and removal of concrete and tarmac surfacing on the land which was ultimately to be returned to agricultural use by replacement of the resultant hardcore with topsoil. It transpired that the cost of carrying out the removal of the concrete and tarmac was out of all proportion to the value of the land after the operation had been completed and hence the council limited their action to removal of the buildings only. Cross J held that by exercising the power under what is now s 91 the local planning authority did not commit themselves to carrying out all the steps required by the enforcement notice as the words 'and take those steps' in the provision did not necessarily mean all the steps required but could be construed to mean any one or more of the steps in question. He also observed in the course of his judgment that the cost of a tree-planting scheme could not be charged to the owners as this was not a step which was required to be taken in order to remedy the breach of planning control.

The specific exclusion of 'discontinuance of a use of land' by s 91(1) seems at first sight to rule out the use of the section in all material change of use cases. That this is a false assumption is now clear from *Midlothian District Council* v *Stevenson* [1986] JPL 913. In this case the local planning authority took enforcement action against an authorised caravan site and specified in the enforcement notice that the steps required to be taken were to remove all caravans, caravan chassis and motor vehicles from the site. The site owner failed to comply with the notice, and objected to the proposed use of the power of entry on the basis that it would lead to discontinuance of the use of the land, a matter specifically excluded by the legislation. It was held that as the steps required in this case were only to remove the caravans etc from the site, this requirement was within the scope of the provision. The fact that such steps might result in the use of the land being discontinued was merely incidental to the legitimate steps which could be taken.

12.4 Recovery of expenses

The person from whom the local planning authority can recover the expenses reasonably incurred by them in exercise of the power of entry is the owner of the land at the time when the entry is made: s 91(1). Recoverable expenses comprise not only the costs of making the entry and taking the steps required to remedy the breach of planning control, but also (under s 36 of the Local Government Act 1974) the establishment charges of the local planning authority, so far as appears to them to be reasonable. By virtue of s 111 of the 1971 Act, expenditure under s 91 is recoverable as a simple contract debt in any court of competent jurisdiction but the expenses do not constitute a local land charge. There is, however, provision in s 91(5) for the making of regulations under which the expenses of a local planning authority incurred under s 91 (but not their establishment charges) can be designated as a local land charge, though this power has not yet been exercised.

The act of carrying out steps required by the enforcement notice will often involve salvageable materials. These belong to the owner of the land. By virtue of reg 16 of the Town and Country Planning General Regulations 1976 (SI 1976 No 1419), s 276 of the Public Health Act 1936 is applicable to these materials. The local planning authority are thus empowered to remove them from the site and after the expiration of at least 3 days from the date of their removal may sell them if they are not claimed by the owner and taken away by him. If the materials are sold the proceeds of sale (less administrative expenses) must be paid to the former owner. They may not be used in direct diminution of the debt owed by the site owner without his consent.

Recovery of expenses must also take into account the possibility that the owner of the land is not a beneficial owner but an agent or trustee for another. In such a case s 294 of the Public Health Act

1936 applies, again by virtue of reg 16 of the Town and Country Planning General Regulations 1976. Under this section, if the apparent owner proves that he is receiving the rent of the premises as agent or trustee for another and has insufficient funds held on behalf of his principal or beneficiary, the liability of the owner is limited to the extent of those funds. The local planning authority may then recover the balance from the principal or beneficiary.

Finally, provision is made by s 91(2) to enable an owner who has been required to make a payment to the local planning authority under s 91(1) to recover the expenses from the person responsible for the breach of planning control. Thus if the land is the subject of a **tenancy** and the breach of planning control was caused by the tenant, the expenses incurred by the owner are, under s 91(2) '. . . deemed to be incurred or paid for the use and at the request of the person by whom the breach of planning control was committed'.

12.5 Exercise of discretion – judicial review

The manner in which a local planning authority should exercise their powers under s 91(1) was reviewed by the Court of Appeal in *R v Greenwich London Borough Council ex p Patel* [1985] JPL 851. In this case the local planning authority mistakenly believed that the owner of the property on which an unauthorised structure had been erected was the person on whom a copy of the enforcement notice was served, who was in fact only a relative. No appeal was made against the notice. It was not until after a prosecution under s 89(1) had failed did it emerge who the true owner was. As the local planning authority then proposed to exercise their powers under s 91 the owner sought judicial review claiming inter alia a declaration that the council were not entitled to carry out proposed demolition works: due to the failure of service he had not known of the enforcement proceedings and had therefore been deprived of his right of appeal to the Secretary of State.

The Court of Appeal held that the failure of service did not render the enforcement notice a nullity, as there were sufficient safeguards in the legislation to deal with defects of service (see ss 88(2)(f), 88A(3) and 243(2)). It was therefore valid and enforceable in a manner which included action under s 91. Neill LJ pointed out, however, that a person who had not been served with a copy of the enforcement notice might nevertheless be in a position to place facts before the local planning authority which might show that (for example) there had been no breach of planning control. It was therefore the duty of the local planning authority to investigate any such facts before implementing s 91, and if the local planning authority unreasonably refused to carry out an investigation then their decision to enter the land and take the steps required to remedy the breach of planning control could be quashed on an application for judicial review.

Chapter 13

Stop Notices

13.1 Introduction

The purpose of a stop notice is, as the name implies, to enable a local planning authority to bring a perceived breach of planning control to a halt sooner than can be achieved through use of the ordinary enforcement procedure. It is a device, backed by criminal sanctions, which operates not only to accelerate the enforcement process but also to counteract the effect on an enforcement notice of the making of an appeal to the Secretary of State under s 88. It will be recalled that under s 88(10) the exercise of the right of appeal has the effect of suspending the effect of the enforcement notice until the appeal is determined by the Secretary of State. A stop notice, therefore, can be served by the local planning authority to counteract the use of an appeal as a simple delaying tactic, as well as to deal with breaches of planning control meriting urgent action. The device was first introduced into the law by the Town and Country Planning Act 1968 and was carried forward to the 1971 Act.

The use of the device is, however, only employed in a minority of cases – those in which the local planning authority are confident of winning any appeal that might be made. This is because should the local planning authority lose the appeal (otherwise than due to a grant of planning permission by the Secretary of State) they may have to compensate an enforcee who has suffered any loss or damage as a result of the stop notice on a claim being made in that behalf under s 177 of the 1971 Act. There is no facility for appeal against a stop notice, which can take effect as little as 3 days after service. A recipient must therefore comply with the notice or seek to show in defending criminal proceedings that the notice was invalid. It is, however, possible to seek judicial review of a stop notice with a view to obtaining a declaration that the notice is invalid.

13.2 Implementation of stop notice procedure

Stop notice procedure is governed by s 90 of the 1971 Act, as substituted by the Town and Country Planning (Amendment) Act 1977 and amended by the Local Government and Planning (Amendment) Act 1981. The enabling provision, s 90(1), is as follows:

Where in respect of any land the local planning authority
  (a) have served a copy of an enforcement notice requiring a breach of planning control to be remedied; but
  (b) consider it expedient to prevent, before the expiry of the period allowed for compliance with the notice, the carrying out of any activity which is, or is included in, a matter alleged by the notice to constitute the breach,
then, subject to the following provisions of this section, they may at any time before the notice takes effect serve a further notice (in this Act referred to as a 'stop notice') referring to, and having annexed to it a copy of the enforcement notice and prohibiting the carrying out of that activity on the land, or any part of it specified in the stop notice.

The appropriate time for implementing this procedure is therefore the period before the enforcement notice on which it is dependent has taken effect ie prima facie during the first period specified in the notice. Where, however, an appeal is made against the enforcement notice to the Secretary of State, the power to serve a stop notice is extended until the appeal is determined since, during that period, the enforcement notice is ineffective.

The provision contemplates that an enforcement notice will have been issued and served before the stop notice procedure is utilised. This does not, however, necessitate two meetings of the local planning authority to obtain the necessary resolutions, for the authority can by a single resolution resolve not only to issue and serve an enforcement notice but also to supplement the enforcement notice with a stop notice: *Westminster City Council* v *Jones*, (1981) *The Times*, 12 June.

It is apparent from s 90(1)(b) that the local planning authority must consider it 'expedient' to prevent the activity which it seeks to prohibit. Some guidance as to the meaning of this word in the present context is given by Department of the Environment Circular 4/87 (Welsh Office 7/87) which was issued following research into the effect of the Town and Country Planning (Amendment) Act 1977. Paragraphs 1–6 of Annex 2 of this Circular advise that stop notice procedure should not be used automatically following service of an enforcement notice, but that expediency depends on whether the breach of control, or the activity comprised in the breach, is so serious that the local planning authority are not justified in waiting for the enforcement notice to take effect or expiration of the period allowed for compliance. Normally a written assessment will be made of the likely consequence of serving a notice which will examine the foreseeable costs and benefits likely to result from taking this action. The assessment should look at the precise effect of prohibiting an activity on the conduct of any business undertaking, and the authority should consult with the enforcee to discover whether he can alter his activities in a manner which is environmentally acceptable.

13.3 Content of the notice

There is no prescribed form of stop notice, but a model form of stop notice is recommended by the Appendix to Circular 4/87. This can be adapted by the local planning authority to meet the requirements of the case in hand. The only statutory requirements are (i) that the notice must specify a date on which it is to come into effect, being a date which is not less than 3 days (nor more than 28 days) from the date on which it is served on any person appearing to have an interest in the land: s 90(3) (this enables successive notices to be served bearing the same date); (ii) that it prohibits the carrying out of any specified activity on the land: s 90(1); and (iii) that it refers to the enforcement notice, a copy of which is annexed to it: s 90(1). The model form of stop notice is reproduced together with the rest of Circular 4/87 at Appendix 1.

In meeting the requirement of s 90(1) that the stop notice must specify the activity which must cease, it is permissible for the stop notice to incorporate the breach of planning control referred to in the enforcement notice (a copy of which must be attached to the stop notice). In *Bristol Stadium Ltd* v *Brown* [1980] JPL 107 the activity prohibited by the stop notice was specified as the carrying out of the operations alleged to be a breach of planning control in the enforcement notice and any other operations so closely associated therewith as to constitute substantially the same operations. The Divisional Court held that the stop notice was valid as the apparent deficiency of particularity in the stop notice could be validated and cured by the fact that the language of the enforcement notice could be relied on to determine the requirement of the stop notice.

In view of the possibility of judicial review of the stop notice particular attention should be paid to the drafting which is used by the local planning authority. The court does, however, permit some latitude to the enforcing authority in specifying the requirements of the stop notice. In *R v Runnymede Borough Council ex p Sarvan Singh Seehra* (1987) 53 P&CR 281 the stop notice specified that the prohibited activity was 'use of the land for the purposes of religious meetings and services and for the purposes of religious devotion otherwise than as incidental to the enjoyment of the dwellinghouse as such'. The applicant sought to have the stop notice quashed on the ground that as the notice failed to specify what was to be regarded as a normal incidence of use of the house in question it was therefore too vague. Schiemann J rejected the application and declined to hold that the degree of clarity of a stop notice should exceed that which is required of enforcement notices. Instead he held that it was permissible to use wording in enforcement and stop notices which incorporate matters of fact and degree even if this left some doubt in the mind of the applicant as to where the line was to be drawn.

The stop notice must be consistent with the enforcement notice on which it is dependent. In *Clwyd County Council v Secretary of State for Wales* [1982] JPL 696 an enforcement notice was served which alleged a failure to comply with a planning condition. Other enforcement notices were issued and served arising from the same development. Stop notices were also served, one of which required a mineral working to cease; annexed to this was the enforcement notice requiring compliance with the condition. Forbes J had little hesitation in quashing the stop notice as being 'hopelessly invalid', as the activity prohibited by the stop notice was not an activity consisting of or included in any matter alleged to be a breach of planning control by the enforcement notice. It must also be very doubtful whether service of a stop notice is appropriate in relation to a breach of a planning condition since non-compliance with the condition is not an 'activity'.

13.4 Scope of the procedure

When the stop notice procedure was first introduced in 1968 it applied only to breaches of planning control of the operational nature, thus excluding material changes of use. This somewhat artificial limitation in its scope was corrected by the Town and Country Planning (Amendment) Act 1977 which expanded the section to encompass any 'activity'. This word is not defined but it would seem from s 90(1)(*b*) that the local planning authority may select a part of a breach of planning control for prohibition by means of a stop notice even though that part may not in itself amount to a breach of planning control. Paragraph 6 of Annex 1 of Circular 4/87 expresses the view that a stop notice can be directed to ancillary or incidental uses of land and even to intermittent or seasonal uses.

A number of matters are excluded from the effect of a stop notice, as identified by s 90(2). This provides that a stop notice shall not prohibit:

(*a*) the use of any building as a dwellinghouse; or

(*b*) the use of land as the site for a caravan occupied by any person as his only or main residence; or

(*c*) the taking of any steps specified in the enforcement notice as required to be taken in order to remedy the breach of planning control.

In addition to these matters s 90(2) also contains a general limitation rule. This provides that a stop notice is ineffective against an activity which started more than 12 months prior to the date of the stop notice (whether or not it has been carried out continuously), unless it comprises or is incidental to building, engineering, mining, or other operations or the deposit of refuse or waste materials. A use of land or buildings therefore loses its potential for stop notice procedure after a year has elapsed since it first commenced. This is so irrespective of whether the use commenced with the benefit of a grant of planning permission for a limited period: *Scott Markets Ltd* v *Waltham Forest London Borough Council* (1979) 38 P&CR 597. In this case the Court of Appeal held (by a majority) that a stop notice was ineffective against a use of land which had previously been authorised by a grant of planning permission for a fixed period of a little less than three years. The 12 month limitation did not run from the end of the period specified in the planning permission but from the commencement of what was then an authorised use.

A further shortcoming in the scope of s 90(2) was exposed in *Runnymede Borough Council* v *Smith* [1986] JPL 592, a case involving an unauthorised caravan site. After an enforcement notice (in respect of which an appeal was lodged) and a stop notice had been served in respect of a site on which a single caravan was situated, a further dozen families came onto the land together with their caravans and vehicles. The local planning authority sought an injunction against the owner of the site for the purposes of seeking to restrain the use of the land for stationing of residential caravans. Millett J refused the injunction holding that the effect of s 90(2)(b) was such that it not only rendered ineffective the stop notice in relation to any caravans on the site at the time of the service of the stop notice but also had the same effect against caravans brought onto the site at a later date. The defendants were therefore not in breach of the stop notice by allowing the site to be used by further caravan dwellers. This did not, however, mean that there was no breach of the enforcement notice upon which the stop notice was dependent and this would once again become effective in the event of an unsuccessful appeal to the Secretary of State.

13.5 Service, duration and registration of the notice

A number of points concerned with the procedural aspects of the use of stop notice procedure require to be noted, together with the question of the 'life' of the notice.

13.5.1 Service

The service requirement is dealt with in s 90(5) and encompasses both personal service and placing of a site notice. The sub-section provides that the local planning authority may serve a stop notice on any person who appears to them to have an interest in the land or to be engaged in any activity prohibited by the notice. This means that in some cases not all parties will be served, so a contractor might be served but not necessarily the owner. But the permissive word 'may' used in the provision is, in effect, compulsive as two further matters are dependent upon a stop notice having been served. Firstly, a prosecution for failure to comply with the requirements of the notice will fail if the defendant can prove that the stop notice was not served on him and that he did not know, and could not reasonably be expected to know of its existence. Secondly, although the local planning authority can put in place a site notice, this can only be done after a stop notice has been served.

If the local planning authority wish to place a site notice on the land this notice must state that a stop notice has been served and that any person contravening it may be prosecuted. Although there is no prescribed form of stop notice, it must also state the date on which the stop notice takes effect and indicate its requirements. Referring to s 90(5) in the course of his judgment in

Runnymede Borough Council v *Smith* Millett J observed that the advantage to the local planning authority of displaying a site notice was that it absolved them from having to prove service of the stop notice upon any person subsequently prosecuted.

13.5.2 Duration

Unlike an enforcement notice, which has continuing effect, a stop notice has a finite life. Under s 90(4) it ceases to be effective on the happening of any one of the following four events:

  (i) the enforcement notice is withdrawn or quashed; or
 (ii) the period allowed for compliance with the enforcement notice expires; or
(iii) notice of withdrawal of the stop notice is served by the local planning authority on persons served with the stop notice. Where a site notice has been placed on the land a further notice of withdrawal must be displayed in place of the original site notice; or
(iv) the enforcement notice is varied by the Secretary of State so that the activities prohibited by the stop notice cease to be included in the matters alleged by the enforcement notice to constitute a breach of planning control.

To these circumstances can be added the possibility that the stop notice may be quashed on an application for judicial review. It should also be noted that even if the local planning authority decide to withdraw a stop notice they may serve another provided the requirements of s 90(1) are observed.

13.5.3 Registration of the notice

If a stop notice is served an entry must be made by the local planning authority in the register of enforcement and stop notices which is maintained pursuant to s 92A of the 1971 Act and art 21A of the Town and Country Planning General Development Order 1977. This register was considered in Chap 5 para **5.5** in the context of entries which are requisite following the issue of an enforcement notice. So far as a stop notice is concerned, an entry must be made within 14 days of the date of service of the notice, of its withdrawal (if applicable), together with a statement or summary of the activity prohibited by the stop notice. If the enforcement notice on which the stop notice is dependent, is quashed or withdrawn then the entries relating to both notices must be vacated. Entries relating to the stop notice must otherwise remain in the register even though the notice has ceased to be effective.

13.6 Prosecution for non-compliance with a stop notice

Failure to comply with the requirements of a stop notice is a criminal offence, in respect of which penalties are prescribed by s 90(7). This provides that an offence is committed by any person who contravenes, or causes or permits the contravention of a stop notice after a site notice has been displayed, or, if a site notice has not been displayed more than two days after the stop notice has been served on him. The maximum penalty for this offence is a fine of £2,000 on summary conviction, but an unlimited fine can be imposed if the defendant is convicted on indictment. Where the offence continues after the first conviction, a further offence is committed and a further fine can be imposed of up to £200 for each day the offence continues (summary conviction) with an unlimited fine if convicted on indictment. By analogy with the decision of the House of Lords in *Chiltern District Council* v *Hodgetts* [1983] 1 All ER 1057 (see para **11.3**) these offences are once and for all offences rather than continuing ones. A single statutory defence is available as prescribed by s 90(8). This provides that it is a defence if the defendant can prove that the stop notice was not served on him and that he did not know and could not reasonably have been expected to know of its existence. This would appear to involve the defendant in having to prove a negative.

A point of particular importance is that a defendant is entitled not only to dispute questions of fact but also the validity of a stop notice in defence to the prosecution. Unlike the position of a defendant in enforcement proceedings, the preclusive effect of s 243(1) does not apply and hence the defendant can rely on any ground whereby the validity of the notice is put in issue. This is principally due to the fact that there is no right of appeal against a stop notice, and hence the notice would only be capable of challenge by an application for judicial review unless it could also be challenged in a court of criminal jurisdiction. In *R* v *Jenner* [1983] 2 All ER 46 an enforcement notice and stop notice were served on the defendant. He failed to comply with the stop notice and was prosecuted in the Crown Court under s 90(7). In his defence he alleged that the activity specified in the stop notice had commenced more than 12 months prior to the date of the notice and hence by virtue of s 90(2) was outwith the scope of the notice. The trial judge held that it was not open to the defendant to challenge the validity of the notice otherwise than by judicial review. On appeal to the Court of Appeal it was held that in the absence of a right of appeal against a stop notice the defendant was not limited to questioning the validity of the notice by an application for judicial review. Moreover in a case such as this judicial review was not a suitable remedy since the validity of the notice involved determination of a question of fact. A prosecution can also be defended on the ground that the stop notice is dependent upon an enforcement notice which is a nullity, as both notices stand or fall together: *Bristol Stadium* v *Brown* [1980] JPL 107.

13.7 Compensation for loss due to a stop notice

Restraint in using the stop notice procedure is in large part attributable to the provisions of s 177(1) of the 1971 Act. This sub-section places local planning authorities under a liability to pay compensation for loss which is caused by service of a stop notice in the circumstances specified by s 177(2). Following amendment by the Town and Country Planning (Amendment) Act 1977, s 177(1) provides as follows:

A person who, when a stop notice under s 90 of this Act is first served, has an interest in or occupies the land to which the stop notice relates shall, in any of the circumstances mentioned in subsection (2) of this section, be entitled to be compensated by the local planning authority in respect of any loss or damage directly attributable to the prohibition contained in the notice (or, in a case within paragraph (*b*) of that subsection, so much of that prohibition as ceases to have effect).

The circumstances identified in s 177(2) as giving rise to a right to compensation in respect of loss or damage are four-fold:

(*a*) if the enforcement notice is quashed by the Secretary of State on any ground mentioned in s 88(2), with the exception of ground (*a*) (grant of planning permission by the Secretary of State); or

(*b*) if the enforcement notice is varied by the Secretary of State (except due to a grant of planning permission) so that the matters alleged to constitute a breach of planning control cease to include one or more of the activities prohibited by the stop notice; or

(*c*) if the enforcement notice is withdrawn by the local planning authority (except if the withdrawal is due to a grant of planning permission in respect of the development to which the notice relates, or for its retention or continuance without compliance with a condition or limitation subject to which planning permission was previously granted); or (*d*) the stop notice is withdrawn.

While ground (*a*) is likely to generate the majority of claims, it should be noted that entitlement to compensation proceeds on the basis that the enforcement notice is a valid one, so that no compensation is payable if the notice is in fact a nullity.

13.7.1 Determining compensation: meaning of 'directly attributable'

Section 177(1) provides for compensation for '. . . any loss or damage directly attributable to the prohibition contained in the notice . . .' It is clear that (i) having regard to the provisions of s 178(1) and (2) the measure of loss is not to be linked to depreciation of value of any interest held in the land and (ii) in accordance with an opinion expressed in the leading case of *J Sample (Warkworth) Ltd* v *Alnwick District Council* [1984] JPL 670, the loss incurred need not be reasonably foreseeable. In this case a developer had partially constructed a house when enforcement and stop notices were served. This had the immediate effect of redeployment of the workforce to another project. They could not be integrated immediately, however, with an attendant loss to the developer of paying wages for idle time. A grant of planning permission was later made by the local planning authority but they refused to withdraw the enforcement or stop notice albeit that they agreed not to prosecute if work restarted. Ultimately the Secretary of State quashed the enforcement notice and an unsuccessful application for costs was made. In addition to the loss due to the payments to the idle workforce the developer claimed (i) the cost of rectifying defects to the property due to deterioration; (ii) the cost of compensating a purchaser of the house who incurred expenditure for temporary accommodation; (iii) loss of interest on the completion moneys due to the developer from the purchaser, completion having been delayed for 6 months; (iv) the cost of appealing against the enforcement notice, the claimant having been obliged to pursue the appeal because the local planning authority refused to withdraw the enforcement notice. The Lands Tribunal allowed the claimant the cost of idle time and all other heads of claim except that relating to the cost of pursuing the enforcement notice appeal. In relation to the final item the Lands Tribunal ruled that the costs of the appeal against the enforcement notice were not directly attributable to the prohibition contained in the stop notice, and that as the matter had already been the subject of an unsuccessful application to the Secretary of State it was inappropriate to award them under s 177.

Very substantial compensation (£527,446) was claimed in *Barnes*

(Robert) & Co Ltd v *Malvern Hills District Council* (1985) 274 EG 733. The applicant, a construction company, carried on business as a developer of houses using profits from one development to finance subsequent activities. A site was acquired with planning permission for 25 houses which was shortly to expire for lack of implementation. By the time the relevant day had passed the developer had only succeeded in pegging out the estate road. When further acts of development were carried out the local planning authority served both an enforcement and stop notice. The enforcement appeal to the Secretary of State was further appealed to the High Court and thereafter the Court of Appeal, which ruled that the planning permission had been successfully implemented before the relevant day and hence there had been no breach of planning control: see *Malvern Hills District Council* v *Secretary of State for the Environment* [1982] JPL 439. The subsequent claim for compensation included (i) interest on delayed receipt of profit on sale of the houses; (ii) charges incurred in financing the original acquisition; (iii) abortive expenditure; (iv) consequential losses of goodwill (in respect of which £200,000 was claimed) and loss of stock relief. Having regard to market forces pertaining at the time of service of the stop notice, the Lands Tribunal awarded only £82,562 finding that the delay in the development programme had not caused the developer a loss as the industry was then in recession. Also there was insufficient evidence to support the claim for compensation in respect of consequential losses as the company's balance sheet did not indicate that the stop notice had disrupted the company's business, though the Tribunal accepted that much of the company's capital had been committed to land acquisition costs. The Tribunal allowed items (ii) and (iii) above, plus sums for dereliction of a bungalow, lost hire of a Portakabin and for architects' fees. Other professional charges were disallowed, as were the administrative and legal costs incurred in resisting the enforcement notice. No interest was awarded on the resultant total sum, calculated from the date building work resumed to the date of the Tribunal's decision, as it was observed that there was no statutory power to award interest.

Two other statutory provisions have to be considered by the Lands Tribunal in determining the compensation payable by the local planning authority. Under s 177(5) the loss or damage which can give rise to a payment specifically includes a sum payable in respect of a breach of contract caused by the taking of action necessary to comply with the prohibition contained in the stop notice. Notwithstanding this provision, s 177(6) allows the calculation of compensation to be reduced to the extent (if any) that the entitlement is affected by the claimant's failure to comply with a notice under s 284 (notice requiring information as to interests in land) or to any misstatement made by him in response to such a notice.

13.7.2 Procedure for claiming compensation

If it is desired to make a claim for compensation under s 177, the section itself merely provides that the claim is to be made in accordance with regulations made under the 1971 Act. The relevant regulations are the Town and Country Planning General Regulations 1976 (SI 1976 No 1419). Under reg 14(1) the claim is to be made in writing and is to be served on the local planning authority either by delivering it to the office of the relevant district council or London borough council, or by sending it to them by pre-paid post. A time limit of 6 months is imposed by reg 14(2)(a) from the date of the decision in respect of which the claim is made; the words 'the decision' refer to the decision to quash, vary or withdraw the enforcement notice, or to withdraw the stop notice. The Secretary of State has a discretion, however, to extend the time limit in any particular case under reg 14(2).

As no prescribed form of claim is in use, the formalities are simply as described above. Thus in making a claim it is not necessary to quantify the amount claimed within the 6 months, as further details can be submitted outside the limitation period: *Texas Homecare Ltd* v *Lewes District Council* [1986] JPL 50. In this case the Lands Tribunal accepted jurisdiction to determine the claim since an initial letter forwarded by the claimant's solicitor to the local planning authority was construed to comprise a claim for compensation (albeit unquantified) as distinct from merely notifying the authority that a claim would be made in the future. The subsequent quantified claim was therefore not out of time.

Chapter 14

Continuing Effect of an Enforcement Notice

14.1 General

When an enforcement notice has been issued and served and its requirements have been carried out it continues in force even though it has been complied with. It does not become 'spent' by virtue of compliance: s 93(1). This section provides that compliance with any requirements of the enforcement notice does not discharge the notice, while s 93(2) goes on to provide that a requirement in an enforcement notice that a use of land shall be discontinued is to be interpreted as a requirement that the discontinuance shall be permanent. Thus if the use is resumed at a later date the original enforcement notice is still effective and accordingly the resumption is a contravention of it. A similar rule applies, by virtue of s 93(3) to reinstatement or restoration of buildings or works which have been demolished or altered in compliance with an enforcement notice. The section has not been judicially considered on many occasions and hence the discussion which follows is necessarily brief. This chapter goes on, however, to consider how the effect of an enforcement notice can be terminated.

14.2 Resumption of an unauthorised use of land

The application of s 93(2) is well illustrated by the events which occurred in *Prosser* v *Sharp* [1985] JPL 717 in which enforcement notices required the cessation of the use of land as a site for a caravan, and the digging up and removal of the concrete hardstanding on which it was situated. The Secretary of State dismissed appeals against the enforcement notices and ultimately the local planning authority successfully prosecuted for failure to comply with them. Subsequently it came to the attention of the enforcing authority that a different caravan had been placed on the site and a further information was laid before the magistrates alleging an offence under s 89(4). The magistrates dismissed the information on the basis that a small wooden hut which was present on the land and which had been renovated by the defendant constituted a 'dwellinghouse' for the purposes of s 22(2)(d) of the 1971 Act and that the use of the site for the stationing of the caravan was incidental to the enjoyment of the dwellinghouse. On appeal by case stated to the Divisional Court it was held that the magistrates were wrong to dismiss the information as they had failed to take proper account of s 93 of the 1971 Act, and that, in any event, the hut was not a 'dwellinghouse'. As the enforcement notices were undischarged by removal of the first caravan they should have convicted the defendant. Stephen Brown LJ observed that the effect of s 93 was such that the enforcement notice could only be discharged by a grant of planning permission.

14.3 Reinstatement or restoration of buildings or works

Where buildings or works have been demolished or altered in compliance with an enforcement notice, the reinstatement or restoration of them without a grant of planning permission is a breach of planning control which is subject to the original enforcement notice. This is the effect of the notice notwithstanding that in the words of s 93(3) 'its terms are not apt for the purpose' as the notice is 'deemed to apply in relation to the buildings or works as reinstated or restored as it applied in relation to the buildings or works before they were demolished or altered'.

The wording of this provision only appears to have been considered judicially in a county court case, *Broxbourne Borough Council* v *Small* [1980] CLY 2638. An enforcement notice was served in respect of a Dutch barn which was erected without planning permission. The structure was demolished, but subsequently the defendant constructed a nissen hut on the same site which was of smaller size compared to the former structure but was put to the same use. The local planning authority took the view that this was a reinstatement or restoration of the barn within s 93(3). As the developer refused to remove it the local planning authority exercised their powers under s 91 of the 1971 Act. After having entered onto the land and demolished the nissen hut they now sought to recover their expenses. The county court judge held that of the words 'if any development is carried out on land by way of reinstating or restoring', the word 'development' referred to the carrying out of a substantial new building enterprise. Of the words 'notwithstanding that its terms are not apt for the purpose', it was held that these meant 'notwithstanding that the building attracted to itself a different purpose or design'. It was further held that s 93(3) was to be considered as a whole and that the words 'reinstated or restored' in the statutory expression 'deemed to apply in relation to the buildings or works as reinstated or restored as it applied in relation to the buildings or works before they were demolished or altered' should not be considered in isolation. Taking this approach the learned judge had no hesitation in holding that the nissen hut was the reinstatement or restoration of the former Dutch barn, and hence the enforcing authority were entitled to recover their expenses.

It must also be noted that it is an offence to carry out any development for reinstating or restoring buildings which have been altered or demolished in compliance with an enforcement notice without a grant of planning permission. This offence, which is contained in s 93(5), applies in lieu of the offences contained in s 89(1)–(4) so it is therefore not an offence to fail to take steps required by the original enforcement notice to demolish or alter the reinstated or restored buildings or works. On summary conviction under s 93(5) a maximum fine of £2,000 may be imposed (level 5 on the standard scale). The offence is not triable on indictment.

14.4 Termination of the effect of an enforcement notice

The provisions of s 93 concerning the continuing effect of an enforcement notice are to be considered in conjunction with those of s 92 which deal with the means by which the effect of an enforcement notice can be neutralised. Under s 92(1), if a grant of planning permission is obtained, subsequent to the service of a copy of an enforcement notice, for the retention of buildings or works for the continuance of a use of land, the enforcement notice is thereby rendered ineffective in so far as it requires steps to be taken for demolition or alteration of those buildings or works or the discontinuance of the use. The notice itself remains in force: it is only its effect which is neutralised to the extent described in the provision. Hence no entry is required to be made in the register of enforcement and stop notices (signifying that the enforcement notice is no longer in force) since such an entry is wholly inappropriate. It will also be appreciated that if the enforcement notice has specified steps to be taken for the purposes of making the development comply with the terms of any planning permission which has previously been granted in respect of the land, or for the purposes of removing or alleviating any injury to amenity which has been caused by the development (see s 87(10)), then these aspects of the enforcement notice will continue in force.

In the case where planning permission is granted for the retention of buildings or works, or the continuance of a use of land without complying with a condition subject to which planning permission was previously granted, then any enforcement notice which requires steps to be taken in order to comply with the condition will, to that extent, cease to be effective: s 92(2). As was pointed out by Lord Widgery CJ in *Dudley Borough Council* v *Secretary of State for the Environment* [1980] JPL 181, this provision enables the Secretary of State to achieve a variation of a planning condition in the course of deciding an enforcement appeal, since by granting planning permission under this section it will be unnecessary to use the power of variation conferred by s 88B(1) and (2).

The manner in which an enforcement notice and a grant of planning permission inter-relate under s 92 was considered in *Havering London Borough Council* v *Secretary of State for the Environment* [1983] JPL 240. A site was used for storage and distribution of building materials in breach of planning control; this attracted an enforcement notice which required the use of the site to cease. The developer responded by making an application for planning permission and by appealing against the enforcement notice. The local planning authority granted planning permission subject to conditions, with which the developer failed to comply, and the Secretary of State then quashed the enforcement notice on the ground that s 92(1) applied. Hodgson J held that the Secretary of State had been right to quash the enforcement notice even though the grant of planning permission was not precisely consistent with it, since the area covered by the notice was the same as the area covered by the grant of planning permission, and the uses involved were consistent. But the fact that there had been noncompliance with the conditions left the local planning authority in the position whereby they would have to issue and serve a further enforcement notice to secure compliance with them. Although this result might not be the most convenient from the point of view of the local planning authority, it was not the effect of s 92 that the enforcement notice would only cease to be effective once all the conditions contained in the planning consent had been complied with.

One of the consequences of the fact that a grant of planning permission only renders an enforcement notice ineffective rather than to nullify it completely is that an enforcee is entitled to pursue an appeal against the enforcement notice to the Secretary of State under s 88. Indeed, it may well be advisable for a person who has an interest in the land to pursue the appeal with a view to ridding the land of the enforcement notice completely. Thus if the Secretary of State allows the appeal and quashes the enforcement notice then the entry of the details of the enforcement notice in the register of enforcement and stop notices must be removed under art 21A(2) of the GDO, with consequent benefits on disposal of the interest in the land. It also means that the Secretary of State retains his discretion to award costs to the appellant against the local planning authority despite the grant of planning permission: *R* v *Secretary of State for the Environment ex p Three Rivers District Council* [1983] JPL 730.

14.5 Withdrawal of an enforcement notice

Once an enforcement notice has been issued and copies have been served by the local planning authority, the notice is only capable of being withdrawn during the period prior to the date on which it becomes effective: s 87(14). In the case where no appeal is made against the enforcement notice this date is the date specified in the notice as the date on which it is to come into effect: s 87(13). Where an appeal is made to the Secretary of State, however, as s 88(10) renders the enforcement notice 'of no effect pending the final determination . . . of the appeal', it follows that the local planning authority are able to withdraw the enforcement notice at any time before the Secretary of State issues his decision on the appeal. Withdrawal may well take place once the appellant's grounds for appeal have become known to the local planning authority.

If an enforcement notice is withdrawn the authority are under a duty imposed by s 87(15) to give notice of the withdrawal to every person who was served with a copy of the enforcement notice. Notwithstanding the withdrawal, the local planning authority are expressly empowered by s 87(14) to issue a further notice if they consider it expedient to do so.

Chapter 15

Enforcement by Injunction

15.1 General

The scheme of enforcement of planning control contained in the Town and Country Planning Act 1971 (as amended), through the medium of enforcement notices and stop notices is not always wholly suitable for the purpose. It fails, for example, to deal satisfactorily with the developer who acts in total disregard for the development control system and who is prepared to pay fines on conviction for offences under ss 89–90. Although a fine of unlimited amount can be imposed on conviction on indictment, there is no power of imprisonment on such conviction. Where the normal enforcement procedures fail to control, the alternative remedy of injunctive relief (which carries a threat of committal for contempt of court) may be sought by the local planning authority. As will be seen, however, it is not essential for statutory remedies to be exhausted before recourse is made to an application for an injunction. Indeed, it would seem that it is not essential to every case that they should even have been implemented.

In the present context the basis of the injunction remedy is the need to uphold and protect a public right, but the scope of the remedy is not clear despite its appearance in the context of enforcement of planning control in *Att-Gen* v *Bastow* [1957] 1 QB 514 over thirty years ago. This slow development is due in part to the advent of the stop notice procedure in 1968 (which only became applicable to material changes of use in 1977) and to the enactment of s 222 of the Local Government Act 1972. This provision has been interpreted by the judiciary as authorising a local planning authority to seek an injunction without the need to seek the fiat of the Attorney-General to authorise relator proceedings. Consequently, this remedy (which is discretionary) has only been regularly requested in comparatively recent times.

15.2 Circumstances for injunctive relief

The circumstances in which injunctive relief can be given and the criteria which are to be applied in determining an application for an injunction are to be deduced (albeit not definitively) from a number of reported cases. These illustrate how the judiciary have progressively expanded the scope of the remedy so that in appropriate circumstances (eg an emergency) the remedy can be treated as a measure of first rather than of last resort. In many instances, however, it will be a long-stop for use where the statutory remedies have failed. The present state of the law can best be appreciated by a chronological approach to the leading cases.

In *Att-Gen* v *Bastow* the defendant was convicted three times for using land as a caravan site in breach of the requirements of an enforcement notice. He did not pay all the fines imposed and was imprisoned for a period as a result of this default. The Attorney-General then brought an action for an injunction on the relation of the local planning authority. The High Court held that when a public right is infringed the court has jurisdiction to grant an injunction, the public right in this instance being (per Devlin J) that '. . . Parliament considers that the public is entitled not to have the land used in ways which may be considered to be unhealthy or offensive'. In deciding that an injunction should be granted, the learned judge ruled that in relator proceedings the court would only refuse the injunction which was sought in exceptional circumstances. But the court was not bound to grant the injunction sought even if a clear and deliberate evasion of a public right is proved. Nor was it essential that the statutory remedies should be exhausted first, though the court clearly placed considerable faith in the Attorney-General's own judgment in assessing this aspect of the matter.

Judicial sympathy for the enforcing authority was demonstrated by an extension in the scope of the injunction procedure in *Att-Gen* v *Smith* [1958] 2 QB 173. In this case the defendant moved the offending caravans from a site in respect of which he had been convicted for failure to comply with an enforcement notice onto another site. He subsequently moved the caravans to a third site. Rather than institute enforcement proceedings for a third time the local planning authority successfully petitioned the Attorney-General to proceed for an injunction on the relation of the council. This injunction was granted despite the fact that no enforcement notice had been issued in respect of the third plot of land. Lord Goddard CJ said that the history of the matter (which included unsuccessful appeals against refusals of applications for planning permission) showed a clear intention by the defendants to act in defiance of the legislation and to use the Act to delay the process of enforcement when it was obvious that the appeals were doomed to failure. The injunction itself was expressed to restrain the defendant from using any land in the area of the local planning authority for unauthorised stationing of caravans. Injunctions on a county-wide basis were granted in the rather similar circumstances of *Att-Gen* v *Morris* [1973] JPL 429: in this case not only was the affected land subject to the injunction but also 'any other land which is not an authorised caravan site within the county'. A request that the injunction be expressed to have effect nationwide was refused by O'Connor J.

The proposition that it is not essential for statutory remedies to be exhausted before an injunction can be granted is based on *Stafford Borough Council* v *Elkenford Ltd* [1977] 1 WLR 324, a case involving Sunday trading in breach of the Shops Act 1950. A conviction under the 1950 Act had been obtained which was the subject of an appeal to the Divisional Court. In addition, an enforcement notice was served which became the subject of an appeal to the Secretary of State. Before either proceedings had been determined the local authority sought an injunction as the illegal trading continued unabated. The Court of Appeal held that the court had jurisdiction to grant an injunction, even though only one conviction for breach of the 1950 Act had been obtained. This was because the defendants had deliberately organised a scheme designed to break the law and that further fines would not be a deterrent. Lord Denning MR went further, however, and added obiter that where there is a plain breach of a statute local councils need not wait for finality before commencing proceedings for an injunction: it was open to them to commence proceedings even before statutory remedies are initiated. The principle to be applied in cases of this nature was stated (at p 328) as follows:

Whenever Parliament has enacted a law and given a particular remedy for the breach of it, such remedy being in an inferior court, nevertheless the High Court always has reserve power to enforce the law so enacted by way of an injunction or declaration or other suitable remedy. The High Court has jurisdiction to ensure obedience to the law whenever it is just and convenient to do so.

Bridge LJ was a little more cautious in that while he agreed with Lord Denning MR he added that it would only be in the most exceptional cases that the court would grant an injunction at so early a stage.

Both the *Stafford* case and some subsequent cases have emphasised a need for a 'deliberate and flagrant flouting of the law' as a condition for injunctive relief. In *Westminster City Council* v *Jones* [1981] JPL 750 the defendants appealed against an enforcement notice on the sole ground that planning permission ought to be granted for the development, an amusement arcade. A stop notice was also served but this was disregarded and criminal proceedings were commenced. Prior to the hearing of the summons the council sought an interlocutory injunction. This was granted by Whitford J since the defendant had proceeded to open the amusement arcade before he had obtained planning permission and there was a deliberate and flagrant flouting of the law and a plain breach of the law. Judicial discretion was exercised in favour of the local planning authority notwithstanding that the trial of the summons was less than a month ahead. Whilst the injunction sought was granted in this case Whitford J accepted that injunctions should not be used to replace the normal development control procedures which had the in-built safeguards of a right of appeal to the Secretary of State and compensation in respect of loss caused by service of a stop notice. It was appropriate to grant an injunction in this case, however, to protect a predominantly residential area from an undesirable use.

The House of Lords adopted the 'deliberate and flagrant flouting of the law' test in another Sunday trading case, *Stoke-on-Trent City Council* v *B & Q (Retail) Ltd* [1984] 2 All ER 332. In the course of his judgment upholding the injunction which had been granted by Whitford J and confirmed by the Court of Appeal, Lord Templeman stated (at p 341)

Where Parliament imposes a penalty for an offence, Parliament must consider the penalty adequate and Parliament can increase the penalty if it proves to be inadequate. It follows that a local authority should be reluctant to seek and the court should be reluctant to grant an injunction which if disobeyed may involve the infringer in sanctions more onerous than the penalty imposed for the offence.

In this case the local authority were faced with the problem of proliferation of illegal Sunday trading and had made efforts to control it by warnings, initiation of criminal proceedings, and by issue of writs for injunctions. The criminal proceedings were not pursued against the present defendants since the local authority took the view that they would not deter them from further breaches since the likely profits from trading were substantially higher than the fines which could be imposed. The House of Lords held that although the local authority should normally prosecute criminal proceedings to their conclusion before relying on civil proceedings, the council were entitled to form the view that these would be ineffective and hence the injunction had been properly granted.

Further relaxation in the requirements seem apparent from the decision of the Court of Appeal in *Runnymede Borough Council* v *Ball* [1986] JPL 288. Here the Court of Appeal rejected the notion that a 'deliberate and flagrant flouting of the law' was always an essential condition for the grant of an injunction. The trial judge had held that there must either be a 'deliberate flouting of the law' or that the case involved an 'inadequate penalty'. The Court of Appeal held that the trial judge had been wrong to hold that total disregard of enforcement and stop notices by gipsies in relation to the site which they had acquired did not amount to 'deliberate and flagrant flouting of the law', but nevertheless an injunction was justified on the further ground that the Green Belt site would suffer from irreparable damage (by laying of hardcore) if an injunction was not granted; the prosecution process would also be too slow for the site would have been fully occupied by gipsies before the proceedings were completed. Finally, in a further decision involving the same local planning authority, *Runnymede Borough Council* v *Smith* [1986] JPL 592 the *Ball* decision was distinguished by Millett J. He declined to grant an injunction in respect of a site used by travelling showmen as it transpired that the stop notice which had been served in that case was ineffective due to the application of s 90(2)(*b*). The defendants were therefore not in breach of the criminal law. As there was no 'deliberate and flagrant flouting of the law' and that there was no irreparable damage (since the defendants were awaiting the outcome of their appeal against the enforcement notice before carrying out any works on the site), an injunction would not be granted.

15.3 Proceedings under s 222 of the Local Government Act 1972

Proceedings for an injunction can be brought by local authorities pursuant to the powers granted to them by s 222 of the Local Government Act 1972. This provision replaced an earlier provision in s276 of the Local Government Act 1933 which was slightly differently worded and which was held in *Prestatyn Urban District Council* v *Prestatyn Raceway Ltd* [1970] 1 WLR 33 not to confer powers to protect the public interest in like manner to the powers of the Attorney-General. It was therefore necessary to petition the Attorney-General to permit a relator action to be brought. The relevant part of the revised provision is as follows:

Where a local authority consider it expedient for the promotion or protection of the interests of the inhabitants of their area
(a) they may prosecute or defend or appear in any legal proceedings, and in the case of civil proceedings, may institute them in their own name . . .

The inclusion of the words 'may institute them in their own name' persuaded Oliver J to hold in *Solihull Metropolitan Borough Council* v *Maxfern* [1977] 1 WLR 127 that the concurrence of the Attorney-General was no longer necessary to permit the local authority to institute civil proceedings for an injunction, a view confirmed by the House of Lords in *Stoke on Trent City Council* v *B & Q (Retail) Ltd*. This is so even if the local authority wish to use the injunction remedy to restrain a breach of the criminal law: *Westminster City Council* v *Jones*. In this case Whitford J ruled that a judgment delivered by Talbot J in the slightly earlier case of *Kent County Council* v *Batchelor* (No 2) [1979] 1 WLR 213 was correct, to the effect that the only restriction on a local authority's power under s222 was that they must act for the promotion or protection of the interests of the inhabitants of their area. The *Batchelor* case involved proceedings for an injunction to restrain an anticipated breach of a tree preservation order, but it was suggested that powers under s222 are limited to cases of great emergency or where the criminal penalty was inadequate to act as an effective control. It was held, however, that any such suggestion (based on the judgments in *Gouriet* v *Union of Post Office Workers* [1978] AC 435) was misplaced. Such considerations would, however, be relevant to the question whether, in the exercise of judicial discretion, the remedy should be granted. Unlike the position applicable to relator proceedings, there is no presumption that the local authority should have the injunction sought.

The power conferred by s222 is limited to local authorities, as defined by s270. This provides that 'local authority' means a county council, a district council, a London borough council or a parish or community council. The common council of the City of London is also included in the scope of s 222 by virtue of a provision to that effect contained in s 222(2). As a development corporation constituted under s 135 of the Local Government, Planning and Land Act 1980 is not a 'local authority' it has no locus standi to seek an injunction under s 222: *London Docklands Development Corporation* v *Rank Hovis McDougall Ltd* [1986] JPL 825.

Proceedings for an injunction will ordinarily be commenced in the High Court by writ or by originating summons under RSC Ord 5 r 4. Such a matter may be transferred to the county court under s 40 of the County Courts Act 1984.

15.4 Committal for breach of an injunction

The sanction for breach of an injunction is primarily committal to prison, although a fine for contempt of court (unlikely to be of much efficacy in the present context) can be imposed. Under RSC Ord 52 r 1 an order of committal can be made by a single judge of the Queens Bench Division of the High Court, unless the proceedings were assigned or subsequently transferred to the Chancery Division, in which case jurisdiction to commit is limited to a judge of that Division. Under Ord 52 r 4 the application for an order of committal must be made by motion stating the grounds of the application and supported by an affidavit; a copy of each of these documents must ordinarily be served personally on the defendant.

That precision in drafting these documents is essential, having particular regard to the injunctive relief already gained, is apparent from the decision of the Court of Appeal in *Chiltern District Council* v *Keane* [1985] 2 All ER 118. The defendant had failed to comply with the requirements of an enforcement notice relating to unauthorised storage of vehicles and caravans, a use which eventually became the subject of undertakings and injunctions, none of which were complied with. The subsequent notice of motion recited that the injunction had previously been granted against the alleged contemnor and alleged a breach of these injunctions without further particularising the matter. The defendant appealed against an order of Goulding J committing him to prison for 2 months claiming that the notice of motion and the subsequent order were invalid. The Court of Appeal held that as personal liberty was involved it was essential that the procedural requirements be strictly observed. These included the drafting of the documents since in their present form they did not make it clear to the alleged contemnor the exact nature of his alleged breach. The difficulty arose from the fact that the undertakings and injunctions in this case covered a wide range of activities; the defendant was entitled to know whether it was being claimed by the local authority that he was in breach of every requirement of the orders made against him or only some of them, and if so which of them. Sir John Donaldson MR considered that every notice of motion to commit must be looked at against its own background, the test for its validity being 'does it give the person alleged to be in contempt enough information to enable him to meet the charge?' Where only one breach was involved, however, it would be sufficient to recite that the defendant had failed to comply with that order.

Chapter 16

Enforcement and Crown Land

16.1 Introduction

The topic of enforcement of development control on Crown land is the subject of separate consideration because in some instances it will be necessary for the local planning authority to invoke a modified scheme of enforcement procedure. This involves the issue and service of an instrument known as a 'special enforcement notice'. The modified procedure is based upon the Town and Country Planning Act 1984 ('the 1984 Act') and the Town and Country Planning (Special Enforcement Notices) Regulations (SI 1984 No 1016), ('the 1984 Regulations') which together prescribe a code for special enforcement procedure which adopts with modifications the enforcement provisions of the 1971 Act.

Notwithstanding the 1984 legislation, the general position of the Crown under the town and country planning code is that the Crown is exempt from the provisions of the 1971 Act in respect of development carried out **by the Crown**. In relation to enforcement of planning control this exemption is the subject of a provision contained in s 266(3) of the 1971 Act. This specifies that 'no enforcement notice shall be issued under s 87 of this Act in respect of development carried out by or on behalf of the Crown after (1 July 1948) on land which was Crown land at the time when the development was carried out'.

Prior to the 1984 Act further exemptions from the effect of the planning legislation were to be implied from application of general principles of law rather than by specific statutory provision. These principles included the proposition that the Crown is not bound by an Act of Parliament unless it is expressly or impliedly included. It was probable that the Crown could not apply to a local planning authority for a grant of planning permission, nor could it validly benefit from such a grant. Nevertheless a person who held an **interest in the land granted by the Crown** was subject to the 1971 Act since by virtue of another provision of the 1971 Act, s 266(1)(*b*), the 1971 Act does apply 'to the extent of any interest . . . for the time being held otherwise than by or on behalf of the Crown'. This means that a person (other than the Crown) who holds an interest in the land (eg a leaseholder) is subject to the full force of the legislation (including enforcement of planning control) but the Crown remains exempt. The reason for this was explained by Lord Denning MR in *Ministry of Agriculture, Fisheries and Food* v *Jenkins* [1963] 2 QB 317, when in commenting upon earlier legislation, he said:

Looking at the whole of the Town and Country Planning Act 1947 I am satisfied that the Crown does not need to get planning permission in respect of its own interest in Crown lands. The reason it is exempt is . . . by reason of the general principle that the Crown is not bound by an Act unless it is expressly or impliedly included.

The general principle has subsequently been amended by s 1 of the 1984 Act which enables the representatives of the Crown to apply for and receive a grant of planning permission. By s 3 of the 1984 Act provision is made to extend the scope of the enforcement aspect of the legislation to persons who do not hold an 'interest' in Crown land. It is to breaches of development control caused by such persons that the special enforcement procedure is relevant.

16.2 Meaning of 'Crown land'

The term 'Crown land' is defined by s 266(7) of the 1971 Act. While most of the instances that will be encountered involve land vested in a central government department, the definition given in the section is much broader. Thus Crown land is 'land in which there is a Crown interest or a Duchy interest'. These terms are further defined as follows:

    (i) 'Crown interest' means an interest belonging to Her Majesty in right of the Crown, or belonging to a government department or held in trust for Her Majesty for the purposes of a government department;

    (ii) 'Duchy interest' means an interest belonging to Her Majesty in right of the Duchy of Lancaster, or belonging to the Duchy of Cornwall.

These lands are administered by what the 1971 Act terms 'the appropriate authority'. This term is also defined in s 266(7); its meaning depends on whether the land is subject to a Crown interest or a Duchy interest. The term embraces four possible bodies. In the words of the provision, 'the appropriate authority' in relation to any land

  (a) in the case of land belonging to Her Majesty in right of the Crown and forming part of the Crown Estate, means the Crown Estate Commissioners, and in relation to any other land belonging to Her Majesty in right of the Crown, means the government department having the management of that land;

  (b) in relation to land belonging to Her Majesty in right of the Duchy of Lancaster, means the Chancellor of the Duchy;

  (c) in relation to land belonging to the Duchy of Cornwall, means such person as the Duke of Cornwall, or the possessor for the time being of the Duchy of Cornwall, appoints;

  (d) in the case of land belonging to a government department or held in trust for Her Majesty for the purposes of a government department, means that department.

16.3 Development carried out by or on behalf of the Crown

No planning permission is needed by the Crown to carry out development on Crown land. Where an act of development is proposed, however, the appropriate authority will normally invoke the procedure contained in Part IV of Department of Environment Circular 18/84 entitled 'Crown Land and Crown Development'. This contains a code for consultation with the local planning authority involving furnishing the local planning authority with a 'Notice of Proposed Development' which is to be treated by the local planning authority as if it were an application for planning permission. The local planning authority will thus issue a 'decision' within eight weeks of receipt of the notice. If this results in disapproval of the 'application' by the local planning authority the decision may be 'appealed' to the Secretary of State for the Environment. By implementing this non-statutory procedure the Crown's exemption from development control is greatly mitigated. The Crown can, however, acting through the appropriate authority apply for a grant of planning permission under s 1 of the 1984 Act. If such an application is successful the grant will only apply to development carried out following a disposal of the land or on grant of an interest in it. Crown land can therefore be disposed of with the benefit of a grant of planning permission to a developer. A purchaser is, however, entitled to carry on using the land for the same purpose as the Crown or to retain buildings or works on the land: see the opinion of Goff J expressed in *Newbury District Council* v *Secretary of State for the Environment* [1977] JPL 373 at p 376. In such a case no planning permission is required and hence any enforcement notice would be invalid.

Since a purchaser is entitled to continue an existing use of former Crown land without planning permission, a particular development control problem arises when the Crown institutes a use of the land which is intended to be temporary but then disposes of the land. Since the Crown did not need to obtain planning permission, a subsequent private owner of the land would take it with the benefit of the intended temporary use being treated as the lawful use of the land and hence with the right to continue it indefinitely. This contrasts with the position obtaining when a temporary use is made of non-Crown land since in such a case a grant of planning permission would be needed for the specific period of the use and the private landowner would have the right to revert (under s 23(5) of the 1971 Act) to the previous use when the temporary period has expired. To overcome this difficulty s 5(1) of the 1984 Act permits the local planning authority to enter into an agreement with the Crown when a material change of use is made or is proposed to be made. The effect of any such agreement is that if the land should cease to be used by the Crown for the purpose specified in the agreement, the 1971 Act is to apply to any subsequent use of the land as if the use specified in the agreement had been the subject of an express grant of planning permission subject to a condition requiring the use to cease on the date on which the Crown in fact ceases to use the land. This means that a prospective purchaser of Crown land subject to such an agreement will not be entitled to continue the existing use of the land without planning permission but will have the right to revert to the use which prevailed before the use specified in the agreement was started.

16.4 Development in right of an interest in Crown land

Where the Crown has granted an interest in Crown land the normal development control provisions apply if the person holding the interest in the land wishes to develop. Thus a grant of planning permission can be obtained in the normal way and the developer is, in general, subject to the normal enforcement procedures: s 266(1)(*b*) of the 1971 Act. To this proposition one exception applies: under s 266(3) it is necessary for the local planning authority to obtain the consent of the appropriate authority before an enforcement notice can be issued under s 87. The grant of consent to enforcement action is a discretionary power and therefore the discretion cannot be fettered by a contractual obligation: *Molton Builders* v *City of Westminster LBC* (1975) 30 P&CR 182.

Since the application of the enforcement provisions of the 1971 Act depends on unauthorised development in right of an 'interest' in Crown land the scope of 'interest' is important. This word is not defined by the legislation but may be taken to include all forms of tenancy. Under s 4(1) of the 1984 Act 'interest' is extended to include a licence in writing to occupy Crown land. Such a licensee is thus brought within the ordinary enforcement procedure, and by s 4(2) of the 1984 the licensee enjoys a right of appeal against an enforcement notice under s 88 and can reply on any of the grounds specified in s 88(2). This is in sharp contrast to the squatter, trespasser or person in possession under an oral licence. Such persons do not have an 'interest' and hence the ordinary enforcement procedure does not apply. It is for application to these cases that the special enforcement provisions introduced by the 1984 Act are intended.

16.5 The special enforcement notice

It will be appreciated that one of the objects of the 1984 Act was to provide a scheme of enforcement in respect of breaches of development control on Crown land where no 'interest' exists which would attract the operation of the ordinary enforcement procedure. Circular 18/84 explains in Part I para 13 that the sort of unauthorised development which had previously proved difficult to control under the town and country planning legislation included 'the stationing of mobile snack bars or refreshment vans on trunk road lay-bys'. Unauthorised caravan sites on Crown land were similarly difficult to control prior to the 1984 Act, otherwise than by way of the site licensing provisions of the Caravan Site and Control of Development Act 1960.

Section 3 of the 1984 Act contains the solution to the problem. It applies 'to development of Crown land carried out otherwise than by or on behalf of the Crown at a time when no person is entitled to occupy it by virtue of a private interest'. Thus the section applies where Crown land is occupied by a person who lacks an interest which would permit application of the normal enforcement procedure. Under s 3(2) the local planning authority may serve a special enforcement notice where it appears to them that development has taken place and that it is expedient to issue the notice and serve copies of it. In exercising their discretion the local planning authority must have regard to the provisions of the development plan and to any other material considerations. No special enforcement notice can be served, however, unless the consent of the appropriate authority has been obtained: s 3(3). Circular 18/84 advises in Part I para 13 that such consent will not be unreasonably withheld.

The statutory provisions regulating special enforcement notice procedure are broadly similar to those which apply to enforcement proceedings under Part V of the 1971 Act. Thus s 3(8) provides that s 88(3)–(10) and s 88A(1) and (2) of the 1971 Act (concerning appeals) apply to special enforcement notices as they apply to enforcement notices issued under s 87, but this subsection empowers the Secretary of State to make regulations which apply other provisions of the 1971 Act to special enforcement notices and appeals as he thinks necessary or expedient, with such modifications as he thinks fit. The Town and Country Planning (Special Enforcement Notices) Regulations 1984 were made pursuant to this power. They provide (reg 2) that the provisions of the 1971 Act which are listed in the Schedule to the 1984 Regulations are to apply to special enforcement notices and to appeals against such notices subject to any modifications also specified in the Schedule. The legislative code applicable to special enforcement notices is therefore to be found in s 3 of the 1984 Act (which contains a number of provisions which are peculiar to such notices) and the provisions of the 1971 Act as modified in the manner specified in the Schedule to the 1984 Regulations.

Reference to this Schedule is essential where a breach of planning control on Crown land occurs which is outside the scope of the unmodified provisions of the 1971 Act. It will be noted, for instance, that s 88B and s 91 do not apply. Particular reference must also be made to s 3(4)–(7) of the 1984 Act which contain the requirements relating to content and service of the special enforcement notice. These requirements are as follows:

16.5.1 Content of the notice

Section 3(4) and (5) requires that the notice must specify:

 (*a*) the matters alleged to constitute development;
 (*b*) the steps which the local planning authority require to be taken for restoring the land to its condition before the development took place or for discontinuing any use of the land which has been instituted by the development;
 (*c*) the date on which the notice is to take effect;
 (*d*) the period within which any step specified in the notice by the local planning authority is to be taken (different periods may be allowed for different steps).

It should be observed that the legislation does not contain precisely the same requirements as are applicable to an ordinary enforcement notice. Thus the latter must require the breach of planning control to be remedied and must state the reasons why it is expedient to issue the notice and the precise boundaries of the land (see para **6.2**). It will be noted, therefore, that the requirements specified by the Town and Country Planning (Enforcement Notices and Appeals) Regulations 1981 do not formally apply. Nevertheless it is clear from para 17 of Part 1 of Circular 18/84 that the Secretary of State expects local planning authorities to act as if the 1981 Regulations had been formally applied to special enforcement notices. No model form of special enforcement notices has been included in the Circular but is available from the Department of the Environment, Tollgate House, Houlton Street, Bristol, BS2 9DJ, or from the Welsh Office, Cathays Park, Cardiff, CF1 3NQ.

16.5.2 Service of copies of the notice

The service requirement is that a copy of the special enforcement notice must be served, not later than 28 days after its issue and not later than 28 days before it is to take effect, on the following parties:

 (*a*) the person who carried out the development alleged in the notice;
 (*b*) any person who is occupying the land on the date when the notice is issued;
 (*c*) the appropriate authority.

An exception applies in the case of service on the person who carried out the development if the local planning authority are unable to identify or trace that person after making reasonable enquiry: s 3(6).

16.5.3 Right of appeal to the Secretary of State

One of the main differences between special enforcement notice procedure and enforcement under s 87 of the 1971 Act is that the grounds of appeal are greatly reduced. Under s 3(7) of the 1984 Act the grounds of appeal are only that

(a) the matters alleged in the notice have not taken place; or

(b) the matters alleged in the notice do not constitute development.

The persons entitled to make an appeal to the Secretary of State are (i) the person who carried out the development alleged in the notice, and (ii) the person who is occupying the land on the date when the notice is issued. These persons have the right of appeal whether or not a copy of the special enforcement notice has been served on them; the appeal must be made before the date specified in the enforcement notice as the date on which it is to come into effect. The local planning authority will normally issue an appeal form when serving a copy of the notice but in default copies of the relevant form can be obtained from the Department of the Environment or Welsh Offices at the addresses specified above. The appeal itself is not subject to a specific code of procedure rules but Circular 18/84 advises that the Secretary of State 'will abide by the spirit' of the provisions of the Town and Country Planning (Enforcement) (Inquiries Procedure) Rules 1981 as if they had been formally applied to special enforcement notice appeals and will expect local planning authorities to do the same: para 17 of Part I.

Appendix 1

Extracts from Departmental Circulars

Circular 109/77

ENFORCEMENT OF PLANNING CONTROL –
ESTABLISHED USE CERTIFICATES

Procedure for certifying an established use of land

16. Since enforcement action can be taken at any time against uses of land (other than as a single dwelling-house) commenced since the end of 1963, persons with an interest in land may wish to establish (notably for the benefit of intending purchasers) that the use to which the land is being put will not be the subject of enforcement action. Section 94 of the Act provides a procedure by which an established use certificate can be obtained from the local planning authority. Section 94(7) of the Act provides that an established use certificate shall be conclusive as respects the matters stated therein for the purposes of an appeal against an enforcement notice served after the date of the application for the certificate.

17. A certificate can be obtained under section 94 (or under section 95 on appeal) only in the following circumstances:

 (i) for a use of land which has secured immunity from enforcement action, ie a use begun before the beginning of 1964 without planning permission and continued since that date; or

 (ii) a use begun before the beginning of 1964 under a planning permission subject to a condition or limitation which either has never been complied with or has not been complied with since the end of 1963; or

 (iii) a use begun since the end of 1963 as the result of a change of use not requiring planning permission and where there has been no change of use requiring planning permission since the end of 1963.

18. In relation to an application for an established use certificate the onus of proof rests with the applicant, but if the local planning authority are satisfied that the claim is made out they must issue a certificate. The manner in which an application for an established use certificate is required to be made and dealt with, the form of certificate, and the procedure for appealing against either the authority's refusal to issue a certificate or their decision to issue a certificate in part only or their failure to give a decision within the specified period are set out in Schedule 14 to the Act and article 22 of the General Development Order. The Order provides that if the information and evidence submitted with an application are insufficient for the purpose the authority may, by a direction in writing, require the production of such further evidence specified in the direction as they may need.

19. An application for an established use certificate may be accompanied by an application for planning permission made in accordance with the provisions of s 32 of the Act to continue the use. The making of such an application is not to be regarded as an admission of doubt about the immunity of a use from enforcement action nor be allowed to prejudice in any way the full consideration on its merits of the claim for an established use certificate. On the other hand, the grant of planning permission will in some instances be acceptable to the applicant and obviate recourse to appeal procedures.

Circular 38/81

PLANNING AND ENFORCEMENT APPEALS

PART III

ENFORCEMENT NOTICES AND APPEALS AGAINST THEM TO THE SECRETARY OF STATE: REVISED PROCEDURES TAKING EFFECT ON JANUARY 11 1982

26. Sections 87(12), 88(5) and 97(4) of the Town and Country Planning Act 1971, as amended by the Schedule to the Local Government and Planning (Amendment) Act 1981, provide the Secretary of State with new regulation-making powers in regard to:
  (1) enforcement notices issued under section 87(1) of the 1971 Act (but *not* listed building enforcement notices issued under section 96(1)); and
  (2) appeals to him under section s 88(1) and 97(1) of the 1971 Act against, respectively, enforcement and listed building enforcement notices.
Following consultation with the Council on Tribunals, the local authority associations and certain professional bodies, the Secretaries of State have made the Town and Country Planning (Enforcement Notices and Appeals) Regulations 1981 (SI 1981 No 1742), which will take effect on January 11, 1982. The relevant provisions of these Regulations apply to all enforcement notices issued by LPAs, under section 87 of the 1971 Act, on and after that date and to all appeals to the Secretary of State against enforcement and listed building enforcement notices, including current appeals which were brought before January 11, 1982.
27. The Lord Chancellor, after consultation with the Council on Tribunals, has made the Town and Country Planning (Enforcement) (Inquiries Procedure) Rules 1981 (SI 1981/1743), which will also take effect on January 11, 1982 and govern the procedures to be followed on all enforcement, listed building enforcement, and established use certificate (EUC) appeals made on and after January 11, for which a public local inquiry is to be held by a Planning Inspector appointed by the Secretary of State. The provisions of these new Rules are closely modelled on the existing Inquiries Procedure Rules for planning appeals and transferred planning appeals (SI 1974, Nos 419 and 420), which are already applied in spirit to enforcement, listed building enforcement and the EUC appeals for which an inquiry is necessary.
28. This part of the circular explains how these new rules and the regulations are intended to operate and the circumstances in which the Secretaries of State will use their new discretionary powers, in section 88(6) and (9), or section 97(5) and (8), of the 1971 Act to dismiss an appeal, quash a notice, or determine an appeal without considering

certain grounds when an appellant or a LPA fails to comply with a relevant requirement of the regulations.

New requirements for enforcement notices issued under section 87(1)

29. Regulation 3 of the Enforcement Notices and Appeals Regulations requires that every enforcement notice issued by a LPA, under section 87(1) of the 1971 Act, shall specify:

   (1) the reasons why the LPA consider it 'expedient' to issue the notice; and
   (2) the precise boundaries of the land to which the notice relates, whether by reference to a plan or otherwise.

The Secretaries of State regard the first of these requirements as an important initial means of enabling anyone served with a copy of an enforcement notice to understand, from the outset, the reasons why the LPA consider it expedient to issue the notice. LPAs were asked, in DOE Circular 109/77 (WO Circular 164/77), to send an informal covering letter explaining why they are taking enforcement action: the new statutory requirement in Regulation 3 takes this a stage further by requiring all LPAs to give such an explanation as a normal part of the process of enforcing planning control. However, in order to avoid creating possible confusion for appellants, LPAs should avoid giving the statement of reasons in close proximity to either the allegation of a breach of planning control, or the specification of the steps required to be taken to remedy the alleged breach. The statement of reasons why it is expedient to issue the notice might most conveniently be given in a separate annex to the enforcement notice.

30. Although the new requirement to give a statement of reasons does not apply to listed building enforcement notices, LPAs are asked to provide a similar statement when they issue such notices if the reasons why the notice has been issued are not self-evident from the statement of the alleged contravention or the steps required to remedy it.

31. As to the requirement in Regulation 3 that the enforcement notice shall specify the precise boundaries of the land to which it relates, the Secretaries of State consider that this is always best done by means of a plan (preferably on an Ordnance Survey base with a scale not less than 1/2500) attached to the enforcement notice, on which the exact boundary of the land is clearly indicated by a suitably coloured outline. If this is insufficient for exact identification of the boundary of the land, the plan should be supplemented by a brief written description, or an accurately surveyed drawing to a larger scale.

32. Regulation 4 of the Enforcement Notices and Appeals Regulations requires that every copy of an enforcement notice served by a LPA, under section 87(5) of the 1971 Act, shall be accompanied by:

   (1) a copy of sections 87 to 88B of the 1971 Act, or a summary of those sections which explains that there is a right of appeal to the Secretary of State against the notice and that any appeal must be made in writing, and gives the grounds on which an appeal may be made to the Secretary of State; and

(2) notification that an appeal to the Secretary of State must be supported simultaneously (or within time-limits imposed by the Secretary of State) by a statement of the grounds and facts on which it is based.

It is for LPAs to decide how best to fulfil this requirement; but the Secretaries of State consider that the best method is to send with every copy of an enforcement notice served on and after January 11, 1982, a copy of the Departments' explanatory booklet about enforcement appeals (entitled 'Enforcement Notice Appeals – A Guide to Procedure') and a copy of the official appeal form. This will ensure that every intending appellant has the same information from the LPA and knows the procedure for appealing. Neither the explanatory booklet nor the appeal form is appropriate for listed building enforcement notices, to which Regulation 4 does *not* apply.

New requirements for appeals to the Secretary of State against enforcement notices and listed building enforcement notices

33. Sections 88(5) and 97(4) of the 1971 Act enable the Secretary of State to make regulations requiring appellants and LPAs to carry out certain procedures at specified times during the progress of an appeal. If those requirements are not carried out, the Secretary of State has certain discretionary powers, in sections 88(6) (9) and 97(5) (8) of the 1971 Act, to enable him to speed up the procedural stages of all enforcement appeals. This does not imply that speed will come before all other considerations; the Secretaries of State recognise that negotiations between the parties to an enforcement appeal often take place while the appeal is in progress and they do not intend to frustrate responsible negotiating procedures – especially when a mutually acceptable compromise will result in withdrawal of an appeal or an enforcement notice. The Secretaries of State intend that appellants and LPAs should regard the new requirements for enforcement appeals as providing an incentive to work jointly towards the quickest possible determination, or some acceptable alternative means of resolving the deadlock produced by the appeal. If this intention is realised in practice, it will be unusual for the Secretary of State to invoke the sanction of dismissing an appeal or quashing a notice because a procedural requirement has not been fulfilled by an appellant or a LPA.

The appellant's statement

34. The key to quicker progress in the procedural stages of all enforcement appeals is for the appellant to provide a better documented and more complete statement of the grounds, as specified in section 88(2) or 97(1) of the 1971 Act, on which the appeal is based and the relevant facts or arguments in support of each ground. The departments have tried to help people making enforcement appeals under section 88, by introducing, on April 1, 1981, an official enforcement appeal form[1] and an

[1] Form DoE 14069 (Revised 1986)
[2] Enforcement Notice Appeals – A Guide to Procedure (Revised 1987)

explanatory booklet[2] giving advice about how an appeal should be presented to best advantage. But many appeal documents still contain incomplete information when they are first submitted. In future, it should be easier for a completely documented appeal under section 88 to be presented at the outset because LPAs must include with the copy of an enforcement notice a statement why it is 'expedient' to take enforcement action. Intending appellants and their agents should therefore consider this statement of expediency most carefully, when they are contemplating an appeal. If they then decide to appeal, they should address their arguments both to the alleged breach of planning control and the LPA's statement of reasons why enforcement action has been taken. If the LPA state that they are prepared to grant conditional planning permission for the alleged unlawful development, an intending appellant should first consider whether instead of appealing, it would be preferable to make a planning application to the LPA for the development in question. If appropriate, this should be discussed urgently with the LPA to establish whether they are prepared to withdraw the notice if an application is made. Alternatively, if it is clear that a conditional permission in the terms indicated by the LPA would not be acceptable, the appeal should state what modified conditions would make it acceptable.

35. For all enforcement and listed building enforcement appeals which are delayed because the appellant provides insufficient information and the department's requests for further information are ignored, the Secretary of State will invoke his new powers, in Regulation 5 of the Enforcement Notices and Appeals Regulations, to require time-limits to be observed. If an appellant fails to provide the required information in response to a request for it, the Secretary of State will formally require him to provide it within a period of 28 days. If this requirement does not produce a satisfactory response, the department will issue a warning letter, one week before the 28 day period is due to expire, to the effect that the Secretary of State may proceed to dismiss the appeal (or determine it only on those grounds of appeal for which he has sufficient information), unless the appellant can show that there are extenuating circumstances genuinely preventing him from providing the required information. If this warning letter fails to produce a satisfactory response within one week, the Secretary of State will proceed at once to consider, in the light of all the information and representations then available to him, whether to dismiss the appeal in accordance with section 88(6)(a) or 97(5)(a) of the 1971 Act; or to determine it, as in section 88(9) or 97(8), without regard to those grounds of appeal which have not been properly and adequately supported by a statement of facts. When an appeal is dismissed under section 88(6)(a) or 97(5)(a), the Secretary of State will not have considered the deemed planning application and any fee already paid by the appellant will be refunded by the department.

36. An appellant's statement is sometimes insufficiently informative or detailed for the purposes of a public inquiry into an enforcement appeal. If so, the Secretary of State will in future make greater use of the power, in Rule 6(5) of the Enforcement Inquiries Procedure Rules, to require the

appellant to serve a written statement of the submission he intends to make at the inquiry. Any such statement will have to be served upon the LPA and the Secretary of State at a specified time in advance of the inquiry date. The Secretary of State will also exercise his power under rule 6(5) in EUC appeals, when the appellant has not provided adequate information in his grounds of appeal.

The LPA's statement

37. Despite the fact that a LPA have, as a last resort, issued an enforcement notice (perhaps accompanied by a stop notice), the Departments sometimes experience great difficulty in obtaining the authority's written statement for the appeal – even when it is relatively straightforward and the parties are proceeding by way of written representations and a site-inspection by a Planning Inspector. Moreover, some LPAs' statements are inadequate as a means of preparing for a public inquiry, with the result that the parties to the appeal and the Planning Inspector who conducts the inquiry spend more time than is necessary at the inquiry.

38. Regulation 6(1) of the Enforcement Notices and Appeals Regulations requires the LPA to serve on the Secretary of State and the appellant a statement of their written submissions on the appeal, which is to include a summary of the LPA's response to each of the appellant's grounds of appeal and a statement whether the LPA would be prepared to grant conditional planning permission, or listed building consent, for the development or works to which the notice relates. To enable an enforcement appeal to proceed satisfactorily, it is essential for the LPA to provide this statement in accordance with the informal timetable set by the departments when they first inform the LPA that an appeal has been received; if the LPA fail to do so, the Secretary of State will exercise the statutory powers referred to in the next paragraph.

39. Regulation 6(2) of the Enforcement Notices and Appeals Regulations requires the LPA's statement of submissions on the appeal to be served:

(1) *in inquiry cases* – not later than 28 days before the inquiry date, unless a later date is mutually agreed by the Secretary of State and the parties to the appeal; and

(2) *in other cases* (*ie* written representations) – not later than 28 days from the date on which the Secretary of State sends the LPA a notice requiring that the statement be served.

If a LPA does not conform to these requirements, the Secretary of State has a discretionary power to quash the enforcement notice, in accordance with section 88(6)(*b*) or 97(5)(*b*) of the 1971 Act. The Secretaries of State consider that it should be exceptional to quash an enforcement notice in these circumstances because the time-limits provide ample opportunity for a LPA's statement to be served before they expire. If the LPA's statement has not been produced one week before the 28 day period is due to expire, the department will issue an urgent warning letter to the LPA, stating that the Secretary of State may proceed to quash the enforcement notice unless they can show that there are extenuating circumstances which have genuinely prevented them from providing the required information. If this warning fails to produce a satisfactory response within one week, the Secretary of State will proceed, immediately following expiry of the 28 day period, to consider whether to quash the notice. If an enforcement notice is quashed in accordance with section 88(6)(*b*) or 97(5)(*b*), the notice will cease to have effect; and any fee already paid by an appellant will be refunded by the department.

Public notification of enforcement appeals
40. The present arrangements for giving public notice of enforcement appeals are now being formalised. Rule 4 of the Enforcement Inquiries Procedure Rules makes the same provision for notification of inquiries into enforcement, listed building enforcement, and EUC appeals as is already made for planning appeals by Rule 4 of the Inquiries Procedure Rules 1974. Regulation 7 of the Enforcement Notices and Appeals Regulations requires the LPA, when the appeal is to be dealt with by written representations, to give notice of the appeal to occupiers of property in the neighbourhood of the appeal site who, in the LPA's opinion, are affected by the breach of planning or listed building control. When giving this notification, the LPA must include in it a description of the alleged breach of control, their reasons for serving the notice (in this case of an enforcement notice served under section 87), the grounds on which the appeal has been made, and a time-limit for interested persons to submit written comments to the LPA. This notification should be given as soon as practicable during the progress of an enforcement or listed building enforcement appeal.

Copy of enforcement notice required by the Secretary of State
41. The revised procedures for issuing enforcement notices since April 1, 1981 (Appendix 1 of Annex B to DOE Circular 9/81; WO Circular 16/81) include a request that a duplicate copy be sent to every person who is to receive a copy of the notice, so that this duplicate copy can be enclosed with any appeal to the Secretary of State. These procedures usually work satisfactorily; but, when they do not, the Secretary of State must be able to obtain a copy of a notice quickly. Regulation 8 of the Enforcement Notices and Appeals Regulations requires the LPA to send the Secretary of State a copy of the enforcement notice not later than 14 days from the date on which he notifies them that an appeal has been made, together with a list of the names and addresses of the people served with a copy of the notice. If the LPA fail to observe this requirement, the Secretary of State has power to quash the notice, in accordance with section 88 (6)(*b*) or 97(5)(*b*) of the 1971 Act. The Secretaries of State consider that it should be most exceptional to quash a notice in these circumstances; if it does seem appropriate to do so, the Secretary of State will give the LPA seven days' notice of his intention and will examine any representations made by the LPA, during that period, that there are extenuating circumstances making it inappropriate to quash the notice.

Revised model enforcement notice

42. The model enforcement notice published in the Appendix to DOE Circular 109/77 (WO Circular 164/77) is no longer appropriate in that form, following the amendments to section 87 of the 1971 Act made by the 1981 Act. Revised model notices and a covering letter from the LPA are published as an Appendix to this circular: these notices are adaptable to deal with other breaches of planning control to which they do not specifically refer.

Appendix

MODEL NOTICE – OPERATIONAL DEVELOPMENT

.... Council (^{a})

TOWN AND COUNTRY PLANNING ACT 1971 (as amended)
ENFORCEMENT NOTICE

.... (^{b})

WHEREAS:

(1) It appears to the .... (^{a}) Council ('the Council'), being the local planning authority for the purposes of section 87 of the Town and Country Planning Act 1971 ('the Act') in this matter, that there has been a breach of planning control within the period of four years before the date of issue of this notice on the land or premises ('the land') described in Schedule 1 below.

(2) The breach of planning control which appears to have taken place consists in the carrying out of the building, engineering, mining or other operations described in Schedule 2 below, without the grant of planning permission required for that development.

(3) The Council consider it expedient, having regard to the provisions of the development plan and to all other material considerations, to issue this enforcement notice, in exercise of their powers contained in the said section 87, for the reasons set out in [the annex to] this notice.

NOTICE IS HEREBY GIVEN that the Council require that the steps specified in Schedule 3 below be taken [in order to remedy the breach](^{d}) [within the period of   days/months from the date on which this notice takes effect] [the period specified in respect of each step in that Schedule.](^{e})

THIS NOTICE WILL TAKE EFFECT, subject to the provisions of section 88(10) of the Act, on ....(^{f})

Issued .... 19 .

Signed ....

(Council's address)

APPENDIX 1

SCHEDULE 1

Land or premises to which this notice relates

(address or description) shown edged [red] on the attached plan(^{g})

SCHEDULE 2

Alleged breach of planning control

(description of operations carried out on the land)(^{h})

SCHEDULE 3

Steps required to be taken(^{j})

(i)
(ii)
(iii)

NOTES TO THE LOCAL PLANNING AUTHORITY:
  (a) Insert the name of the Council issuing the notice.
  (b) Insert the address or a description of the land to which the notice
       relates.
  (c) See paragraph 29 of DOE Circular 38/81 (Welsh Office Circular
       57/81).
  (d) Or, as the case may be, having regard to section 87(7)(a) and (b)
       of the Act. Where steps are required to be taken for more than
       one of the purposes provided for in section 87, the purpose for
       which each step is required should be specified in Schedule 3.
       Steps may be required as alternatives.
  (e) If a single period is to be specified, by which all the required steps
       must be taken, insert it here. But if a series of steps is required to
       be taken, with a different compliance period for each step, the
       appropriate period should be clearly stated against each step (in
       columns if more suitable) in Schedule 3.
  (f) The date selected must not be less than 28 clear days after all the
       copies of the notice will have been served (see s 87(5) of the Act).
  (g) See paragraph 31 of DOE Circular 38/81 (Welsh Office Circular
       57/81).
  (h) Where the works being enforced against are on only part of the
       land identified in Schedule 1, their position should be shown on
       the plan.
  (j) Specify the actual steps to be taken with, if appropriate, the
       compliance period for each step. The requirements should be
       clear and precise. See also notes (d) and (e) above.

MODEL NOTICE – MATERIAL CHANGE OF USE

.... Council(^{a})

TOWN AND COUNTRY PLANNING ACT 1971 (as amended)
ENFORCEMENT NOTICE

.... (^{b})

WHEREAS:

(1) It appears to the .... (^{a}) Council ('the Council'), being the local planning authority for the purposes of section 87 of the Town and Country Planning Act 1971 ('the Act') in this matter, that there has been a breach of planning control after the end of 1963(^{c}) on the land or premises ('the land') described in Schedule 1 below.

(2) The breach of planning control which appears to have taken place consists in the carrying out of development by the making of the material change in the use of the land described in Schedule 2 below, without the grant of planning permission required for that development.

(3) The Council consider it expedient, having regard to the provisions of the development plan and to all other material considerations, to issue this enforcement notice, in exercise of their powers contained in the said section 87, for the reasons set out in [the annex to] this notice.(^{d})

NOTICE IS HEREBY GIVEN that the Council require that the steps specified in Schedule 3 below be taken [in order to remedy the breach](^{e}) within [the period of   days/months from the date on which this notice takes effect] [the period specified in respect of each step in that Schedule.](^{f})

THIS NOTICE SHALL TAKE EFFECT, subject to the provisions of section 88(10) of the Act, on ....(^{g})

Issued 19   .

Signed ....

(Council's address)

SCHEDULE 1

Land or premises to which this notice relates

(address or description) shown edged [red] on the attached plan(^{h})

SCHEDULE 2

Alleged breach of planning control

(description of the material change of use alleged to have been made)([j])

SCHEDULE 3

Steps required to be taken([k])

(i)
(ii)
(iii)

NOTES TO THE LOCAL PLANNING AUTHORITY:

(a) Insert the name of the Council issuing the notice.
(b) Insert the address or a description of the land to which the notice relates.
(c) Where section 87(4)(c) of the Act applies insert 'and within the period of four years before the date of issue of this notice.'
(d) See paragraph 29 of DOE Circular 38/81 (Welsh Office Circular 57/81).
(e) Or, as the case may be, having regard to section 87(7)(a) and (b) of the Act. Where steps are required to be taken for more than one of the purposes provided for in section 87, the purpose for which each step is required should be specified in Schedule 3. Steps may be required as alternatives.
(f) If a single period is to be specified, by which all the required steps must be taken, insert it here. But if a series of steps is required to be taken, with a different compliance period for each step, the appropriate period should be clearly stated against each step (in columns if more suitable) in Schedule 3.
(g) The date selected must not be less than 28 clear days after all copies of the notice will have been served (see s 87(5) of the Act).
(h) See paragraph 31 of DOE Circular 38/81 (Welsh Office Circular 57/81).
(j) If the new use is a mixed use, include all the uses comprising that mixed use.
(k) Specify the actual steps to be taken with, if appropriate, the compliance period for each step. The requirements should be clear and precise. See also notes (e) and (f) above.

MODEL LETTER

IMPORTANT – THIS COMMUNICATION AFFECTS YOUR
PROPERTY

Dear Sir or Madam

TOWN AND COUNTRY PLANNING ACT 1971 – SECTION 87

ENFORCEMENT NOTICE

LAND OR PREMISES AT . . . .
. . . .

    1. The Council have issued an enforcement notice relating to the above
land and I now serve on you a copy of that notice, in view of your interest
in the land. [Copies of the notice are also being served on others who, it is
understood, have interests in the land.]

    2. Unless an appeal is made to the Secretary of State, as described
below, the notice will take effect on . . . . 19....
and you must then ensure that the required steps for which you may be
held responsible are taken within the period(s) specified in the notice.

    3. If you wish to appeal against the notice, you should first read
carefully the enclosed booklet entitled 'Enforcement Notice Appeals – A
Guide to Procedure.' Then you or your agent should complete the enclosed appeal form and send it, together with the extra copy of the
enforcement notice enclosed herewith and the appropriate fee of £   ,
to the address shown on the appeal form. Your appeal must be *sent* to the
[Department of the Environment] [Welsh Office] *before* the date given in
paragraph 2 above as the date when the notice takes effect, *ie*
        19 .

Circular 18/84

CROWN LAND AND CROWN DEVELOPMENT

Section 3 Control of development on Crown land

13. Section 3 applies to development of Crown land carried out otherwise than by or on behalf of the Crown at a time when no person is entitled to occupy it by virtue of a private interest. An example of such development is the stationing of mobile snack bars or refreshment vans on trunk road lay-bys. Where it appears that such development has taken place after the passing of the Act, ie 12 April 1984, subsection (2) empowers the local planning authority to issue a 'special enforcement notice' if they consider it expedient to do so, having regard to the development plan and other material considerations. Subsection (3) requires the consent of the appropriate authority to the issue of the notice (but Government Departments and other Crown bodies will not unreasonably withhold such consent).

14. The notice is required to specify the matters alleged to constitute development and the steps which the local planning authority require to be taken for restoring the land to its previous condition or for discontinuing any use instituted by the development (subsection (4)). It will also specify the date on which it is to take effect and the period within which the required steps are to be taken (subsection (5)).

15. Copies of the notice are to be served on the person alleged to have carried out the development (save in a case where, after reasonable inquiry, the local planning authority are unable to identify or trace him), on any person occupying the land when the notice is issued, and on the appropriate authority. The copies have to be served not later than 28 days after the notice is issued and not later than 28 days before it takes effect (subsection (6)).

16. Subsection (7) gives the person alleged to have carried out the development and any person occupying the land – whether or not they have been served with a copy of the notice – the right to appeal to the Secretary of State before the notice takes effect. But an appeal can be made only on the grounds that the matters alleged in the notice have not taken place or do not constitute development to which the section applies.

17. Subsection (8) secures that the provisions contained in or having effect under sections 88(3) to (10) and 88A(1) and (2) of the 1971 Act shall apply to special enforcement notices and appeals against those notices, and enables the Secretary of State, by regulations, to apply other provisions of the 1971 Act. These regulations are set out in the Town and Country Planning (Special Enforcement Notices) Regulations 1984, SI No 1984/1016, which are accompanied by their own explanatory memorandum. The Secretary of State does not at present intend to apply formally to 'special enforcement notices' and appeals the relevant provisions in the Enforcement Notices and Appeals Regulations 1981 and the

Inquiries Procedure Rules 1981, which relate to ordinary enforcement notices issued under section 87 of the Town and Country Planning Act 1971. Instead, he will abide by the spirit of those provisions, as though they formally applied to 'special enforcement notices', and will expect local planning authorities and appellants to do likewise.

18. Model 'special enforcement notices' and appeal forms are obtainable, if required, from the Department of the Environment, Tollgate House, Houlton Street, Bristol BS2 9DJ, or from the Welsh Office, Cathays Park, Cardiff CF1 3NQ.

Circular 20/85

TOWN AND COUNTRY PLANNING ACT 1971: ENFORCEMENT APPEALS AND ADVERTISEMENT APPEALS

1. As part of the Government's continuing commitment to improving the efficiency and effectiveness of the planning appeals system, and to reducing the time taken to process and decide appeals, the Secretaries of State for the Environment and for Wales have reviewed the present administrative arrangements for dealing with enforcement appeals (made under section 88 of the Town and Country Planning Act 1971) and advertisement appeals (made by virtue of Regulation 22 of the Town and Country Planning (Control of Advertisements) Regulations 1984). This Circular sets out the revised arrangements which will apply to these types of planning appeal, *with effect from* 1 *October* 1985. There has been consultation with the local authority Associations, the Council on Tribunals in regard to advertisement appeals, and other interested organisations about the proposed changes.

Revised procedures for making enforcement appeals
2. The revised procedures for local planning authorities (LPAs), when issuing enforcement notices, and for appellants and their agents, when submitting appeals to the Secretary of State against enforcement notices, are explained in appendix 1 to this Circular. In summary, the main changes are:—

(1) LPAs are no longer asked to inform the recipient of an enforcement notice how much will have to be paid by way of a fee for the deemed planning application, if an enforcement appeal is made: instead, the Department or the Welsh Office will calculate the appropriate fee in each case, and require the appellant to pay the fee after the appeal has been submitted to the Secretary of State;

(2) a revised enforcement appeal form and explanatory appeals booklet (entitled 'Enforcement Notice Appeals – A Guide to Procedure') have been produced and should be brought into use *with effect from* 1 *October* 1985: all copies of previous enforcement appeal forms and explanatory booklets should then cease to be used; and

(3) *with effect from* 1 *October* 1985, enforcement appeals are to be sent to the Department of the Environment's office in Tollgate House, Bristol for appeals involving land in England (instead of being sent to Seymour House, Hemel Hempstead): there is no change in the arrangements for submitting appeals involving land in Wales, which are sent to the Welsh Office.

The time-limit for making an effective enforcement appeal
3. Section 88(1) of the Town and Country Planning Act 1971, as amended by the Local Government and Planning (Amendment) Act 1981, provides as follows—

'A person having an interest in the land to which an enforcement notice relates may, at any time before the date specified in the notice as the date on which it is to take effect, appeal to the Secretary of State against the notice, whether or not a copy of it has been served on him.'

In the past, it was considered that, provided an appeal was sent (for example, by posting it by first-class post) to the Department's office before the date specified by the LPA for an enforcement notice to take effect, the appeal was validly made in accordance with the provisions of section 88(1) of the 1971 Act. However, following the judgment of the High Court on 28 November 1984, in the case of Lenlyn Limited v Secretary of State for the Environment and the Royal Borough of Kensington and Chelsea, a stricter view is now taken of the time-limit for making an effective enforcement appeal. The Court's judgment in the *Lenlyn Limited* case states that, to be valid, an enforcement appeal *must be received by the Secretary of State before the date on which the related enforcement notice is specified to take effect.* Since an enforcement appeal is usually the only way in which the recipient of an enforcement notice can challenge the LPA's action in issuing the notice, it is vital that all intending appellants are made aware of this absolute time-limit, which the Secretary of State has no discretion to vary, for making a valid appeal.

4. The revised enforcement appeal form and the explanatory booklet about appeals (which are still to be sent to the recipient of every copy of an enforcement notice issued by LPAs) have been revised to emphasise the strict time-limits when the Secretary of State will apply to enforcement appeals submitted to him. *LPAs are therefore requested to ensure that only copies of the revised appeal form and explanatory booklet are distributed with enforcement notices issued on and after 1 October 1985.*

Appendix 1

Procedures for issuing Enforcement Notices and submitting Enforcement Appeals to The Secretary of State

1. This Appendix explains the procedures to be followed by LPAs, when issuing enforcement notices under section 87 of the Town and Country Planning Act 1971; and the procedures for appellants, when submitting an appeal under section 88 of the 1971 Act, against an enforcement notice. Similar procedures are applicable to established use certificate (EUC) appeals, made under section 95 of the 1971 Act, and they are mentioned where appropriate in this Appendix.

Fee payable for a deemed planning application
2. Under Regulation 8 of the Town and Country Planning (Fees for Applications and Deemed Applications) Regulations, a fee is normally

payable for deemed planning applications arising from enforcement appeals, appeals against decisions on applications for EUCs and any application for an EUC 'called in' by the Secretary of State. The appropriate fee is payable to the Secretary of State, *not* to the LPA. Payment of the fee should be made immediately it is requested by the Secretary of State: this will normally be some three to four weeks after the initial appeal has been submitted to the Department of the Environment or the Welsh Office.

Provisions for calculation of the fee and for refunds
3. The fee for deemed planning applications arising from enforcement and EUC appeals is calculated in exactly the same way as the fee for the corresponding planning application; and there are the same exemptions, except that there are no exemptions similar to those for revised applications. However, for a deemed application, in consequence of an enforcement appeal, a refund is due if the related enforcement notice is withdrawn by the LPA at any stage; and, in the case of both types of deemed application, refunds are due if the related appeals are withdrawn before the date of the public inquiry, or the date of the site-inspection which is made when the written representations appeal procedure is being used. In addition – and this reflects the fact that the fee is solely for considering a deemed planning application (not for considering appeals or EUC references as such) – a refund is due if:—

    (1) an enforcement appeal succeeds on any of the grounds (b) to (f) in section 88(2) of the Town and Country Planning Act 1971, unless the appeal involves stationing a residential caravan on land;

    (2) an EUC is granted by the Secretary of State, on appeal or a reference to him, or he modifies, on appeal, a certificate already issued;

    (3) an enforcement appeal is rejected as invalid, or is formally dismissed for lack of facts in support of the grounds of appeal within a prescribed period;

    (4) an enforcement notice is quashed and the appeal allowed by the Secretary of State because the LPA have failed to submit prescribed information within a prescribed period;

    (5) an enforcement notice is found to be invalid, or to contain a defect which the Secretary of State cannot correct on appeal; or

    (6) on an EUC appeal, the Secretary of State determines that he has no power to grant planning permission under section 95(3) of the 1971 Act.

Submitting an appeal and arrangements for paying the required fee
4. When a copy of an enforcement notice is served on a number of individuals, an appeal to the Secretary of State by one person will suspend the effect of the notice for all of them, until that appeal is determined. Everyone who appeals against one enforcement notice will be required to pay the appropriate fee; but intending appellants are free to arrange for one of them to appeal, or to continue the appeal, on all the relevant

grounds, while the remainder withdraw their appeals. When there is only one appeal, only one fee is payable. However, if that appellant subsequently withdraws his appeal after the statutory appeal period has expired, the enforcement notice immediately becomes effective; and all the other recipients of the notice would lose their protection from possible prosecution for breach of the requirements in the notice. Care must also be taken to ensure that all the grounds of appeal are pleaded at the outset, as it may not be possible to add additional grounds later.

5. One effect of charging for deemed planning applications in this way is that anyone who carries out unauthorised development will not be able to obtain planning permission for it, after the event, without paying any fee which would have been due on a prior planning application. However, if an appellant has already applied to the LPA for planning permission before the enforcement notice was issued, and has paid the appropriate fee, and providing his application or an appeal to the Secretary of State against its refusal had not been determined on or before the date of issue of the enforcement notice, the Fees Regulations provide that he will not need to pay a further fee for his 'deemed application'. This provision is intended to prevent an appellant from having to pay twice for an application to regularise unauthorised development.

Assessing whether enforcement action is expedient or not

6. LPAs should not initiate enforcement action solely with a view to securing payment of a fee. *The advice in paragraph 15 of DOE Circular 22/80 (WO Circular 40/80) still applies; that is, enforcement action should only be taken when it is clearly justified on planning grounds and there is no suitable alternative means of remedying a clear breach of planning control.* If the LPA consider it unlikely that they would grant planning permission for the development, they should warn the 'developer' or his agent that they may be compelled to issue an enforcement notice, and that any appeal to the Secretary of State against the notice will attract a fee for the deemed planning application for the development in question. When enforcement action has to be considered in these circumstances, the advice in paragraph 15 of Circular 22/80 (WO 40/80) still applies *and an enforcement notice should only be issued as a last resort.*

7. When the LPA consider that they would be likely to grant planning permission for an operation or use of land which appears to involve a breach of planning control, they are advised to proceed as follows:—

    (1) notify the 'developer' or his agent that there is an apparent breach of planning control (which might create difficulties in regard to any subsequent intention to dispose of the land) and state whether (and on what conditions) the authority would be likely, in present circumstances, to grant planning permission for the development involved;

    (2) invite the 'developer' or his agent to comply with the statutory planning requirements by submitting an appropriate planning application for determination by the LPA; and

    (3) if the 'developer' or his agent declines to submit a planning

application, warn him that the development is apparently unlawful and will remain at risk of enforcement action if planning
permission is not obtained for it.

When it appears from discussion with a 'developer', or from the
planning history of the land, that it may have an 'established use' which
would be immune from enforcement action, the 'developer' or his agent
should be invited to apply to the LPA for an established use certificate. If
the LPA eventually decide that enforcement action is expedient, a copy of
any formal notification, as at sub-paragraph (1) above, should be securely
attached to the enforcement notice.

Fees payable when more than one enforcement notice is issued

8. In accordance with the provisions of the Fees Regulations, a fee is
payable in respect of the deemed planning application on an appeal
against each enforcement notice issued by the LPA. The amount of the
fee payable depends upon the precise development to which the notice
relates. When one notice is issued, alleging a number of different activities
(either changes of use or operations) which fall either within more than
one category of development, or in the same category of development
specified in Part II of Schedule 1 to the Fees Regulations, the amount of
the fee payable is the highest amount calculated. However, when more
than one enforcement notice has been issued in respect of activities on the
same site, and appeals are lodged in respect of more than one of these
notices, a separate fee is payable in respect of the development to which
each of those notices relates. For that reason, LPAs are reminded of the
advice contained in paragraph 6 of DOE Circular 26/81 (WO 39/81) about
the practicability of embodying in a single enforcement notice allegations
of one or more breaches of planning control involving the same land.

*Administrative procedure for service of enforcement notices on interested
persons*

9. At the same time as every copy of an enforcement notice is served in
accordance with section 87(5) of the 1971 Act, LPAs are asked to:—
   (1) enclose a copy of the official enforcement appeal form, to be used
       in the event of any appeal to the Secretary of State against the
       notice;
   (2) send a duplicate copy of the enforcement notice (and any en-
       closure) to the recipient, so that he can send the copy to the
       Secretary of State with any appeal which may be made; and
   (3) enclose a copy of the latest version of the DOE/Welsh Office
       explanatory booklet about enforcement appeal procedures.

10. LPAs are also asked to ensure that any advice they may give to
intending appellants indicates that any enforcement appeal made to the
Secretary of State *must be received at the address indicated on the appeal
form before the date specified by the LPA for the enforcement notice to take
effect.*

Circular 4/87

SECTION 90 OF TOWN AND COUNTRY PLANNING ACT 1971: PROVISIONS AND PROCEDURES FOR STOP NOTICES

1. We are directed by the Secretary of State for the Environment and the Secretary of State for Wales to refer to the provisions, in section 90 of the Town and Country Planning Act 1971 (as amended by section 1 of the Town and Country Planning (Amendment) Act 1977), which enable local planning authorities (LPAs) to serve a stop notice, in addition to an enforcement notice under section 87 of the 1971 Act, when it is essential to halt an unlawful activity on land immediately.

2. The LPA's discretionary power to serve a stop notice is not subject to an appeal to the Secretary of State, so that neither the Department of the Environment nor the Welsh Office have access to reliable information, from the planning appeals process, about the practical effects of the revised stop notice procedures introduced by the 1977 Act. (The revised procedures are stated in the Appendices to DOE Circular 82/77 (WO 122/77) issued to local authorities in August 1977.) Accordingly, the Department of the Environment arranged for a research project to be carried out by independent consultants who examined all stop notices served, and decisions whether to serve a stop notice, taken by a representative sample of LPAs in England during the five-year period from 1 January 1978 to 31 December 1982. One of the consultants' recommendations was that 'best practice' of those LPAs with the most experience of using the stop notice procedure effectively be made available to all LPAs, with a view to minimising the uncertainty of some LPAs about the scope and extent of their powers to serve a stop notice, and the procedures for deciding whether to serve a notice and implementing a decision to do so.

3. The Annexes to this Circular provide comprehensive guidance about the statutory provisions for stop notices and the operation of stop notice procedures, as follows:—

    Annex 1: the main statutory provisions;
    Annex 2: the practical operation of stop notices;
    Annex 3: the liability for compensation arising from service of a stop notice.

The Appendix to the Circular provides a model stop notice form which LPAs are invited to use, subject to any modification they regard as essential for their own purposes.

4. Apart from increasing the maximum daily penalty for a continuing offence under section 90(7) of the 1971 Act, the Housing and Planning Act 1986 makes no amendment to the stop notice provisions in the 1971

Act. This Circular is therefore confined to describing the relevant existing provisions. It is not considered that it will have any effect upon local authority manpower resources and expenditure.

5. DOE Circular 82/77 (WO 122/77) is cancelled.

ANNEX 1

STOP NOTICES: THE MAIN STATUTORY PROVISIONS

1. The main statutory provisions for the service of a stop notice are in sections 90 and 177 of the Town and Country Planning Act 1971, as amended by the Town and Country Planning (Amendment) Act 1977 and the Local Government and Planning (Amendment) Act 1981. There are related provisions for the service of 'information notices' in section 284 of the 1971 Act, as amended by the 1977 and 1981 Acts.

The power to serve a stop notice
2. Section 90(1) of the 1971 Act enables the local planning authority (LPA) to serve a stop notice prohibiting any specified activity which is, or is included in, a breach of planning control alleged in an enforcement notice (issued by the LPA under section 87 of the 1971 Act). A stop notice may be served on any person who appears to have an interest in the land to which the notice relates, or who appears to be engaged in any activity prohibited by the notice. The LPA must annex to the stop notice a copy of the related enforcement notice.

3. The LPA must specify in the stop notice the date when it is to take effect. This effective date must not be less than three, nor more than 28, days from the date on which the stop notice is first served on any person.

Public notification of service of a stop notice
The LPA may publicise the fact that a stop notice has been served by displaying a 'site notice', in accordance with section 90(5) of the 1971 Act, on the land to which the stop notice relates. If a site notice is displayed, it extends the effect of the stop notice to any person who carries out on the land any activity prohibited by the notice.

5. A site notice publicising a stop notice must state:—
   (1) that a stop notice has been served;
   (2) that any person contravening the stop notice may be prosecuted for an offence under section 90 of the 1971 Act; and
   (3) the date on which the stop notice takes effect and the LPA's requirements in the notice.

Scope of the prohibition in a stop notice
6. With the exceptions indicated in paragraph 7 below, a stop notice may prohibit any, or all, of the activities which comprise the alleged breach of planning control in the related enforcement notice. Thus the prohibition may be directed at a use of land which is ancillary, or

incidental, to the main use of the land specified in the enforcement notice as a breach of control; or it may be directed at a particular activity taking place only on part of the land specified in the enforcement notice; or it may be directed at an activity which takes place on the land intermittently or seasonally.

7. A stop notice may *not* prohibit:—

(1) the use of any building as a dwellinghouse;

(2) the use of land as a site for a caravan occupied by any person as his only or main residence (for this purpose 'caravan' has the same meaning as it has for the purpose of Part I of the Caravan Sites and Control of Development Act 1960);

(3) the continuation of any activity which began more than twelve months earlier, unless that activity is, or is incidental to, building, engineering, mining or other operations, or the deposit of refuse or waste materials (thus a stop notice relating to 'operational development' can be served at any time before the operations are completed);

(4) the taking of any steps required for the purpose of complying with the LPA's requirements in an enforcement notice.

In consequence of the limitation mentioned in sub-paragraph (3) above, a stop notice cannot prohibit an activity which is intermittent or seasonal, if the activity first took place more than twelve months earlier.

Power to withdraw a stop notice

8. The LPA may withdraw a stop notice at any time (without prejudice to their power to serve another notice) by giving notification of the withdrawal to everyone who was served with the stop notice. If a site notice was displayed on the land specified in the stop notice, a notice of the withdrawal is to be displayed in place of the site notice.

Cessation of the effect of a stop notice

9. A stop notice ceases to have effect when:—

(1) the related enforcement notice is withdrawn by the LPA, or is quashed on appeal to the Secretary of State under section 88 of the 1971 Act;

(2) the period the LPA have allowed for compliance with the related enforcement notice expires (at that point the prohibition in the stop notice will be effectively superseded by the requirement specified by the LPA in the enforcement notice);

(3) notification is first given of the LPA's decision to withdraw the stop notice.

10. When an enforcement notice is varied (on appeal to the Secretary of State under section 88 of the 1971 Act) so that the alleged breach of planning control no longer includes a particular activity which is prohibited in the related stop notice, the prohibition in the stop notice ceases to have effect in so far as it relates to that particular activity.

Penalties for contravention of a stop notice

11. When a person contravenes, or causes or permits the contravention of, a stop notice served on him (or for which a site notice has been displayed on the land), he commits an offence which is open to prosecution by the LPA under section 90(7) of the 1971 Act. The maximum fine on conviction for an offence in the Magistrates' Court is £2,000; and there is an unlimited fine on conviction on indictment. A further offence (for which there is a continuing daily penalty, on conviction) is committed if the initial offence is continued after conviction of it.

12. It is a defence for any person prosecuted for an offence under section 90(7) of the 1971 Act who can prove that the stop notice was not served on him and that he did not know, and could not reasonably have been expected to know, of the existence of the stop notice.

Challenging the prohibition in a stop notice

13. There is no right of appeal to the Secretary of State against the prohibition in a stop notice; and the merits of the LPA's decision to serve a stop notice cannot be examined in the course of an appeal to the Secretary of State, under section 88 of the 1971 Act, against the related enforcement notice. The validity of a stop notice and the propriety of the LPA's decision to issue a notice may be challenged by means of an application to the High Court for judicial review, made in accordance with the Rules of the Supreme Court, or by way of the defence to a prosecution brought by the LPA under section 90(7) of the 1971 Act.

Provisions for serving 'information notices'

14. Section 284(1) of the 1971 Act, as amended by the 1977 Act, enables the LPA to serve a requisition (referred to in this Circular as an 'information notice') for information they require in order to enable them to issue an enforcement notice, or serve a stop notice (as well as certain other types of notice or order). The LPA's request to supply information must be made in writing to the person at whom it is directed; and must allow 21 days, or such longer period as the LPA may allow, from the date of service of the notice for the required information to be provided.

15. The requirement in an information notice may only be directed at the occupier of the premises to which it relates, or any person who directly or indirectly receives rent for the premises.

16. The matters on which information may be required by an information notice are as follows:—

    (1) the nature of the interest in the premises of the person on whom the notice is served;

    (2) the name and address of any other person known to him as having an interest in the premises;

    (3) the purpose for which the premises are being used;

    (4) the time when that use began;

    (5) the name and address of any person known to the person on whom the notice is served as having used the premises for that purpose;

(6) the time when any activities being carried out on the premises began.

These matters of information are intended to comprise all the questions of fact likely to arise when the LPA's officers are considering what further information they need in order to decide whether a breach of planning control has occurred; and, if so, when it began. For example, the information which can be required under sub-paragraph (6) will help to decide whether the 'four-year rule' for operational development (in section 87(4) of the 1971 Act) applies, or whether the service of a stop notice is prevented because the activity taking place on the land began more than twelve months ago.

Penalties for failing to comply with an information notice.
17. Any person who:—
   (1) without reasonable excuse, fails to comply with an information notice served on him; or
   (2) having been required by a notice to give any information, knowingly makes any mis-statement,
is guilty of an offence and is liable to prosecution by the LPA in the Magistrates' Court under, respectively, subsections (2) and (3) of section 284 of the 1971 Act.

ANNEX 2

THE PRACTICAL OPERATION OF STOP NOTICES

Use of the power to serve a stop notice
1. Section 90(1) of the 1971 Act enables a local planning authority (LPA) to serve a stop notice in order to reinforce the requirements of an enforcement notice (issued under section 87 of the Act), when they consider it 'expedient' straightaway to prevent the continuation of the breach of planning control alleged in the enforcement notice, or the carrying on of any 'activity' which is included in the breach of control. The intention of these provisions is that the discretionary power to serve a stop notice should only be used in circumstances where the breach of control, or an activity comprised in the breach, is so serious that the LPA are justified in not waiting for the enforcement notice to take effect (as provided in section 87(13) of the 1971 Act), or for the expiry of the period allowed for compliance with it (as provided in section 87(8) of the Act).
2. Since the effect of serving a stop notice will usually be to halt the breach of control, or the specified activity, almost immediately, LPAs should ensure that a quick and thorough assessment of the likely consequences of serving a stop notice is available (preferably, when the decision is not delegated to officers, in the form of a report submitted by Planning Officers who are thoroughly familiar with the locality and the detailed operation of the alleged breach of control taking place on the land) to the Committee or officer who will authorise service of the notice.

The assessment should examine the foreseeable costs and benefits likely to result from a stop notice.

Cost/benefit assessment for stop notices

3. The costs arising from serving a stop notice will usually be confined to the firm or individual who is thereby prevented from carrying on the activity prohibited by the notice, although there may occasionally be some costs to the local economy. The costs to a firm may vary from having to modify a production process, at little or no additional cost (at one extreme), to the complete cessation of a business (at the other), with consequent loss of jobs, failure to complete contracts, or bankruptcy. The precise effect of prohibiting a particular activity should always be carefully examined. For example, preventing storage in the open of raw materials or finished products may have an immediate and serious effect upon a production process relying on those raw materials, or on the availability of the storage area for the finished product. Even if the practical effect of the stop notice falls short of disrupting a production process, it may nevertheless have the effect of adding appreciably to a firm's costs, so that the finished product is priced out of its home market; or the firm can no longer compete effectively with other firms in a wider market. Since section 90(1)(b) of the 1971 Act enables a stop notice to be directed either at the entire breach of control or at a specified activity, the LPA should ensure that a stop notice's requirements do not prohibit anything more than is essential to safeguard amenity in the neighbourhood.

4. Before deciding to issue an enforcement notice, and subsequently to serve a stop notice, discussion should take place with the person carrying on the activity to ascertain whether there is any alternative means of production or operation which would overcome the objections to the activity in an environmentally acceptable way. If an acceptable alternative means of production or operation would require the grant of planning permission, in order to carry it on lawfully, the LPA should take the initiative in inviting a planning application; and, if possible, in co-ordinating a suitable grant of permission with the service of the stop notice.

5. The benefits of serving a stop notice will usually be readily apparent as an improvement in amenity in the neighbourhood. However, some attempt should always be made to estimate the number of people who are likely to benefit, and how adversely their amenities will be affected if a stop notice is not served (on the assumption that the enforcement notice will eventually take effect on expiry of the compliance period specified in it).

6. In certain defined circumstances the costs of serving a stop notice may also include the cost to the LPA of any payment of financial compensation arising from the provisions of section 177 of the 1971 Act. (The liability to compensation is described in Annex 3.)

The twelve-month limitation period for stop notices

7. Section 90(2) of the 1971 Act effectively imposes a twelve-month

limitation period on the service of a stop notice for any activity which involves a 'use' of land. In practice, this means that, when a use began after the end of 1963 but it has already been taking place for more than twelve months, the LPA may issue an enforcement notice directed at the use of the land which is alleged to be in breach of control, but any related stop notice may only prohibit such activities or activity (if any) as began in the preceding twelve months. For this purpose, an activity might be a completely new 'ancillary' activity (not itself involving a material change of use of the land); or the 'intensification' of a use specifically identified as an activity which began during the past twelve months.

8. Seasonal or intermittent activities sometimes present special difficulties for LPAs in deciding whether to serve a stop notice. Because the twelve-month limitation period applies equally to this type of activity, a stop notice cannot be served for a seasonal or intermittent activity which *first* began more than twelve months earlier.

9. The twelve-month limitation period for stop notices does not apply to 'operational development', or to the deposit of refuse or waste materials. Thus, for example, where a new building or engineering operation began more than twelve months earlier, in connection with a use of land which is not 'immune' from enforcement action, but only later reaches the stage at which prohibition of any further building or engineering works is justified, the LPA may serve a stop notice for that purpose.

Effective service of a stop notice

10. Unlike the provisions in section 87(5) of the 1971 Act, for serving a copy of the related enforcement notice, there is no statutory requirement that a stop notice shall be served on the owner and occupier of the land, or on any other person who has an interest in the land. It follows that the validity of a stop notice cannot be challenged on the ground that it has not been served on someone who ought to be served with it. Instead, section 90(5) of the 1971 Act enables the LPA to serve a stop notice on any person who appears to them to have an interest in the land, or to be engaged in any activity prohibited by the notice. Thus, for example, when an enforcement notice is directed at a breach of planning control involving building operations to rebuild substantially a dilapidated and abandoned dwellinghouse in a rural locality, and the owner of the land cannot be contacted, the LPA may serve the stop notice on anyone who is actually engaged in carrying out the building works which are prohibited by the notice. However, normal administrative practice should be to locate any owner and occupier of the land and arrange for the stop notice to be served on them also, as with an enforcement notice.

11. Additionally, section 90(5) of the 1971 Act enables the LPA to display a 'site notice' on the land for which a stop notice has been served, notifying the fact that a stop notice has been served and that any person contravening it may be prosecuted for the offence which is created by section 90(7) of the Act. The 'site notice' should give the date when the stop notice takes effect and indicate its requirements. This procedure is an

especially effective way of surmounting the problems LPAs sometimes meet in establishing exactly who is reponsible for an alleged breach of control.

12. If a site notice has been displayed on the land, and the LPA decide to withdraw the stop notice to which it refers, they should arrange for the display of another notice on the land (in place of the site notice), notifying the fact that the stop notice has been withdrawn.

Period in which a stop notice may be served
13. Section 90(1)(b) of the 1971 Act provides that a stop notice may be served before the related enforcement notice takes effect. Section 87(13) of the Act effectively requires the LPA to specify the date on which the enforcement notice shall take effect. However, if there is an enforcement appeal to the Secretary of State, section 88(10), of the Act suspends the effect of the enforcement notice until the appeal against it is finally determined or withdrawn. It follows from these provisions that, when there is an appeal against the related enforcement notice, the LPA may serve a stop notice at any time during the currency of the enforcement appeal.

Prosecution for an offence
14. When a site notice has been displayed for a stop notice, it is an immediate offence for anyone to contravene, or to cause or permit the contravention of, the prohibition in the stop notice, once the stop notice takes effect. When a site notice has not been displayed and the stop notice has been served on a person, it is an offence for that person to contravene, or to cause to permit the contravention of, the prohibition in the stop notice for more than two days after the stop notice has been served on him. Prosecution for an offence under section 90(7) of the 1971 Act is usually in the Magistrates' Court.

Information notice procedures
15. The LPA's power in section 284 of the 1971 Act to obtain information about uses of land is expressly intended for exercise of their functions under the Act. Accordingly, this power should only be used where the LPA have prima facie evidence of a breach of planning control and they are seriously contemplating the issue of an enforcement notice, or the service of a stop notice. The power may also be useful when the LPA contemplate making a discontinuance order under section 51 of the 1971 Act.

16. While a person who is served with an information notice must give a truthful reply, he cannot reasonably be required to provide information beyond what is within his own knowledge, or what he can reasonably find out. He is not obliged to engage in research, to produce witnesses, or to seek legal or other professional advice. Any information given in reply to a notice will form part only of the stock of relevant information which the LPA will have to consider before deciding what action may be appropriate to deal with an alleged breach of control. Sometimes, the information will

help to confirm that enforcement action is expedient (possibly accompanied by a stop notice): on other occasions, it will show a different use or activity from what had been suspected, or even confirm that there is no breach of control on the land. If the reply to an information notice results in doubt about the use of the land, a site-inspection will usually be essential to resolve the doubt and ensure that any subsequent enforcement decision is taken on a sound basis.

Administrative procedures for dealing with stop notices

17. Once the LPA have decided to serve a stop notice, it is essential that they should be capable of implementing their decision speedily and effectively. There should always be a clear understanding (preferably stated in administrative instructions) about the respective responsibilities of the local authority's Planning Department and Legal Department for the necessary preparatory work (including the service of an information notice), the formulation of the terms of the stop notice, the arrangements for serving it and how its practical effect will be assessed (including the need to bring a prosecution quickly if the notice is ignored). Since the service of a stop notice is a relatively infrequent event for many LPAs, it will usually be convenient and economical to maintain the essential knowledge and experience of stop notice procedures in a small group of planning and legal officers, or to confine it to the LPA's enforcement officer (if one is employed). When the decision to serve a stop notice has been taken, action to implement it must have priority.

18. The service of a stop notice should always be recorded in the enforcement and stop notice register which LPAs are required, by section 92A of the Act, to maintain.

19. The procedures for service of notices, specified in section 283 of the 1971 Act, apply to the service of a stop notice. In particular, a stop notice should always be identifiable by the recipient as a communication of the first importance. If the notice is served by postal delivery, the envelope containing it should clearly state that it is an urgent and important communication; and it should be sent by recorded delivery service.

ANNEX 3

THE LIABILITY FOR COMPENSATION ARISING UNDER SECTION 177 OF THE 1971 ACT

1. There is quite widespread misunderstanding about the circumstances in which the local planning authority (LPA) may become liable for the payment of compensation for an activity which has been prohibited by the service of a stop notice. The available evidence is that compensation has only had to be paid infrequently and by relatively few LPAs.

2. The circumstances in which a right to compensation may arise, for loss or damage directly attributable to the prohibition specified in a stop notice, are defined in section 177(2) of the 1971 Act, as follows:—

(1) when the related enforcement notice is quashed on any ground
other than ground (a) in section 88(2) of the 1971 Act (that is,
planning permission is granted for the development alleged in the
enforcement notice, or a condition or limitation imposed on a
grant of planning permission is discharged). In effect, this means
that the enforcement notice was defective and has therefore been
quashed, either because it failed to identify correctly a breach of
control or what had taken place on the land, or the alleged breach
was 'immune' from enforcement action, or the issue or service of
the notice was defective in some other way;

(2) when the related enforcement notice is varied, on appeal to the
Secretary of State, on any ground other than ground (a) in section
88(2) of the 1971 Act, so that the breach of planning control
alleged in the enforcement notice ceases to include any activity or
activities prohibited by the stop notice;

(3) when the LPA withdraw the related enforcement notice for any
reason other than their decision to grant planning permission for
the development to which the notice relates, or for the retention
or continuance of the development without complying with a
condition or limitation on a previous grant of permission;

(4) when the LPA withdraw the stop notice.

Consequently, no liability for compensation arises if an enforcement
appeal to the Secretary of State succeeds *only* on ground (a) in section
88(2) of the 1971 Act; or if planning permission is granted, in consequence
of the deemed planning application arising from an enforcement appeal,
by the Secretary of State or a Planning Inspector.

Making a claim for compensation for loss due to stop notice
3. Anyone (whether served with a stop notice or not) who had an
interest in, or occupied, the land when an activity on it was prohibited by a
stop notice is entitled to claim compensation from the LPA for the loss or
damage which is directly attributable to the prohibition specified in the
stop notice. Any claim for compensation must be made to the LPA within
six months of the decision giving rise to the claim, or within such longer
period as the Secretary of State may allow.

The extent of payment by way of compensation
4. The extent of any compensation payment is confined only to loss or
damage directly attributable to ceasing an activity prohibited by a stop
notice. However, this may include damages awarded for breach of contract due to action taken in order to comply with the terms of a stop
notice. In assessing the amount of any compensation, account will be
taken of the extent to which the entitlement to compensation arises from
the claimant's failure to provide the LPA with information required by an
information notice (under section 284 of the 1971 Act), or to any mis-
statement of the facts which has been made to the LPA in reply to an
information notice.

Disputed claim for compensation

5. Any disputed claim for compensation arising under section 177 of the 1971 Act is to be referred for determination by the Lands Tribunal.

APPENDIX

Model form of stop notice for use by local planning authorities

IMPORTANT: THIS NOTICE AFFECTS YOUR PROPERTY

TOWN AND COUNTRY PLANNING ACT 1971

.... Council

To .... (name of intended recipient of the notice)

Whereas:

(1) The .... Council, being the local planning authority for the land to which this notice relates, have issued an enforcement notice (dated............), under section 87 of the Town and Country Planning Act 1971, alleging that there has been a breach of planning control on the land described in Schedule 1 to this notice; and

(2) The Council consider it expedient to prevent, before the expiry of the period allowed for compliance with the requirements of the enforcement notice, the activity alleged to constitute or form part of the alleged breach of control.

Notice is hereby given that the Council, in exercise of their power in section 90 of the 1971 Act, now prohibit the continuation of the activity specified in Schedule 2 to this notice.

A copy of the related enforcement notice, issued under section 87 of the 1971 Act, is annexed to this notice.

This notice shall take effect on .... (date) when all the activity specified in Schedule 2 to this notice shall cease.

Dated ....   Signed ....
                                     Chief Executive/Secretary

[Address of Council]

Schedule 1

The land or premises to which this notice relates comprises land at .... (address or brief identifying details of the land), shown edged red on the annexed plan.

Schedule 2

The activity to which this notice relates is [operational development consisting of .... [1]] [the use of the land for the purpose of .... [2]] [the continuing breach of Condition No .... on the planning permission granted on .... (date)[3]].

[1] for use when the prohibited activity is 'operational development'.
[2] for use when the prohibited activity is a material change of use of the land, or is an activity comprised in a change of use.
[3] for use when the prohibited activity is the breach of a condition imposed on a grant of planning permission.

Appendix 2

Good Practice at Planning Inquiries

(Appendix F of the Chief Planning Inspector's Report January 1985–March 1986)

Introduction

1. The task of Inspectors at planning appeals or similar inquiries is to obtain the material necessary to make an informed and reasoned decision or recommendation. To do this they hear evidence from the parties and may also seek such other additional information as they consider necessary. Inspectors must be satisfied before the inquiry ends that they understand what the subject of the inquiry is and what the relevant arguments and submissions are. They need also to ensure that the parties are satisfied that their cases have been understood and that they have had a fair hearing. While Inspectors must always act in accordance with the principles of fairness, openness and impartiality set out in the Franks Report they are also responsible for ensuring that the inquiry is run efficiently and that inquiry time is not wasted. Thus they will seek to avoid inquiry time being spent on matters which are not in dispute or where, in their view, sufficient evidence has been heard to establish a point at issue, or on matters where expert witnesses can reach agreement more quickly or easily prior to the inquiry.

2. The great majority of planning inquiries are completed in 1 day and there is little scope for saving time at these, but nevertheless some of the points made in the following paragraphs apply to all inquiries. There are however each year a substantial number of longer running inquiries where time could be saved at the inquiry, and this would in turn help to reduce the time required by the Inspector to prepare his report or decision letter, and hence speed up the final decision.

Preparing for the inquiry

3. Adequate preparation by the parties and by Inspectors is essential, and present practice frequently does not allow this to take place. Some improvements can be achieved by changes in the Inquiries Procedure Rules, and these are under review, but what is needed is basically a willingness by the parties to disclose their case in advance to each other

213

and to the Inspector. At present pre-inquiry statements submitted by local planning authorities and by appellants (when requested to do so) are intended to provide the other parties and the Inspector with the gist of the cases to be presented. Too often they fail to do so; they tend to be couched in very general terms and contain none of the substance of the case that will be presented at the inquiry.

4. In this respect they tend to be less satisfactory than the statements produced for informal hearings. The Code of Practice for Informal Hearings requires both parties to produce comprehensive statements 3 weeks before the informal hearing. These ensure the Inspector knows in advance what the cases are and enables him to open the hearing by identifying the issues in the appeal and summarising the main arguments on each. This practice is welcomed by the parties and is indeed one of the reasons why informal hearings are popular with parties and with Inspectors.

5. Pre-inquiry meetings are found to be useful in advance of inquiries which are expected to last more than a week or so. They provide an opportunity for the Inspector to obtain agreement on the scope and date of submission of pre-inquiry statements, on the exchange of proofs of evidence in advance, on witnesses meeting to agree material before the inquiry starts and on inquiry programming. When such meetings have been held it has on occasions resulted in witnesses for the appellant and local planning authority submitting an agreed statement of facts together with documents, plans and suggested planning conditions prior to or at the commencement of the inquiry. This is good practice which could with benefit be adopted in those cases where pre-inquiry meetings are not held.

6. Even though many statements are at present of limited use in assisting the Inspector or the parties to prepare for the inquiry, they can on occasions serve to encourage the parties to enter into negotiation. But if the statements are served close to the 28 day limit before the inquiry the time available for negotiation is limited and the Inspectorate is often faced with last minute requests for adjournment or late cancellations. While it is clearly desirable to resolve matters without the expense and delay involved in a public inquiry, late cancellations or adjournments impose costs on the Inspectorate, and prevent other appellants having their case brought forward. Hence it is good practice for pre-inquiry statements to be exchanged as early in the appeals process as possible.

7. Inspectors have the discretion to permit additional evidence. But the last minute introduction of a material consideration intended to catch an opposing party off-guard, is not 'good practice'. In some circumstances it may lead to an adjournment and this in turn could result in a successful application for costs against the offending party.

At the inquiry

8. The Inquiries Procedure Rules provide for the appellant (and the applicant in Section 35 call-in cases) to present their case first, and to have the last word, but this often means that more ground is covered by the

appellant than is necessary. If it appears that the local planning authority case is going to deal with only a limited number of points, it may be advantageous for that case to be heard first. Then the appellant has only to adduce evidence in response to the local planning authority's case, and any additional material requested by the Inspector.

9. There are also some inquiries where there are a number of discrete issues, each requiring complex technical evidence to be submitted and tested. In such cases it can be useful for each issue to be dealt with in turn. These cases have to be identified well in advance, pre-inquiry meetings arranged and agreement of the parties obtained to present their cases on a 'topic' basis. This can result in appreciable savings in time, both at the inquiry and in preparation of the Inspector's report; the practice is strongly commended in every appropriate case.

Opening submissions

10. Short opening statements lasting no more than 20 to 30 minutes outlining the cases to be presented by witnesses are all that is required if there has been adequate exchange of information in advance. It can be very useful in multi-day inquiries if all the principal parties provide such statements on the first morning, when there tends to be maximum press and public interest, as these statements help those present to understand what the inquiry is all about.

Presentation of evidence

11. It is generally the task of the advocate to ensure that when there is more than one witness, proofs are consistent, and do not cover the same ground. At the inquiry sufficient copies should be available for the parties, if not circulated in advance, and for members of the public present: copies of plans and photographs which are submitted should also be made available or, preferably, displayed so that they can be easily seen.

12. The major criticism of proofs is that they are too long and many could with advantage be shortened with more use made of annexes to provide the detailed evidence, for example, extracts of policy statements, tables and statistics, historical background, etc. It is particularly useful when complex or technical evidence is submitted for summaries containing the salient points to be prepared and for only these to be read out in evidence. Copies of the whole proof should of course be available to the parties and the public, and the witness would be open to cross- examination on all the evidence he has submitted.

Cross examination

13. Cross examination can be helpful to the Inspector and the inquiry in for example:—

> **Testing** the validity of the facts and assumptions on which cases are based to expose any defects,

Exploring how the application of policies would forward the objectives they are intended to achieve,
Identifying and **narrowing** the issues which are in dispute.

14. Cross examination is much less useful when it is directed to persuading a professional witness to change an opinion for example on aesthetic matters, or in attempting to establish inconsistencies in wording of policies which are not intended to be construed as statute.

15. Where Inspectors find cross examination irrelevant or repetitious, they should and do indicate this; they must also ensure that the cross examination does not lead to intimidation of the witness.

16. At many inquiries however the difficulty faced by Inspectors is that of one side not having the skills or experience to probe and test the evidence of opposing witnesses. In such cases the role of the Inspector has to become more inquisitorial. They need to establish what weight is to be given to evidence submitted, to assess how realistic are the assumptions and on what forecasts they are based. In doing this they must be thorough, though of course always impartial, but unless they are given proofs in advance they may be at a serious disadvantage.

Re-examination

17. Re-examination should not be used to introduce new evidence, nor in general should questions be put in such a way as to suggest the desired answer.

Participation by interested persons and groups

18. On occasions interested persons and groups may seek to introduce material irrelevant to the inquiry or consider that repetition will add to the strength of their case and Inspectors must discourage this. In general however groups and individuals with similar cases do respond well to requests for co-operation, for example nominating one of their number as a spokesman. This good practice is to be encouraged.

Conditions

19. Parties are now expected to submit suggested conditions which would be attached to planning permissions if granted and it is becoming more common for the parties to discuss these in advance and obtain a measure of agreement. However the opportunity should be taken at the inquiry to resolve remaining disagreements.

20. It must be emphasised that Inspectors do not take submission of suggested conditions by local authorities to indicate any weakness in their opposition to the proposed development. Inspectors have been making this point clear when opening the inquiries as there have been cases when local residents have construed the measure as a 'sell out' by the local planning authority.

Closing submissions

21. Closing submissions can be of great value particularly in multi-day inquiries when covering a multiplicity of topics and issues. Not only do they summarise the case for the parties as they have emerged from cross examination and re-examination but logically ordered summaries can also provide Inspectors with a framework for the report. Some advocates have been providing Inspectors with copies of summaries of the closing submissions and increasingly Inspectors will ask for these to be provided if possible.

Acknowledgment:
The material contained in appendixes 1 and 2 is reproduced with the permission of the Controller of Her Majesty's Stationery Office.

Index